Also in Plains Histories

America's 100th Meridian: A Plains Journey, *by Monte Hartman*

American Outback: The Oklahoma Panhandle in the Twentieth Century, *by Richard Lowitt*

Children of the Dust, *by Betty Grant Henshaw; edited by Sandra Scofield*

The Death of Raymond Yellow Thunder: And Other True Stories from the Nebraska–Pine Ridge Border Towns, *by Stew Magnuson*

From Syria to Seminole: Memoir of a High Plains Merchant, *by Ed Aryain; edited by J'Nell Pate*

"I Do Not Apologize for the Length of This Letter": The Mari Sandoz Letters on Native American Rights, 1940–1965, *edited by Kimberli A. Lee*

Nikkei Farmer on the Nebraska Plains: A Memoir, *by The Reverend Hisanori Kano; edited by Tai Kreidler*

Railwayman's Son: A Plains Family Memoir, *by Hugh Hawkins*

Rights in the Balance: Free Press, Fair Trial, and *Nebraska Press Association v. Stuart, by Mark R. Scherer*

Ruling Pine Ridge: Oglala Lakota Politics from the IRA to Wounded Knee, *by Akim D. Reinhardt*

As a Farm Woman Thinks

As a Farm Woman Thinks

Life and Land on the Texas High Plains, 1890–1960

Nellie Witt Spikes
Edited by Geoff Cunfer
Plainsword by Sandra Scofield

Texas Tech University Press

This book is typeset in Filosofia. The paper used in this book meets the
minimum requirements of ANSI/NISO Z39.48-1992 (R1997). ∞

Designed by Kasey McBeath

Library of Congress Cataloging-in-Publication Data
Spikes, Nellie Witt, b. 1888.
    As a farm woman thinks : life and land on the Texas high plains,
1890–1960 / Nellie Witt Spikes ; edited by Geoff Cunfer ; Plainsword
by Sandra Scofield.
        p. cm.—(Plains histories)
Summary: "Selected weekly columns by Nellie Witt Spikes, published
in small-town Texas newspapers from 1930–1960, describe farm life
on the Texas Panhandle, along with the region's culture and natural
history. Organized topically and then chronologically, with commentary by the editor; contains historical photographs"—Provided by
publisher.
    Includes bibliographical references and index.
    ISBN 978-0-89672-710-6 (hardcover : alk. paper) 1. Texas
Panhandle (Tex.)—Social life and customs—20th century. 2. Llano
Estacado--Social life and customs—20th century. 3. Spikes, Nellie
Witt, b. 1888. 4. Women farmers—Texas—Texas Panhandle—Biography.
5. Texas Panhandle (Tex.)—Biography. 6. Farm life—Texas—Texas
Panhandle—History—20th century. 7. Frontier and pioneer life—Tex-
as—Texas Panhandle. 8. Natural history—Texas—Texas Panhandle.
I. Cunfer, Geoff, 1966– II. Scofield, Sandra Jean, 1943– III. Title.
        F392.P168S66 2010
        976.4'8—dc22   2010021762

Printed in the United States of America
10 11 12 13 14 15 16 17 18 / 9 8 7 6 5 4 3 2 1

Texas Tech University Press
Box 41037 | Lubbock, Texas 79409-1037 USA
800.832.4042 | ttup@ttu.edu | www.ttupress.org

Dedicated to my grandmother,
Pauline Mantz Cunfer

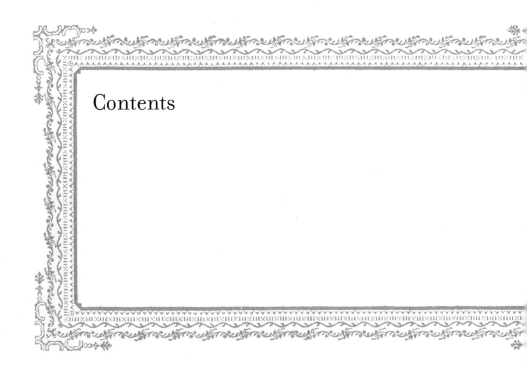

Contents

Illustrations

Maps

Acknowledgments

Many people contributed to the creation of this book, starting with archivists and museum staff who have preserved the evidence of past lives across the decades and into a third century of Euro-American experience on the southern plains. All of the text and photographs in this volume are available thanks to the dedication of local historians and archivists who cared to find them, preserve them, and make them available to the public. The Southwest Collection of Texas Tech University holds many documents, newspapers, photographs, clippings, and interviews related to Nellie Witt Spikes's life and to Crosby County history. Most of the material presented here came from that valuable institution. I especially appreciate the help of Southwest Collection archivist Janet

M. Neugebauer, whose book *Plains Farmer: The Diary of William G. De-Loach, 1914–1964* served as an inspiration for this one. Jennifer Spurrier was helpful in arranging access to historical newspapers on micro-film, and Patricia Perry efficiently corralled a large photo reproduction order. I would also like to acknowledge the help of Donna Harris of the Ralls Historical Museum and the staff of the Crosby County Pioneer Memorial Museum in Crosbyton, who made available many of the photographs included here.

Once the newspaper columns were on hand, there was a lot of typing to be done. I am especially appreciative of the care and effort expended by three students at Southwest Minnesota State University who transcribed many a long article from fuzzy photocopies and bleary microfilm: Jody Grismer, Lisa Peterson, and Jenna Greenwood. I also appreciate the photographic processing assistance provided by Janet Timmerman and Hannah Waack. All of my colleagues at the Center for Rural and Regional Studies at Southwest Minnesota State University were supportive and encouraging as this project meandered forward.

My colleagues at the University of Saskatchewan's History Department have also been interested proponents of this book. In particular I owe a deep debt of appreciation to Merle Massie, whose expert editorial knife whittled the manuscript to manageable size and got it moving toward completion. Gina Trapp helped with the proofreading. I also appreciate the useful suggestions of two anonymous reviewers, of editors Judith Keeling and Karen Medlin at Texas Tech University Press, and of copyeditor Noel Parsons, all of whom improved the final product considerably. Finally, I thank my family: my wife, Victoria; children, Patrick and Claire; and parents, Barry and Patricia, for their steady support of my work.

GC

Plainsword

By the time your kids are half-grown, they are likely to call your childhood the olden days. I recall my daughter looking up from reading *Anne of Green Gables* and asking me if I remembered what it was like back then. Not quite, I said, and I told her about hurrying home from swimming lessons to listen with my parents to "People Are Funny" on the radio. I told her about squeezing colored ooze from a packet into pale margarine to turn it yellow. Not long after, we visited my grandmother in Wichita Falls and taped her telling us about carrying hot potatoes in her coat pockets when she walked to school on frigid Oklahoma mornings. When she died, her meager collection of old photographs came to me, with her social security cards, one for each marriage.

A couple of years ago here in Missoula, Montana, archivists

in a federal program came through town and issued an invitation to old-timers to tape five-minute memories. I wondered how the takers would choose what to tell. I wondered if immigrants—a lot of Hmong have settled here—would think their memories counted.

We are, all of us, witnesses to our lives. Some events are too big to forget, some too terrible to remember. Most memories are fragmentary, filed away too long to be clear and accurate. Our past wavers like laundry on the line in a breeze; there is hardly room for it in the busyness of daily life. But, think of the past or not, it accrues in our becoming. And, if we set aside our bias that the ordinary doesn't matter, if we take the time to reflect and, better yet, share our memories, we recognize that all along we have been keepers of our past.

No wonder we like to read memoirs and letters, journals and diaries. No wonder we are grateful to people whose urge to remember and to understand made them carve out time to record. We went to school and learned about the big picture we call history; it is a different experience to hear what people on the ground have to say. For all the heroes and villains, the battles and triumphs, life is quotidian. History

is created as each calendar page is turned. When we can look back and learn what those old days were really like for someone, we tap the vast reservoir of common living, our humanity. We leave the thrill of celebrity and commercial entertainment for a while to appreciate the courage and persistence and plain pleasures of individuals and communities. Thank goodness someone saves the scraps that make up our history. Thank goodness someone cares.

As a Farm Woman Thinks exists because the Southwest Collection of Texas Tech University archives thousands of documents and other artifacts about Southwestern life, because regional historical museums collect and keep safe photographs and papers that might have been destroyed and forgotten, and because Geoff Cunfer appreciated the importance of Nellie Witt Spikes's writings and did the work of organizing them for contemporary readers. From the early 1930s to the close of the 1950s Spikes wrote columns for her local newspaper and other newspapers of the region, recording her observations of daily life as well as her astonishingly detailed accounts of pioneer life as far back as the late nineteenth century. The columns comprise a vibrant history told from a unique perspective—that of a woman who lived, worked, and thrived in West Texas while it was changing from million-acre ranches to small ones, to dryland farms, into the prosperity brought by irrigation.

Consider the child, Nellie Witt, four years old, climbing up onto the wagon seat as her extended family set out from Parker County in north central Texas in 1892. The family lore was mostly Southern. Among the family artifacts was Confederate money, emblematic of the men's experiences in the Civil War. Two hundred fifty miles and twenty days later they arrived in Crosby County on the edge of the Llano Estacado— the frontier. Most of the rest of her life would be spent laboring on a farm, often in harsh circumstances. It would be a long time before carts and buggies and horses made way for cars, a long time before electricity, phones, and indoor plumbing arrived to ease her burdens. Her husband did not stop farming until he was eighty-two years old; that was when the couple moved to town.

Nellie Witt Spikes's memories and observations of almost seventy years of life on the plains are remarkable for their specificity, liveliness, affection, and pride. She loved her kin, her neighbors, the fruits of their work, and she loved the land. Nothing was too small, too particular, for her to remark upon. Her columns are a treasure trove of West Texas language and habits, a veritable natural history of the area's vegetation and climate, and an exhaustive rendering of farm life on the plains in good and bad times, wartime, old and modern days. She is so exuberant, so confiding, I can only think of her as Nellie.

Were some times hard? You bet. She gives you sandstorms and blue northers you'll hope you never meet. She sees fields flooded and crops drooping in drought. She recounts an endless litany of chores: feeding and milking and killing and rendering animals; making clothes and quilts; raising, cooking, and canning food, and so on. She was proud of her work and her life, and she had the optimist's gene: she always looked on the bright side. When old-timers died, she missed and mourned them, but she celebrated their lives and thought of them as heaven bound. When storms turned skies black and laundry froze on the line, her heart lifted at the first ray of sunlight.

The topics of the columns, and there are hundreds, are often familiar: the old one-room schoolhouse, the weather and the work, the fun of dances and parties and Christmas festivities. Yet they are so particularized by Nellie's spot-on descriptive skills, every column is fresh. She writes about the little memories that make her life so vivid. There was the time she made her own dress form from gummed brown paper and had to be cut out of it with a slice down the form's back. The time she thought she put too much soda in the cornbread and discovered she had used washing detergent. The time during the war, when there was no room for waste, and she spilled kerosene on a sack of flour and they ate it anyway. How her neighbors give her rhubarb and call it "pie-plant." Her father exclaiming "plague-take-it!" when the stovepipes stuck.

Nellie lived a life of the senses. She observes colors and shapes of fruits, flowers, trees, and skies. Her little farmhouse, she says, looked like yellow cheese on the prairie. She smells the air and the aroma of food and flowers. She basks in spring sunshine and feels her toes in cool mud. In the summer she treads Blanco Canyon, gathering wild plums for jelly. She was a woman who woke up and embraced each day, took her duties in stride, and sought joy in nature, friendship, family, and her sense of belonging to her world. She had the gift of good health.

I had a neighbor for twenty-odd years, transplanted from Oklahoma to Oregon, who had written down every significant purchase of her married life. (Think washing machines, cars, toasters, winter coats, storm windows, carpets.) She had boxes of steno pads in which the purchases were itemized. When I asked her why she did it, she said when she looked at an entry, she could remember the day and a host of memories, and besides, she took pride in her thrift.

Similarly, Nellie looks at her father's ledgers from his general store and from the briefest notes conjures up the purchaser and often the occasion. Though she was a woman who as a farmer lived in relative isolation most of her life, she felt connected to people near and far, alive and gone. She felt grounded in geography and climate and history. So when she sat down in her kitchen to write, she was the reader's friend and the region's scribe.

Nellie had a poet's soul. She loved flights of language, sought the full-hearted phrase, strived for lyricism. The contemporary reader may sometimes find her a bit fanciful, but her fancy brings home time and place and the swelling of her heart. She must have been a generous friend, grateful for company, glad to do her share to prepare for gatherings, gentle with young and old. Though she led a white woman's life, she expresses, a bit sentimentally, her appreciation for the Mexicans who were to her kind, beautiful, exotic, and hardworking. She mentions black men who worked for her family whom she regarded with respect and affection. I can only think that if she saw injustice she would have said so; my guess is she wasn't looking. She liked to see the best in things. She loved the land and remembered how it used to be before the playas were drained and the grasses turned over, but she was proud of what settlers accomplished, and she took change in stride.

We must remember these columns were all written before the 1960s and all that that decade broke open in our society. Nellie's life was an old way, not just of living, but of seeing. In her kindness, though, I read no condescension. In her pride I read no arrogance. Perhaps her optimism and enthusiasm really did make her see the best in people; maybe she had the best of acquaintances. She did not look far beyond her familiar life for diversion or concern. She was truly rural, and this volume honors her for probing, understanding, and sharing that perspective.

I hope curious children will have a chance to learn about the old days from her. I hope adult readers will enter the spirit of her writing (generous, celebratory, honorable) and enjoy the amazing range of experience she conveys. I hope if there is a heaven, she is enjoying flowering mesquite and wild plums.

Sandra Scofield
Missoula, Montana

As a Farm Woman Thinks

Introduction

Nellie Witt was four years old—exactly—the day her family left their home in north central Texas to move to the frontier on the edge of the Llano Estacado. It was on her birthday, May 4, 1892, that her parents made their final rounds, turned the cattle out of the corral, said goodbye to a handful of friends and neighbors gathered to see them off, and stopped at the family graveyard (where their firstborn, Nellie's older sister, had been buried at age two). The wagons were already packed, full of dry corn to feed the animals and cured bacon and ham to feed themselves. The ox-drawn prairie schooners also carried the family's most valued possessions: a well-worn Bible, tintype photographs, locks of children's hair, Confederate Army memorabilia, seed packets carefully wrapped from the garden, and, treasure of treasures, a marble-topped bureau.

In the party were Nellie's parents, John M. Witt and Margaret Jones Witt, plus her one-year-old brother, Lowell. Her grandparents, Mr. and Mrs. George D. Jones, led the procession, and their nearly grown children, Nellie's aunts and uncles, filled out the group. It was a multi-family, multigenerational migration. The 250-mile journey over a rutted road took twenty days. At night the family camped alongside the trail or at nearby creeks. Oxen pulled the wagons, and the family had a few horses, but their main concern was a small herd of cattle trailing along behind.

First, one of the cows lost the bell around her neck, causing some dismay. Then the party nearly fell victim to a scam designed by ranchers to relieve migrants of their cattle at rock-bottom prices. As they moved west through heavy and uncomfortable rains—on one occasion Grandmother Jones exclaimed she would go mad if it did not stop raining—they heard from oncoming travelers of a "quarantine line" beyond which cattle were not allowed to pass. The quarantine was designed to prevent livestock infested with ticks, carriers of Texas fever, from entering West Texas. As Nellie's mother made dinner in camp one night, a group of men rode in to enforce the quarantine. They asserted the cattle could not continue any farther west but offered to buy the small herd at a very low price. George Jones, anticipating a confrontation, had his guns visible and invited the men to sit down—"and gentlemen, when I say set, I mean set," he instructed them. He let them know that he knew most of the ranchers in the area and knew there was no such quarantine law on the books, and that unless they presented legal documents demonstrating their authority, they should leave. The men left and did not return, and the family took its dozen cows on to West Texas.

After three weeks on the trail the Caprock Escarpment loomed on the western horizon, growing slowly as they approached. The oxen dragged the wagons up the three-hundred-foot hills leading to the high plains of the Llano Estacado, and they emerged in a wonderland: a vast prairie, flat as a bedspread, green grass waving in the wind, spotted with small blue lakes brimming with water and populated by an abundance of birds and wild game. The summer sky was a brilliant blue and immense over the minimalist landscape. Decades later, writing about their arrival that day, both Nellie and

Nellie Witt Spikes's world: the Llano Estacado. The southern lobe of the Ogallala Formation, shown here in gray, outlines the Llano Estacado—the high, flat tableland of the southern plains. Spikes's birthplace in Weatherford, Parker County, seems far to the east in her reminiscences. Today it is an easy four-hour drive across the rolling prairie. Map data from ESRI Data & Maps v. 9.3 (2008), drawn by Geoff Cunfer.

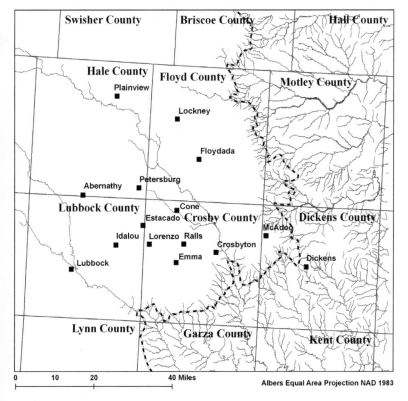

Crosby County, Texas, and environs. The heavy dashed line marks the Llano Estacado's caprock escarpment, with well-drained eroded plains to the east and flat, virtually undrained grasslands to the west. Map data from ESRI Data & Maps v. 9.3 (2008), drawn by Geoff Cunfer.

The John Witt house after it was moved to the south part of Emma, Texas, in 1902. *Left to right:* Lois Witt, Jeff Spikes, Joe Witt, John Witt in door, Edna Witt, Margaret Witt, Eli Jones with fiddle, baby Jim Witt in buggy, Lowell Witt, George Jones with Guy Witt in front, Nellie Witt. Photo courtesy of Southwest Collection, Texas Tech University, Lubbock, SWCPC 291 E1 #4.

her uncle, Frank Jones, commented on the impression made by their first view of the high plains. They felt they had reached the promised land.

It was only the latest in a series of promised lands that had led the Jones and Witt families ever westward through more than a century. The Joneses had come from Virginia, as far back as anyone could remember, moving to Murfreesboro, Tennessee, early in the nineteenth century, then to Texas in 1852. Nellie's great-grandparents made that move with their six sons and six daughters. All six of those young men, including George Jones, served in the Confederate Army and survived the Civil War to return to Texas, where they took up cattle ranching together. The family had been in Parker County, Texas, for several decades when George and his wife, plus several married children and their families, decided to move west to Crosby County.

John Witt, Nellie's father, had

been born in Missouri and had moved to Bell County with his family at age fifteen and then to Parker County, where he married Margaret Jones. John and Margaret Witt would live in Crosby County for a dozen years before moving west again, first to Hereford in the Texas Panhandle in 1905, then to a homestead near Portales, New Mexico, in 1907. Millions of American families followed a similar course during the nineteenth century, drifting generally westward from frontier to frontier and farm to farm as better opportunities beckoned.

Illustrative of American mobility in the late nineteenth century is the family's trajectory once they arrived on the Llano Estacado. Several of them turned around and went straight back to Parker County. Among these were Nellie and her younger brother, who traveled back with their mother to their old home place, where they lived for another two years before moving to Crosby County permanently. Nellie's father, John Witt, stayed in Crosby County, where he began making a new home for the family. After three weeks her uncle, nineteen-year-old Frank Jones, was already homesick for his young wife and their baby boy, left behind in Parker County. He

proceeded to the nearest railroad station and took the train home, covering in several hours the distance that had just taken twenty days by ox-drawn wagon. He stayed with his wife, Ella, and son, Roy, through the summer and fall, then they all moved to Crosby County in October 1892, traveling halfway by train, then overland for the last 150 miles. In 1894 Nellie's mother, who had since given birth to a third child, moved the family to Crosby County and set up house with her husband and three young children. They lived in Emma, where they opened and ran the Witt Hotel, providing room and board to visitors, especially those coming to town for business at the county courthouse. Later, John Witt purchased a share in a general store in Emma. It was there that Nellie grew up and went to school.

Emma was a town created almost entirely by newly arrived settlers from Parker County. When the Witts and Joneses arrived in the area they did not land among strangers. As is typical with migrants, they moved to where others from home were moving. In the course of only a few years several hundred people moved from Parker County to sparsely settled Crosby County, where they quickly became the politically dominant force. There had been a handful of ranchers and their cowboys in the area in the 1870s, then a group of Quakers from several eastern states created the town of Estacado in 1879. By 1886, when Crosby County was organized, Estacado had over one hundred people, eventually growing to nearly five hundred. The Quakers outvoted the cowmen and made Estacado the county seat for a dozen years before the migration from Parker County in the early 1890s displaced it. The Parker County immigrants created Emma and promptly outvoted the Quakers to move the county seat there. They also elected the first sheriff in the county, Felix Franklin, a distant relative of the Joneses. Nellie grew up in Emma in its heyday, when the town boasted several hundred residents and was booming.

The Parker County migration brought a strong Southern culture to West Texas. These were people who remembered the Civil War. Many of the older generation had fought in it—both of Nellie Witt's grandfathers were Confederate veterans—and some had been slaveowners in the East Texas cotton country and elsewhere. Most of the new arrivals were Baptists or Methodists, mirroring predominant Southern religious af-

filiations, and they voted for Democrats as did the rest of the "Solid South." They brought a culture to West Texas that was in contrast to the two they found when they arrived: the austere, pacifist, Republican, and strongly antislavery Quakers and the free-wheeling cattlemen and cowboys. It helps to understand the subsequent cultural development of West Texas when one realizes that the earliest settlers were more likely to identify themselves as Southern rather than Western. That cultural legacy sets West Texas apart from its nearby neighbors, Hispanic New Mexico and Kansas, which was settled mainly by northerners and veterans of the Union Army.

When those newcomers arrived they found a place that was very different from their recent home. Most impressive, it was wide open. The high plains seemed unbounded, virtually flat to the horizon in all directions. Here the sky was immense, the landscape of only minor consequence. When Nellie's uncle Frank Jones first arrived, he set out for a mirage, bucket in hand, thinking it a nearby lake where he could collect water. He never reached it, then shot his gun at wild game impossibly distant, thinking the animals were well within range, all

Felix Franklin, first sheriff of Crosby County, 1888. Photograph courtesy of Crosby County Pioneer Memorial Museum, Crosbyton, Texas, °434.

to the amusement of more seasoned plains people. They did not understand the geology of their new home, but the immigrants had driven their oxen up onto an ancient formation. The Llano Estacado is the flattest part of the very flat Great Plains. It is the remnant of a broad plateau that once sloped gently away from the Rocky Mountains all the way to the Mississippi River. Over millions of years the elements etched away at this surface from the west, south, and east, slowly eroding hundreds of feet of soil and rock. Natural erosion continues as the escarpment face moves inward toward the center at the rate of an inch or two a year. The Llano Estacado is a giant, flat island surrounded by a wash of eroded, hilly plains one hundred to five hundred feet below. The junction between eroded plains and high plains is stark: a high, jagged, red and green canyoned wall. That was the escarpment that the weary Jones and Witt oxen climbed at the end of their journey.

The caprock surface is so flat, and rainfall so scarce, that no river or stream flows regularly across the Llano Estacado. When occasional heavy rains overwhelm a locality, the water accumulates in one of the thousands of shallow playa lakes that dot the countryside or flows off rapidly through draws, depressions that lead into canyons along the edge. The water in the playa lakes stays there until heat and evaporation return it to the air or it seeps into the ground, while runoff water in the draws and canyons forms the headwaters of several Texas rivers, including the Brazos and the Colorado.

Crosby County straddles the intersection of high plains and eroded plains, with most of the county up on the high, flat tableland. The Caprock Escarpment slices through the southeastern corner of the county, and the area below the escarpment remains relatively rugged ranch country, interspersed with an occasional field of dryland crops. Besides the exposed landscape, the climate in Crosby County was also quite different from that of their former home, even though it was only 250 miles farther west.

Parker County was wetter, known for its cotton, corn, cattle, and hogs. The Llano Estacado is a dry land— averaging only eighteen inches of rain per year—where even drought-hardy wheat and sorghum crops often struggled to survive. In later years Nellie commented about the load of corn and cured pork the family brought west for feed and food: "Little did the folks in the wagons know that the corn and the good hog meat would not be known for many years in the west." Covered by hundreds of miles of shortgrass prairie, the plains were best suited to cattle ranching, according to accepted wisdom of the times. Settlers ridiculed the occasional farmer who tried to grow cotton there in the late nineteenth century. The Parker County migrants moved to the plains to be small ranchers, not small farmers. That was one reason bringing their dozen cattle across the "quarantine line" was so important to the Jones and Witt families in 1892—those animals were the beginnings of the herd that they expected would form their primary economic activity, equivalent to the garden seeds carefully wrapped in paper packets inside the wagons.

Not until the early years of the twentieth century did people on the

Witt and Spikes General Merchandise, Emma, Texas, 1895–1905. *Left to right:* Ollie, Eddy, Dink, Logan, Cotton, Bedingfield, Hank C. Smith (seated in chair), A. J. Botts, Leatherwood. Photograph courtesy of Southwest Collection, Texas Tech University, Lubbock, SWCPC 291 E9.

Llano Estacado begin trying seriously to grow crops as their main livelihood. Between 1905 and 1920 the largest ranches in the region made a calculated decision that they could earn more money by selling their land in small parcels to newly arrived farmers than by raising cattle on extensive ranges. As immigrants poured in by the thousands and as railroad lines extended to haul produce to distant cities, ranches sold small plots of land on a rising real estate market.

Nellie participated in that transition from open range to fenced farmland. Soon after her father opened his general store in Emma in 1895, he took on a partner, Joseph Jefferson (Jeff) Spikes, and renamed the place Witt and Spikes General Merchandise. Although a generation older, Jeff fell in love with his partner's young daughter, Nellie, and, according to her account, waited for her to grow up. In 1905, when Nellie was seventeen, her parents took

Nellie Witt Spikes with her book *Through the Years: A History of Crosby County, Texas*, ca. 1952. Photograph courtesy of Ralls Historical Museum, Ralls, Texas.

advantage of the booming real estate market in Emma and sold their general store. They moved to Hereford, Texas, about ninety miles to the northwest in the Texas Panhandle. The family lived there for just over a year before moving west again, to a homestead near Portales, New Mexico. While in Hereford, Nellie enrolled in business courses at Panhandle Christian College, but she studied for only a few months. On December 27, 1906, she married Jeff Spikes at Hereford. She was eigh-

teen; he, thirty-nine. Despite their difference in age they had a long life together and had been married fifty-six years when he died in 1964 at age ninety-six.

A few days after their marriage Nellie and Jeff moved back to Crosby County, even as her parents and younger siblings made plans to migrate to New Mexico. They joined Jeff's family near the community of Cone on a farm that straddled the boundary between Crosby and Floyd Counties. Nellie moved into a house that Jeff had built for her, so new it still smelled like fresh-sawn lumber. Together they raised a family and made a life on that farm for forty-three years. Having arrived in the early 1890s as part of the transition from large, sparsely settled corporate ranches to thousands of small nester ranch families, Nellie and her husband then participated in the next major social, economic, and environmental transition in the region, the advent of small family crop farms.

In fact, Nellie Witt Spikes lived through half a dozen major transitions in the lives of West Texas residents. She observed major changes, not only on the Llano Estacado and the southern plains, but in American rural life generally. Between 1890 and 1960 West Texas shifted from large ranching to small ranching and then to dryland crop farming. It suffered the drought, dust storms, and depression of the 1930s and then the irrigation revolution of the 1940s and 1950s that brought true prosperity to regional farmers for the first time. Nellie also experienced the remarkable changes in everyday rural life that characterized the twentieth century throughout the nation. Farm families shifted from horse power to tractor power and replaced buggies and wagons

with automobiles. Farm homes acquired indoor plumbing, electricity, and phone service. Farm wives produced less and less of their families' subsistence needs—milk, eggs, meat, canned garden produce, and so on—at home and began buying food from grocery stores. Nellie recalled, "The first time I ever bought lard, I apologized to the merchant. A farmer was not much, who could not raise his own meat and lard." It was a poignant reflection on changing expectations. In dozens of ways the modernization of rural homes changed daily life for people. Nellie Witt Spikes lived through—and wrote about—all of these dramatic changes. Her newspaper columns offer a secret spy-hole into the past, one that reveals a place and a time that no longer exist.

Nellie and Jeff had three children: Lowell, born in 1908, and Wilma and Wilda, twins born in 1910. It wasn't until after her children were grown, in the mid-1930s, that Nellie embarked on her writing career. She penned weekly articles about rural life and the history of her beloved plains and canyon country, writing them between chores on the farm, rushing to meet the deadline when the mail carrier would arrive to collect her article for delivery to the newspaper office in town. She sent occasional articles to small local newspapers beginning about 1934, then began writing weekly under the title "As a Farm Woman Thinks" in 1937, when she was forty-nine years old. The articles appeared in four weekly newspapers: the *Ralls Banner,* the *Lorenzo Tribune,* the *Floyd County Hesperian,* and the *Crosbyton Review.* She wrote columns for more than twenty years until 1960. Her column also appeared in *Crop and Stock* magazine, published in Lubbock, and on one occasion she wrote a series of articles for the *Fort Worth Star Telegram.* In the early 1950s Nellie, along with her sister-in-law, Temple Ann Ellis, wrote and self-published *Through the Years: A History of Crosby County, Texas.* Completed in 1952, it is typical of county histories created across North America and includes biographies of prominent county families and individuals, numerous black-and-white photographs, and stories focusing on the region's pioneer past. The women fronted four thousand dollars for the publication and sold it themselves to local residents.

The two decades of newspaper columns authored by Nellie Witt Spikes create a detailed, lyrical, and engaging portrait of rural life in early-twentieth-century Texas. In them we meet friends, neighbors, and family and learn about the great adventures and mundane routines of life on a frontier as it quickly developed into a modern agricultural society. The columns are especially evocative. Reading them, we find ourselves sitting next to Nellie on a friend's porch, strolling down a dusty small-town Main Street, or trudging behind a rattling covered wagon across endless rolling prairie. The present volume revives Spikes's writing from a file of old newspaper clippings buried for half a century in the archives. It brings her historical knowledge, love of the plains, and literary flair to a broad audience for the first time.

This book is by no means comprehensive. Collected here are only a small selection of Spikes's best columns. The Southwest Collection at Texas Tech University in Lubbock holds scores of clippings of the columns, plus microfilm editions of the local newspapers that ran them. I read as many as I could find and identified several hundred for serious consideration. I looked especially for columns with evocative writing about topics of special interest, topics that eventually coalesced into the thematic chapters presented here.

The original newspaper columns skip quickly through multiple topics. In any given week Spikes might include a favorite poem, a memory of Old Emma, a description of a visit to a dear friend, and commentary about recent activities at her own farm. I faced an editorial choice: to reproduce the full columns as originally composed or to break them up into thematically unified pieces. Ultimately, I chose the latter. Only in that way could I bring coherence to the wide range of topics she addressed and focus on the best examples of her writing. Ellipses in the text indicate where I have removed text from the original. I also engaged in wholesale copyediting. Even the most professional big-town newspapers are full of typographical errors, and small-town papers often ran with skeleton staffs. The original newspaper clippings were replete with skipped and jumbled words, misordered lines, and a profusion of spelling, punctuation, and grammatical errors. Rather than clutter the text with brackets, parentheses, and a blizzard of *sic* notations, I simply cleaned up the text as I went. Likewise, the paragraph breaks in the present text do not follow the random indentations of the original newspapers. I was careful not to remove colloquialisms, dialect, and any nonstandard usage that appeared intentional.

Though Spikes occasionally uses terms or phrases that today are instantly offensive, there is no evidence in her text that she intends them as pejorative or insult, rather that without any serious consideration she has simply used words that have slipped into the colloquial. These I have left alone, not only to be faithful to her text, as any historian should be, but also to reflect the West Texas culture of the day. That, I feel, is my obligation.

The book is arranged topically first, then chronologically, with the aim of evoking the complex mix and sweep of life in one place and at a particular time. Within chapters columns appear in chronological order, and chapter arrangement was meant to be roughly chronological as well. Thus, the chapter "Settling the Llano Estacado" comes early, "Drought and Dust Storms" later, and "The Modernization of Farm Life" near the end. But interspersed among these more time-specific chapters are others that span the years, such as Nellie's writings about "Small Town Life," "Women's Work," and "Natural History of the Llano Estacado." Two short chapters round out the list: "Portraits" includes descriptions and life histories of some of the more memorable characters from Crosby County's past, while "A

Poetry of Place" collects short and long items in which Spikes drifted into poetic prose.

Nellie Witt Spikes's 1892 covered wagon journey to the Llano Estacado was the defining event in her life. That experience imbued her with a sense that she lived in the midst of a great historical story and needed to record and celebrate it. An awareness of momentous events carried out by regular people continued through the remainder of her life as she saw the plains and the nation changing quickly. Her articles provide the modern reader with a window into life in a place and a time that has passed, but that established the cultural foundation of the modern southern plains.

Settling the Llano Estacado

The origin of the name Llano Estacado, Spanish for "Staked Plains," is uncertain. Some say that conquistador Francisco Coronado was so lost on the vast, flat plain in 1541 that he instructed his men to drive stakes into the ground to mark their route, easing their way back to New Mexico. Others say that the name refers to the ubiquitous yucca plants, which push up a tall flower stalk, or "stake," every year. Or perhaps the Caprock Escarpment resembled a staked palisade. Whatever the source of the name, it reminds us that there was already a long and rich cultural tradition on the southern plains when Anglo-Americans began arriving there after the Civil War. These new settlers knew little about the thousands of years of Indian cultures that had succeeded one another on this land or about the several centuries of Spanish-speaking Mexicans and New Mexicans who were

long familiar with this place. To Nellie Witt, her family, and the hundreds of newcomers streaming into
the region in the 1880s and 1890s
this was virgin land, an enormous
blank slate on which they could, and
would, inscribe their own way of life.

Nellie arrived with the first generation of American pioneers, and
those "old settlers" were a favorite
subject of her weekly newspaper
articles. In many columns she described her own family's epic migration story and that of others through
firsthand and secondhand accounts.
She knew many of the pioneers
personally, visited with them, asked
pointed questions, and described
the process of making a new home
on the Llano Estacado. Throughout
the selections below, her stories
combine a precision of detail with
considerable pride in the place—the
homes, the ranches, the farms, the
towns—that these men and women
created from the ground up.

April 13, 1934

House cleaning days had come
again and I was in the attic at work.
I picked up an old daybook to dust
it. Idly I began to turn the pages.
Memories came floating in. Gone
were the days of depression, motor
car, airplanes and picture shows. I
was a little girl again in a little town

named Emma. Perhaps you would
like to go back with me to those
faraway early days at Emma and read
this history with me.

I began wondering, why was the
town located where it was and why
was it started? My questions were
answered like this: Estacado, the
town built by the Quakers, was the
first county seat. Ab Benedict filed
on a section of land near the center
of the county and laid off a townsite.
He gave everyone, both cowboys
and settlers, a deed to ten town lots,
and got Stringfellow and Hume to
move their store to Emma. Gleaton
Produce Co. at Ralls is located in
this old building, and if old houses
could talk, it could tell us of dances
in it at Emma when the counters
were pushed back, the proprietors
gone home, and the crowd stayed till
morning. Judge J. N. Murray, who
was printing the *Crosby County News*,
moved from Estacado to Emma and
built the first home there. A school
building of two rooms was built and
served the town for both school and
church house until about 1905. R. N.
Martin put in a store, Arch Paschall
started the saloon and Mrs. Kate
Jones the hotel.

In the fall of 1891 the county seat
was voted to be moved to Emma, as
it was nearer the center of the county. Mr. Cousineau, who lived in the
brakes south of Emma, contracted

to move the courthouse. It was torn down, the lumber moved and put up in its original form. A rock jail was then built. As there was a post office in Texas named Crosby, Tiny Hume, one of the town's promoters, suggested the name of Emma in honor of his sweetheart. Levi Jones, son of the hotel proprietor, a young man of twenty-one, looked around and said, "Boys, we need a graveyard. We will have to ship in an old 'codger' and let him die to start one." But alas! Levi started to take his gun off a load of mesquite wood, which he had hauled from the brakes; the gun was accidentally discharged and Levi started the graveyard. J. W. Holt gave two acres of land for it.

Ben Norwood put in a general merchandise store on the north side. Mr. Dry bought him out. My father, J. M. Witt, bought in with Mr. Dry. The store became laughingly known as "Wet and Dry." At the time my memories of Emma begin, Jeff and John Spikes became partners with Witt. Dry moved to New Mexico. Nearly all business was done by credit. A man had things charged till he sold some cattle or hauled a load of freight to pay off. The nearest railroad towns were Amarillo, 125 miles to the north, and Colorado City, the same distance to the south. Our banking business was done at Amarillo, cattle herds driven

there to ship, and freight hauled from there. J. K. Millwee wrote the bank for a check book. Not getting it, he wrote a check on a shingle. Needless to say, when the bank got it, they sent him a check book.

April 20, 1934

Now it may be somewhat of a surprise to the ones who get their idea of a cowboy from the Wild West thrillers and picture shows that always feature the cowboy dressed in chaps, with two guns, drinking and shooting up towns, to read of one, Brooks Terrell, buying collar buttons; another, Walter Blue, ties and fancy half-hose, as they were called; and another, Jeff Spikes, a toothbrush.

Tues. 8-30-1898. Miss Lou Elkin in town buying eight yards calico, hair pins and braid. Once when the rainmaker had forgotten us and the grass was the color of Uncle Marion Reed's good sourdough biscuits, Miss Lou said she was going to buy her horse, Dandy, some green goggles so he would think he was eating green grass. How we all loved Miss Lou, later Mrs. O. B. Kelly, and how we miss her! A new baby in the Jones family. Frank Jones to 10 yards cotton flannel, 5 yards outing, 5 yards lawn and safety pins. . . . Mosquitoes must have been bad as

Stringfellow and Hume, Emma, Texas, ca. 1900. Photograph courtesy of
Crosby County Pioneer Memorial Museum, Crosbyton, Texas, 0293.

I read that Clabe Simpson is buying pennyroyal. E. Luce in town from near Tap. My! He bought six boxes of pills, $2.50. Here must be a party. Lee Noble 1 pint bay rum. Wax, 5c. Jim Kidd, four cigars. . . . I do not see much profit in the following, but anyway the poultry business was good. S. M. Walker, by 1/2 dozen hens, $1.20. . . .

Rev. Paul Bentley from Canyon City on his circuit as Methodist pastor. He was a large man with a booming voice and always sang "When The Roll Is Called Up Yonder I'll Be There." I could just feel the world coming to an end and could hear the roll being called. Yes, Bro. Bentley has answered roll call, and I am sure he answered, "Present." Oh, yes! Methodist circuit riders, Baptist ministers and preachers of other faiths. Was it not largely to your influence that the saloon only stayed about two years?

Summer of 1899. Tom Franklin in town after supplies. 50 lbs. meal, $2.25; 50 lbs. flour, $1.50; 7 lbs.

beans, 45c; 10 lbs. lard, $1.00; 5 gals. coal oil, $1.75; 16 lbs. sugar, $1.15; 17 lbs. bacon, $1.70. I can see his old white-top buggy with Red and Property tied on the west side of the courtyard fence. How I recall the big pots of mush cooked for his wolf dogs, for he hunted wolves in the big ranch pastures. The picture in Mr. Hargrave's window is the picture of one he raised. H. B. Murray to 1 collar, 10c. I wonder if that were not the one Hal had on the time the boys were shooting fireworks and Hal's collar, being celluloid, was set afire. . . . I can see the old drummer (no traveling salesman then), Mr. Villipeg, showing his harness and what was new in sidesaddles.

Oh, how fast my tears fall and the lonely feeling in my heart as I see names of my girlhood friends in the handwriting of my dear father and realize that they are gone. Their names have grown dim on the yellow pages, but I hope someday to read their names in God's daybook, and the things they will be credited with will read: loyalty, faith, generosity, love and courage.

B. W. Mitchell, crackers and 1 can sausage. Sept. 1899. St. Louis Cattle Co., 3 gallons lick $1.75. Crosby $5.00 per Billy Weatherby. We know that Uncle Billy had plowed the courtyard with Ole Deck. How we all wanted to know the history of Uncle Billy, but the only information he gave to his closest friends was that he was born in Maine, soldiered in the Civil War for the North, lived in New Mexico, married a Mexican woman, who was, he thought, a "dang good woman." But when he wanted to come to West Texas, she would not, so he came on.

People were trusted then. Witt and Spikes let people who were passing thru the country sleep in the store on bad nights, and read this: Bill, the jail bird (as it is on the pages) to tobacco, and John, the jail boy, to morphine, laudanum, 1 bottle pills. Not only one entry, but all thru the year. They were in jail. . . . Horses cheap: Elijah James, by 1 horse, $12.50, by 1 bike, $10.00.

Christmas of 1899. The big cedar in the courtroom made gay with its loads of presents. Bright silk hand- kerchiefs on every limb. Dolls, toy pistols, vases (every girl must have gotten at least one pair), autograph albums, picture albums, mustache cups with "To Father" on them. Here are some things bought: Condie Carmack to 1/2 dozen work boxes; John Wheeler, 1 writing desk. Do you still have it, Leta? Money for fireworks. R. H. Blue, fireworks, $3.00; Will Simpson, fireworks, $1.50. John Wheeler, to cologne, 10c.

Historians build their narratives of the past from primary documents, written accounts that date to the time of interest. In these early columns Spikes consulted a primary document—the daily account book from her father's turn-of-the-century dry goods store in Emma, Texas—then embellished it with personal memories of the people mentioned there. Items the store purchased appear with the annotation "by," and items it sold show "to." Thus, the notation "1-19-01—J. A. Noble by 8 1/2 dozen eggs to gloves for Carl" means that on January 19, 1901, J. A. Noble sold the store 102 chicken eggs and purchased a pair of gloves.

April 27, 1934

Emma had a good nine-months school every year. Instead of getting diplomas, we took state examinations for teacher's certificates. Mr. Woody was principal in 1900–1901. Boys on one side of school room; girls on the other, with long recitation benches in front. I sat near a window. How many times I saw the C. O. Thomas and A. Kidd children coming in their two-wheeled carts. From nine miles west Jones children came in an old buggy. Poor old Nubbin and other school horses! The Detwiler girls came six miles, the Smyer children seven, and the Bedingfields six. The long, cold drives in open-top buggies! Here comes Paul Poulson riding in a slow jogtrot on his blind mare. His stirrups were too short and his legs too long. Milton Burleson on his black pony. Nothing could daunt these children of early settlers in their efforts to learn. The Witt boys from six miles west in their old rattle-trap.

Do you remember the bucket of water in the corner and how the boys would get permission to pass the water in time of "books." You would pour some on your new shoes that were hurting your feet after their long summer vacation of being bare. Germs were unknown to us then and we all drank from the same dipper. Literary societies (how the boys hated them), spelling matches and school entertainments. How John Bedingfield could recite "Bingen on the Rhine" and Rena Murphy "Curfew Shall Not Ring Tonight." How we sang "God Be With Us Till We Meet Again" on the last day of school till no eyes were dry. . . .

5-12-1900—Condie Carmack to wax 10c, candy 10c, perfume 25c, gloves $1.25. I turn a few pages. Condie's name again, but this time—to lace 20c, 1 lb. starch 10c, 1 paper pins. From now on there are items of dry goods, but no more perfume and wax. . . . J. W. Boyle, attorney, to buggy and driver $2.50. Must have gone to Lubbock to court. George Mayes to 1 bottle hair vigor $1.00. Although the fight was begun early in life, we can see that Mr. Mayes lost. R. N. Martin to shoe blacking. The picture of Mr. Martin blacking his boots, getting ready to go to Sunday School and church is clear. How he rang the school bell calling the people to worship on Sundays and Wednesday nights. Few times he failed to be there as superintendent of Sunday School. Faithfulness will be written after his name.

Fall coming on. Lee Clark to 1 cane knife. Sorghum was then the main crop. Look here! H. C. Smith to 5 spittoons $1.00! We know by this that Uncle Hank had many, many people who made his home headquarters during dull work season. Christmas sales begin. Bob Smith to 1 handkerchief 85c. Must have been a silk one. Marsh Wheeler to 5 jew's harps 25c, 7 sticks wax 25c. Marsh must have organized a jew's harp band. 1-19-01—J. A. Noble by 8 1/2 dozen eggs (Aunt Lucy always sent something to sell) to gloves for

Carl. No light bread then. Freighters would buy some at Canyon City when they had to, but they called it "gun wadding." And no wonder; the crust so tough, the middle like a sponge.

H. S. Smyers to 5 gallons gasoline $1.60, 5 gallons coal oil $1.60. Hardy Witt, 1 pair boots $7.00. There was going to be a dance and Hardy wanted shoes. But Uncle Jim told him he could dance in boots and then he would have them for his new job on a ranch. . . . Fiddler Robertson to pneumonia medicine.

Can you see a little schoolhouse near Robertson with me as teacher? I asked the class which race of people we belonged to. Bryant Robertson snapped his fingers and waved his hand. "The human race," he almost shouted. Well, perhaps we do. Didn't we have a fine time playing town ball, the times we were not digging the ball out of a prairie dog's hole? LaBarque was the name of the school.

4-5. Big dance in the courtroom. Albert Burleson, Walter Angel, Lee Blanchard, Joe Lindsay and Fred Spikes buying candy, wax and perfume. Some of the fiddlers then were Chad Gott, Coke Fullingim, Bud English, C. A. Reagan and "Uncle Dink" Logan. How the music of Wagner's "Hell among the Dogies" and other popular music poured from the courthouse windows. "Swing your partners, do-si-do, promenade all." How much we used that old courthouse. Big meetings were held there. Were you in the courtroom that still, hot night when the wind struck during prayer, bringing the heavy shutters around, breaking the glass and sounding like the crack of doom? Picnics were held there. Speeches being made in the courtroom. Boys and girls going up and down stairs. Women sitting in the offices, talking and looking after children. Beeves being barbecued on the east side, broncs ridden and the tournament run. Lemonade with no ice, made with a few lemons and citric acid. No ice cream. No bananas, no carnival, merry-go-round or ferris wheel. And then the thrill when district court met. Pat Murphy calling, "Oh yez, Oh yez. The District Court is now in session." How grand the district officers looked.

J. J. Tipton 1 bottle colic cure. J. P. Long, D. C. Littlefield and Mr. Chapman from north part of county. J. N. Zumwalt by 5,770 pounds of freight $28.80—50c per 100. 5-29—four slickers sold. Boys getting ready to go up trail. Prairie hay good. Joe Brown to mower and rake $70.00. Emma with an elocution teacher. J. H. Babb to $8.00 to pay Miss

Dorsey for lessons for his children. . . . A. D. Meyer, the German, who wanted Mr. Witt "to send me for a gun." V. A. Leonard, Jim McNeil and Kinchen Carter buying groceries. Like shadow and sunshine, joy and sorrow follow each other through the pages. 7-16. C. A. Reagan, 120 feet of coffin lumber. I would watch the carpenters make the coffins in Father's store. Black plush for the grown people, white for the young. What a sad little company of people standing in the Emma graveyard singing the old songs and listening to the preacher saying "ashes to ashes."

May 4, 1934

3-13-1902—J. W. Carter to 1 yard cassimere, 1 yard outing, 5 coffin screws. Just three items, but they tell of a tiny baby's death. What high ideals of right and love of beauty did Mrs. Carter have and express.

Matt Davis, 1 puff comb. Seems funny now, but we tangled our hair or used "rats" to make it puff, and held it in place with a puff comb. What good times we had when we visited the Davis family. Mrs. J. H. Wheeler buying dry goods. Mrs. H. S. Smyer, 1/2 yard allover lace, 2 1/2 yards ribbon. "Aunt Dell" is a fine example of the friendliness and hospitality that has made the Plains noted. Mrs. A. Poulson, who made a real home in a dugout. Mrs. Detwiler and Mrs. Jim Witt who kept us cheered and laughing during hard times. Mrs. Kidd, who taught us music. Can't you just hear Mr. Kidd saying, "Now, Kate, play 'Old Zip Coon'"?

R. N. Martin, to lace. The scent of honeysuckle, Martha Washington and Seven Sisters roses comes to me. We carried water a while from Mr. Martin's. Many a time I went home with zinnias, or honeysuckle and roses. Dear Mrs. Martin. I hope you knew the joy you gave a little girl. The *Crosby County News*. What a pleasure to go to the Murray home. The printing press was in one room. The smell of printer's ink, the kindness of Mrs. Murray in answering our questions and showing us the type remains in my memory.

Mrs. Mertie Ishamel, to 1 dress pattern—not a paper pattern but ten yards of material. Aunt Mertie was

really a help in need. . . . Ruby Ellis, by 2 1/2 dozen eggs 25c. Mrs. Gillon still sells eggs, but I doubt if she gets the thrill she did when she sold her first ones. Mrs. Temple Ellis and mother, Mrs. J. W. Spikes, in town. Mrs. Ellis's father was known as "Cap'n" Spikes; he was buried in the Emma cemetery in the early days of Emma.

As the men were gone on the cattle drives two or three months and were hauling freight from Canyon City, salt from the salt flats or Colorado City, the women and children who lived in the country were alone a great deal. Neighbors far apart, the high winds in spring and howling blue northers in winter tried the spirits of these pioneer women. When the prairie fires swept over the plains, carried by a high wind, the snowstorms raged and wolves and coyotes howled and barked, these pioneer women taught their children courage.

The editor of the *Ralls Banner* commissioned several columns from Spikes in the spring of 1934, making use of her local knowledge. They ran in a six-part series about the history of Emma, Texas, but she apparently did not write again for the paper until three years later. Her first known column under the heading "As a Farm Woman Thinks" appeared in the *Floyd County Hesperian* on April 22, 1937.

It was an interesting choice of titles, borrowed in full from another pioneer farm girl who developed a literary career late in life.

Laura Ingalls Wilder, before she penned any of the *Little House* books, wrote a regular column for the *Missouri Ruralist* that was sometimes entitled "As a Farm Woman Thinks." The newspaper columns, appearing between 1911 and 1924, were her first public writing. At age forty-four, living on a farm in Missouri, Wilder responded to an editor's request and sent in a single column. She wrote sporadic columns for the paper for four years, then from 1915 to 1921 her articles appeared almost weekly under the heading "The Farm Home." From 1921 to 1924 Wilder penned weekly columns entitled "As a Farm Woman Thinks" before moving on to write for national literary magazines and then to author her famous series of children's books based on her own experience of pioneer life.

A little over a decade after Wilder's columns appeared, Spikes borrowed the title for her own column. The parallels in their lives are interesting. Though a generation apart in age, both women began writing in their forties, only after their children were grown and had moved away. Both wrote about contemporary farm life but gave disproportionate attention to topics of pioneer settlement. We don't know whether Spikes or one of her editors selected the title for her columns. She never mentioned reading Wilder's work. But it seems unlikely to be a coincidence, and it may be that Spikes saw Wilder as a model for her own, more modest, literary career.

October 28, 1937

Mr. and Mrs. Bob Smith from the Rock House were pleasant visitors in my home Sunday. How swiftly the time passed while we talked of the old, dear days when we were young and the west was new. Bob told an interesting bit of early-day history. Uncle Hank Smith kept supplies for the buffalo hunters. While he and Aunt Hank Smith were away on a visit, Uncle Charlie Hawes and a man named Jacobs kept the store. At four o'clock one afternoon nine outlaws came riding up, dismounted and entered the store and began asking questions. "Mister," they addressed Mr. Hawes, "Better lay that six shooter on the counter." Uncle Charlie pulled it off and handed it over. The man buckled the belt around his own waist. "That is a

Hank C. Smith, ca.
1895. Photograph
courtesy of Crosby
County Pioneer
Memorial Museum,
Crosbyton, Texas,
0303.

pretty fine pair of shop-made boots you have on old man, better hand them over also," and Uncle Charlie handed them over just as you or I would have done. The outlaws took what they wanted, then mounted the stairs to the rooms above, going through Aunt Hank's trunk, taking cherished pieces of jewelry and treasured relics. The outlaws carried off several horses. Two of the horses came back and the robbers returned for them. Uncle Charlie Hawes and Jacobs were in the upstairs rooms, buffalo guns ready to shoot. Mrs. Jacobs begged and pleaded "Don't shoot at them; they will come back and kill all of us," then went into hysterics. The robbers drove the horses away once more. State rangers followed the outlaws into New Mexico, and had a fight with them, but Aunt Hank never saw her jewelry again nor Uncle Charlie his good boots.

Charlie Hawes with horse, ca. 1900. Photograph courtesy of Crosby
County Pioneer Memorial Museum, Crosbyton, Texas, 0422.

When Spikes calls people "aunt" and "uncle," she doesn't mean that they were really her relatives. Paired with their first names, these were titles of respect and affection for older women and men in the community. At a certain age Charlie Hawes ceased to be "Mr. Hawes" and became instead "Uncle Charlie." Married women sometimes took their husband's first name, so Hank C. Smith and Elizabeth Boyle Smith eventually became "Uncle Hank" and "Aunt Hank." Turns of phrase like this provide clues about gender relationships and about the way that people brought elderly neighbors symbolically into the family, just at the time of life when they might need extra help to get along. Anthropologists refer to such practices as "fictive kinship."

December 30, 1937

Monday December 27, 1937. Today is my wedding anniversary. Thirty-one years ago in the morning, a young, blue-eyed girl climbed into a loaded wagon beside her tall, slim husband and waved to a tear-dimmed father and mother as they stood on the porch of their little home. The four tough mules strained in the harness, and the wagon, with a loaded wagon trailed behind, started down the muddy road from Hereford to Crosby County, the county where the young girl had grown to young womanhood before moving to Hereford. Inside the covered wagon were the few possessions the girl had. Quilts, doilies, and dresser scarfs worked with her patient hands. Shining silver wedding gifts and her trunk with the vases, work boxes and albums that had been given her at many happy Christmas times. They were side by side with the new iron bed, the shiny varnished table, the pretty green flowered dishes, the new iron skillet, the black bread pans. A lighted lantern kept the girl's feet warm; the young husband walked most of the time to keep the mules moving along. Four days the wagons creaked and slid over the muddy roads. Early in the morning the ground was frozen, white frost

on the mules' backs. By ten o'clock it became a sloppy, slithery endless trail over the bare prairie. At the end of the fourth day a light gleamed from a tiny window pane, the tired mules held their long ears forward at the sound of barking dogs. The long journey was over. . . .

A new house began to take shape near a windmill on the prairie. The new table, the pretty green-flowered dishes were soon moved into the two-room house, which looked like a piece of yellow cheese in the pale winter sunlight. A packing box with cream cheesecloth curtains, the embroidered dresser scarf, on top some shelves for the vases and the doilies. Gay pictures were hung on the bare pine walls, a box of treasured books nailed near. A new home had begun. And into this home came little children, a curly-haired boy and tiny twin girls. Happiness and peace spread their wings over the prairie home. Friends and relatives came and spent happy hours.

The years passed quickly. School and work and play. College days. Three laughing young people home for holidays and summer vacations. The boy got a doctor's degree, married a young nurse at Scott and White's hospital, where he was an intern. A new home branched off from the old. A sweet baby girl laughed and cooed at the father and mother. One of the twins married a slim, brown-eyed boy. Another happy home began. And today. The last of the three is being married to the man of her choice, a curly-haired, laughing boy, and another fine son will pat me on the shoulder and call me mother.

And Dad's and Mother's anniversary will be celebrated with a double celebration next year. And another happy home is founded from the old. "How can you stand giving up your children," my friend pitied me. "No I do not give up my children. They still love me, and each of the three has given me someone else to love, and a new daughter and two more sons will love and honor me as the years pass and my hair begins to whiten and my steps to falter. And I have the granddaughter so precious, so dear. No I have not given up my children. The little home that looked like a piece of yellow cheese has now become old and sedate. The blue-eyed girl and the tall, slim husband have begun to feel the passing of the years, but the children will come to the old home again and we shall laugh and talk of the good old days. Friends will sit by our fire and warm themselves by the grateful heat as we warm our very souls by the love we have for one another. I shall dream and hear childish voices from the past and the fragrance of other happy days will linger round our home, like perfume in an old bottle. "It Takes a Heap of Livin' to Make A House a Home." Thank you, dear God. I have had the livin'.

Here Spikes presents the American Dream as manifested on the rural frontier of the Great Plains. Though she refers to her "few possessions," the list of material goods she took into her marriage is quite impressive, suggesting a comfortable middle-class life. By 1906, when Spikes married, the United States was rapidly industrializing and urbanizing. In 1920 more than half of Americans lived in urban rather than rural communities. In cities prosperity meant a good job and moving up in the company. But on the plains, farming could still bring upward mobility, increasing material wealth, a college education, and professional employment for grown children.

April 7, 1938

We bring home so many things from a visit. Pleasant memories, happy hours spent with friends and relatives. My mind and heart are full. There are plants, given by flower-loving friends, to set out; there are rocks to place in my rock fence. A smooth, flat rock from my mother's old homestead in Parker County. I will sit on it and dream of the past. I shall see a small cemetery on the side of a tree-covered hill. Inside of the rock wall lie the bones of the Jones family that have been sleeping there many years. The tiny grave with the marble headstone is that of my little sister, Emma Frances, that I never knew. Mother and I could not hold back our tears as we knelt there.

Another rock will be placed on my fence that came from Spikes's Prairie, in Kaufman County. Again as I look at it I will walk with my husband and the old Negro who was born on the Spikes land. We will stand under the shady oak trees and peer down in the old cistern that supplied the needs of a large family. The old home has burned down, the turned brick from the chimney marking the spot. It was my first time to be in Kaufman County. What a beautiful place it was. Flowing streams bordered with beautiful trees. Grapevines swinging their fragrant blossoms, red woodbine glowing with beauty amidst the shining green leaves. The prairie land, and under the trees was a carpet of clover and tiny wildflowers.

But the most beautiful sight we had was the love and pleasure we saw in the eyes of my husband's people he had known in his boyhood days and had seen for the first time in forty years. How welcome we felt in the big high-ceiling houses. We sat by the fireplace where wood was burning, ate biscuits cooked on a wood stove. We sniffed the pleasant scent of burning hickory and oak; looked at our sun-tanned faces, made by the burning winds of the prairie, in mirrors of marble-topped bureaus. We gathered dark, damask roses, blue flags, and sweet wild pinks, in the country where many of the Spikes and the Fox families are waiting for the last day.

Stopped at the Negro school where children were playing at recess. Talked with the proud young Negro professor. Held a tiny little black baby in my arms. We shall remember a tiny old man working in a garden of beautiful flowers, tying up a honeysuckle that was white and sweet with blooms, giving us lovely roses, taking us in his room and showing us pictures of his family. A Bible and a woodbox, two rocking chairs and braided rugs. The room looked as if his wife had only left it and would be gone a few minutes, but in the flower-covered cemetery near the old town, the good, sweet wife was awaiting the time when the husband would also leave the peaceful room, never to return.

June 9, 1938

Memories: The old hotel at Emma kept by Mother and Father. We started in with two rooms. How grand we felt when we got a regular boarder and added a tiny room and porch. Our guest was J. Wilson Boyle, a good-looking young Scotchman just arrived from Scotland to practice law in Emma. You wonder why the hotel was so small? Emma was a very small place. Ranch people came to town for supplies and ate but didn't stay all night. District court was the main event at Emma for hotel needs. Father built two more rooms and a long hall connecting them with the rest of the house. It seemed to me the house was very large. A balsam vine grew on the porch and shaded it from the sun. Four-o'clocks bloomed around the sides. Drummers came in big white-top hacks, gave the children candy

and dimes. Dignified judges and lawyers ate at our table. Rich ranch men from their northern homes did not fill us with awe. We felt as good as they. A bride and groom stayed all night, cowboys' spurs clinked on our floors. Suppers for big dances at the courthouse were spread on our table.

July 21, 1938

Old clothes are sorted, the best ones to go into hooked rugs, others to be used in plays put on by the neighborhood. Old relics, a cavalryman's sword, used by my husband's father in the Civil War. The first shackles bought by Crosby County (the story goes that a man tried to escape with them on), old rawhide hobbles and spurs, two old gunbelts worn by sheriffs of long ago, a dressing case, some Confederate money, buffalo and antelope horns. These I shall lend to the Museum at Tech. The pile I want to keep grows faster than the things I shall burn. My face is dirty, for how could I help the tears that fell as I lived again the days that were? Each article I picked up tells me a tale. . . . But the past is gone and the present is here with its joys and its problems. It does one good once in a while to spend a day with the past.

December 22, 1938

A Christmas at Emma: Nellie sat at her desk in the back of the schoolroom near the window, but her thoughts were not on the history book open before her. In vain did the picture of General Lee with his sword and uniform appeal to her. The picture she usually found so interesting, for had not Grandpa fought with him in the Civil War? It was the last school day before Christmas. The door to the outside was opened and a cool breeze stirred the cedar on the "Merry Christmas" in an arch over the door, bringing a whiff of spicy fragrance. Nellie looked with pleasure and satisfaction around the room she had helped decorate. Letters had been cut from the cardboard on the backs of the tablets and covered with cedar. The clock on the wall, which never struck the time, bore a wreath. The problems of X, Y, and Z, the many figures of multiplication, the circles and angles of geometry had been erased from the boards, and the tiny dots made from the stencils had been followed with colored crayon, and behold there was Santa Claus coming down the chimney (Nellie wondered just how nice a fireplace would be). Reindeers pranced on snowy lawns, red holly berries glowed from the green pictured wreaths round each blackboard that held the scenes of Christmas.

After the songs for the Christmas program and the speeches had been practiced, school was dismissed for the holidays. Nellie ran all the way home to finish her presents. There were the floor pillows to be stuffed with cotton. The one for Jeff was made of a huck towel with Swedish weaving; the one for Uncle George was made of watermelon pink and green tenerif wheels. The spectacle cases for the grandparents were labeled. A lovely card all covered with shiny tinsel and bearing a merry greeting was ready for teacher's name. There were the doilies embroidered with silk thread for Mother, the mustache cup with the flowers and words "for Father," the gifts for brothers and sisters all ready.

Christmas Eve found Nellie with a laughing jolly bunch of boys and girls, seeing who could say "Christmas Eve Gift" the quickest and get a present, carrying tubs of labeled gifts to the tree for the merchants. Across the hard, windswept street, over the steps of the courtyard, up the stairs to the dignified courtroom where solemn judges keep court but where now busy women were decorating the tree. Under the capable direction of Mrs. Alice Brown, pink and blue and white and red tissue paper turned to fluffy chrysanthemums and gay poppies. Strings of white popcorn and strings of red cranberries festooned the tree. Wads of cotton and stars made from cardboard were covered with tinfoil from the tobacco plugs. Yellow and red apples swung from cords.

But it was at night that the tree blazed away in all its beauty and splendor. The tree was a magic tree, covered with sleepy dolls and china dolls with pink cheeks and black hair, with bugles and drums and balls. The light from the candles caught the gleam of the gold of watches and chains, the gold and silver of collar and cuff buttons and stick pins for ties, the brilliant sets in the bracelets, the pearly tints of the pearl pen staffs with their pens of gold. Silk handkerchiefs of every hue looked like gorgeous tropical flowers. Silk and satin cravats, soft, wooly fascinators, warm hoods and nubias, crocheted wristlets of silk and wool hung from the branches. Nothing was wrapped; that would have taken from the beauty of the gift.

And I wish you could have seen the things stacked under the tree. No one, not even a visitor, was left out.

There were enough mustache cups to keep a hundred mustaches out of the coffee. Stacks of plates, cups and saucers for the mothers, work boxes, dressing cases, albums both autograph and photograph, enough to hold all the verses that could be made and thought of, and enough to hold all the pictures the West ever knew. There were tea sets and vases, dozens of them. Vases that looked like silver and gold to be put on the organs, ones like regal lilies, oriental ones, little squat ones, tall and slender vases, enough to fill every mantle where there was a girl. And there were the vanity sets for the dressers. Two big bottles for the cologne, three flat dishes for goodness knew what, a jewel box, a hair receiver, a box for the powder and one for the puff. Dishes for common pins and dishes for hair pins, there never was a dresser large enough to hold all that vanity set. (Nellie did not have a dresser, and Father made a shelf for hers.)

After the speeches by the boys and girls and the Christmas songs Santa Claus came, saying "Hello" to all the good little boys and girls, then giving of the presents took place. Soon the benches and the floor around the people were holding the things that had graced the tree. The gold watches and chains shone from red and blue wool dresses, stick pins were stuck in cravats, silk hand-kerchiefs knotted around brown necks. Firecrackers popped, people jumped, the stove in the corner was as round and as red in the middle as Santa himself. The fiddlers tuned up the fiddles for the breakdowns and the waltzes, the schottisches and the gay polkas. The long wail of a lobo and the staccato barking of coyotes came into the room when a window was opened for air. The smells of fruit, cigarettes, cologne and spicy cedar filled the room. Snow began falling, made blobs of white on the yellow-lighted windows, the stove grew redder, the dance music livelier, the dancers more gay. Fathers and mothers gathered up sleepy children with dolls and toys hugged tight in little arms and with little stomachs filled with Christmas goodies, gathered up toys and dishes and gifts, went down the stairs and home.

After the gay holidays the cowboys would have to go back to the lonely line camps and to the ranches, pull poor cows out of the bog, cut ice on the creeks; the freighter would have to make his hard lonely trips for freight; the merchant would go back to selling flour and bacon and calico, the mothers to ordinary duties; the children would have to go back to school, erase the beautiful scenes from the boards and put on the dull figures, but tonight it was Christ-mas, and time seemed to stand still a few hours for the glad, joyous mer-rymaking.

May 4, 1939

Yesterday we went back, back to our childhood days and the ranch of my husband when he batched. We stopped for Mr. and Mrs. Marsh Wheeler. Then as Jeff and Nellie and Marsh and Esther we were young again. We stood by the hole in the ground that long ago was the dugout home, first of Jeff and then of Marsh and Esther, walked down the washed out path down the steep hill to the spring, picked up a step that had broken off a buggy, got rocks for our fence from the old dugout, one from near the spring and one from the Yellowhouse River that was not far away.

Jeff roamed around, picked out the places where he had his lot, his chickens, saw the place where he had his bed outside the dugout on hot summer nights. Lived again the fright he had when something bit his finger and saw it was a pole-cat. Wondered why he could find nothing to throw, only a biscuit, as there were small rocks all around.

He recalled he moved his bed back in the dugout and shut the door that hot night. He saw the place where the vicious lobo had caught a little white-faced calf lying in the soft, grey-green sagebrush. Heard again its frightened pitiful cries and the bawling of its mother.

Esther pointed out the places in the dugout where she had her two beds, her organ, kitchen cabinet, table and cookstove. We wondered how they were all gotten in such a small place. She told of tying her two children in the dugout while she climbed up and down the steep hill for buckets of water, and she said, "We kept as clean those days as we do now." Taking the two children in a buggy to spend the day at Emma fifteen or so miles away or crossing the canyon to visit with friends on the other side were common experiences. Oh, a sweet, brown-eyed mother, helping build a home in a place that would look so lonely to some. Counting nothing a hardship, only glad for a home and family, rocking babies in a cane-bottomed chair on a dirt floor and singing lullabies while overhead a coyote howled.

Gathering beautiful flowers to adorn her dugout home, the dainty pink kramerics, blue bells and soft yellow buttercups and white daisies put in a blue bowl or a brown glass hob-nailed pitcher. Watching the plum patches turn from a fragrant snowy white to green leaves partly hiding red balls of juicy, delicious plums. I could see the young mother making batches of clear red jelly and rich preserves, turning the purple black canyon grapes gathered in Plum Creek into jam, making pies of green grapes and purple mulberries, frying the tender quail and baking the prairie hen in the wood stove. Seemed that the hills and hollows held an echo of her sweet voice singing old hymns as her busy hands took time to play on her organ. And perhaps the blue haze on the hills was a memory of the smoke that poured from the old rusty stovepipe on the earth-covered dugout roof.

We gathered small rocks, red and purple, black, green, yellow and brown. Found a black jet button that had once been on a dress Esther's mother had worn. Picked up a piece of a blue dish, heard Marsh and Jeff tell of the old building place of a vanished ranch, the LANC over in Lanc Draw, saw Buzzard's Roost Hill, where Indian arrows are found. Oh it is said that people are getting old when they live in the past. Well I don't mind so much getting old.

The history of settlement and farm making in West Texas differs from that in other plains states. While farmers in New Mexico, Colorado, Kansas, Nebraska, and the Dakotas could acquire free land from the federal government under the Homestead Act, Texas farmers could not. When most western territories achieved statehood, the federal government acquired ownership of their unclaimed lands, hundreds of millions of acres that entered the public domain. The U.S. Congress and president then controlled the distribution of public land through sales or grants, eventually making much of it available free to homesteaders.

Texas, however, had been an independent nation for nine years before petitioning Congress for entry into the United States in 1845. When it joined the union, Texas retained state ownership of its unsettled western lands. Thus, privatization of West Texas was up to the state legislature, not the U.S. Congress. In 1882 the state made a spectacular trade: a new capitol building in Austin in exchange for a large part of the Texas Panhandle. The cash-poor state paid a Chicago consortium in land for the construction of its beautiful granite capitol. That land became the XIT Ranch—said to stand for "ten in Texas"— stretching across ten Texas counties. For two decades the XIT ran cattle on its three-million-acre domain.

By the early 1890s, when the Jones and Witt families rolled up onto the caprock, all of West Texas was owned by private ranches. There was no free land for farmers on the Texas plains; they had to purchase or rent property from large landowners. Farmers plowed up West Texas for crop agriculture later than they did the rest of the Great Plains. Intensive farm settlement came to Kansas and Nebraska in the 1870s, to the Dakotas and Montana between 1900 and 1915. Rapid conversion of ranchland to farmland began only about 1905 in West Texas, continuing into the 1930s. The southern plains were in many senses the last agricultural frontier in the United States, the last chance to start a new farm in the great West.

July 6, 1939

The fourth of July, 1939. The fourth of July 1904. . . . I had been in Plainview during the month of June 1904 . . . attending a teachers' in-

stitute, as I was to teach a little rural school the coming winter. Perhaps I had not learned much in the hurried review we had been given, but I had made new friends, learned the ways of a larger town than the one I had grown up in, and the new game of tit-tat-too. I was sixteen, and this was my first time to be away from home for so long a time. Father and my little brother of some seven years came in a wagon for me the second of July, and that night it rained and rained on an earth already wet from many rains.

Next morning Father bought his supplies for the fourth, as there was to be a picnic at Emma. A box of lemons, some citric acid to help out on the lemonade, two boxes of oranges and a stalk of bananas, boxes of candy and firecrackers were loaded in. We set out from town in a trot, but soon the team slowed down to a slow walk in the soft roads. The freight road was deeply rutted and wound around lakes of clear blue water, where it got softer and softer. The horses balked. Father was not a good hand with horses. We unloaded the picnic things and I drove across the hundred yards of soft, boggy ground. Then the things had to be carried and loaded in the waiting wagon.

Three times the hard work was repeated during the day. Friends came by in a surrey going to the picnic. They asked me to go on with them and get to Emma that night.

Papa implored me to go on, but I was grown, so I thought, and saw my responsibility. I sorrowfully watched the matched team take my friends swiftly on. The hot sun made the ground steam, the horses plodded on. The sun sank farther down. The shadows of the wagon and team stretched out like gigantic animals that had trod this same land so long ago. Not a house in sight. Then the distant scenes were wrapped in a soft, dark mantle that finally hid all the earth. The stars came out. Frogs croaked from the lakes. Oh, how I wanted to see my mother! A light gleamed from a window, dogs began barking; oh, there was Coke Fullingim's house. A good supper, a soft bed and a glad welcome we found there.

Early the next morning we reached Emma, the lemonade stand was soon up and I was selling lemonade, "ice cold lemonade," the boys teased as they passed, "made in the shade and stirred by an old maid." I remember the dress I wore, a light tan linen with embroidered red clover leaves all over the material. Broncs were eared down, saddled and ridden till the boy was thrown or the horse was tamed. Orators told of the Great and Glorious Fourth from the courtroom, cowboys on swift cow ponies rode the tournament. Rings were hung on arms nailed to posts and the boys caught them on long sticks as their ponies raced swiftly by. By night the dancing began in the courtroom and lasted till the dawn of another day.

December 7, 1939

I remember one Christmas long ago. Mother, myself, my brother Lowell and little sister Edna were nine miles from Emma where my father had a job in a store for a short time. The one-room house was set on the prairie, with only a windmill and a little wire lot. We were poor in money but, I realize now, rich in the things that count. Mother made a funny rag doll that slid down a plank, our old hen laid an egg and Mother made some cookies. Late in the afternoon we saw Father walking across the prairie, nine long, lonely miles, that we children should have a little Christmas. Next morning we found the doll and a few apples, oranges, and some stick candy in our cotton stocking. Oh Mother, dear, living, and Father, who has left us, the things were meager but the richness of the gifts of love has given us courage and pleasure through all these many years.

March 7, 1940

By a fortunate chance we had dinner with an old friend, J. D. Caldwell. Not many are left that were here when he pulled up to the caprock in a covered wagon to make his home on the plains. He settled at Estacado in 1888. Had a little store, was a barber and carpenter. The lumber for the new courthouse was hauled from Colorado City; Clayton was the contactor. His folks got sick, he quit to go home. White, a brother-in-law of Caldwell's from Dallas, took the job. His folks got sick and he left. Judge Swink was the county judge. He said, "Caldwell, can you build that courthouse?" "I think I can," was J. D.'s reply. "Do you know you can?" the old judge insisted. And Caldwell could and did. It was begun the first of May 1888 and took four months to finish. Capt. Weedin, a Confederate soldier, and a man named Smith helped. Dignified, the new courthouse, white as the summer clouds, stood on the green, treeless prairies, a house of justice in a brand new country.

But a new enterprise beckoned J. D. Caldwell. He loaded his family and furnishings and his house on four wagons and moved it as it stood to Lubbock County in 1890.

Courthouse at Estacado, Texas, 1888. *Left to right:* E. B. Covington, Jeff King, two unidentified men, Thornton Jones, William Standefer, R. N. Martin, and Hank C. Smith. Photograph courtesy of Crosby County Pioneer Memorial Museum, Crosbyton, Texas, 0951.

Two towns had been started. North and South towns. J. D. went on with his story of that time: "We went to see Judge Covington over in Crosby County to which we were attached for judicial purposes. He told us if we would start another town and get 150 signers, who they were he did not care, we could get the county organized. Otherwise we would have to get 150 bona fide names of voters to organize with two towns. Now, many herds were coming through. Every time we got a few names. Names on that petition were from men from the Rio Grande to Montana."

July 11, 1940

When I was a child, Mother had a contraption called a Turkish bath-tub. The patient undressed, took his seat on a chair under which some cotton saturated in alcohol was set afire. The round, rubbery bath-tub was pulled down over his head leaving only the head sticking out. Wet towels were wrapped 'round the head. Then the patient was left to his fate, which seemed imminent death by being roasted alive. Such intense heat one never felt before. Sweat poured from the body. But you could not get out without help, and the helper had left the room and seemingly could not hear your wails and pleadings. But the next day, the soreness in your body made from playing wolf-over-the-river or blackman too strenuously had left, and you felt light, clean and free.

January 30, 1941

As I write my thoughts go back many years to a little frame schoolhouse known as LaBarque, which was near where the Robertson school now is. When I go down to that community I cannot place where the little schoolhouse once stood, as the waving prairie grass has been plowed up and even the little lake that once held water for the patient school horses is now planted in cotton or maize. I looked in vain for the shinnery that came close to the south of the school. And where the teacher with the aid of pupils picked up kindling, loaded it on the rickety topless buggies and carried it in triumph near the house. The wild range cattle that turned and ran as the school hours came are gone, and soft-eyed Jerseys do not look up as the bus passes. The prairie dogs no longer bark defiance as they stand ready for quick entrance into their holes deep in the ground, no longer

is the whirr of the prairie hen heard as the hunters shot at them or the buggies scared them up.

LaBarque stood on the prairie, not a house closer than a mile or more. It had done duty as a schoolhouse in the Murphy neighborhood and had been moved for the benefit of more children. Mr. Detwiler named the school for one he had known in Missouri. How thrilled was I that warm, sunshiny fall day in 1905 when I rang the bell for my few pupils to come in to books. I was not much older than some of my pupils, just sixteen. The desks were homemade. Coats, hats and dinner buckets were placed in the back. As the lessons were heard, there would come many sounds from the raised windows, the barking of prairie dogs, the bawl of a cow for her calf, and once in a while the wailing of a loafer wolf or the staccato barks of coyotes. The worn out school horses stood patiently tied to the buggies; Old Nubbin the Jones children drove; Jug, if I remember right, the Robertson children, Fred, Earl, Bryan and Mable, worked to their buggy. These horses switched at flies and mosquitoes in warm weather and stood shivering, tails to the cold north winds, in winter. I think it would be fine to erect a monument to these old school ponies and the boys and girls who worked them and went long miles through the wind and cold.

Let us look at everything, for it will not be many more years you will have a chance to see these old days first-hand from the people who lived them. Look! there in that buggy at the old suggans made from the worn out wool clothes of the family, the harness that barely holds together with wire, the short whip or stick that the horse was urged along to greater speed. We will go inside and listen to the classes recite. On a long bench before teacher's desk the fourth grade geography class sits, two girls on one end, two or more boys on the other crowding and pushing when teacher is supposed not to be looking. They hold up their hands as questions are asked, popping eager fingers if they think they know the answer. Two little girls in the first reader, Mary Witt and Mable Robertson, are drawing queer pictures on the blackboards, and other pupils are more interested in them than in their open books. Felix Jones is having a hard time with an arithmetic problem that the girl teacher cannot work and will have to get help with over the weekend. From first grade to the tenth the classes run, one teacher to the whole long list of classes.

But we must put our books away for it is dinner time. Lids are pried off tin buckets and the contents spread on the benches, the whole family eating together. Fried steak, boiled beef sausages and fried potatoes between biscuits, boiled eggs to be cracked on someone's noggin, maybe pickles or a dish of black-eyed peas with pods of hot pepper, wild plum jelly and pre-serves with black jam of the canyon grapes had their place in the bucket with the spread of yellow tomato preserves. . . .

But gracious sake, we must finish that dinner and go play town ball, the girls with Felix Jones, the big boy, against all the other boys. Pick up that "barn door" bat if you are a girl and a small round stick, prob-ably an old hoe handle, if you are a boy, and hit that little fast rubber ball a mighty lick and run and run and make an eye with all your side hollerin' and jumping up and down. Well, too bad, the next ball goes down in a prairie dog hole. Everyone wants to get down on their knees and peer into the hole, hoping the ball can be reached and the game go on. But no, we will have to wait till tomorrow till a grubbing hoe can be brought and the ball dug out. Anyway the alarm clock is going off, so that means books again, and we sit quietly again, listen to the prairie

wind bringing sounds to our ears
that should be hearing the children
recite and bringing the smell of
green grass and of wild blossoms
in the spring to our noses that had
been smelling the coal in the stove
and the scent of burned grass from
the prairie fires through the winter.

We must pack up our books, put
the lid on the dinner bucket, take
home the alarm clock and the pitted
rubber ball, say farewell to the old
school ponies and the Taylors, the
Witts, the Joneses, the Robertsons,
the Carnahans, the Kidds, and the
Garrisons. The prairies are plowed
up, the school building has blown
away in a little tornado, the bones of
the horses have long been bleached
by the same sun that warmed the
horses when alive, the children have
grown up, and the teacher sits with
happy and lovely memories of the
old LaBarque School.

February 20, 1941

The district court at Emma is in session. The dignified judge and all the
lawyers are in town with the ranch-
men, the nesters and the cowboys.
Mother is cooking dinner in the Witt
Hotel. Coffee is pouring into the cup
of the fast-turning old coffee mill.
I am turning, Mother is rolling out
tender crusts for pies. A bit of flour

is on her flushed cheeks as swiftly
the dough is moulded into a tin plate
for its filling of delicate egg custard.
The baby plays at her side, catches
at her apron strings as she bends to
put the pies in the hot oven of the
black range stove. Deftly she rolls
out biscuits by the dozens, stirs the
drying potatoes. The majesty of the
law must grind away in the courts,
but its grinders must be fed.

July 10, 1941

A thin, pearly mist, the ghostlike
wraith of the recent rains, rose from
the lakes and wound across the
fields and prairies over the draw this
morning. The sun rises clear, only
a small cloud of gold trying to hide
his morning splendor. We take heart
again. Maybe we will have enough
dry weather to get the wheat cut and
some weeds killed. We never saw
such a time, do we old-timers shake
our heads and say? When we went
around full overflowing lakes long
ago, we were in wagons and buggies
and there were no fences to hinder.
Small patches of cane and maize and
kaffir did not need so much attention as now. Rains did not paralyze
everything as they do now, as there
was not much place to go. True, the
freighter unhooked trail wagons and
left them by the side of the road,

Margaret Jones Witt
as a young woman,
ca. 1882. Photograph
courtesy of Crosby
County Pioneer
Memorial Museum,
Crosbyton, Texas,
2309.

coming into town with a few necessities. I remember one summer when horses' feet bogged down out on the prairie. When Uncle John and Aunt Mary Taylor moved to Emma they were met some fifteen or twenty miles away. We still laugh about how their chairs were bogged down to the cane-bottomed seats as the travelers sat by their campfire to eat their dinner. . . .

It is time to go a—plum hunting, but we are afraid the roads are washed out. I close my mind to everyday worries and take my blue ruffled sun bonnet and pile in a wagon with Father and Mother and a bunch of children and go creaking away to the canyon. How long the miles seem and how slow the horses trot. We grab mesquite beans when the wagon goes near, suck the sweet bitter juice and spit it out. There is a rivalry about who will see the canyon first, and as we fuss and argue, we lose out. The blue haze softens the bright green of the canyon hills, an eagle soars slowly overhead, making a deep purple shadow over our white wagon sheet . . . .

Draw up close, for we are ready for dinner. Get a tin plate and cup while Mother dishes out fried crisp bacon, corn simmered in bacon grease and potatoes cooked with onions. Reach in the dutch oven and pull out a tall sourdough biscuit light as a happy thought, brown as our faces. Clear and fragrant is the coffee in our silver cups, hot and untainted by sugar or cream. Sweet is the sorghum that Uncle Jim made as we eat under the wagon sitting in the sand made cool by the shade.

What is the matter? The sunbonnet has soared away with its own strings for wings, the wagon has vanished around the hazy hills. Father has passed off to another land; the children are all men and women, with many problems, but the plums still gleam like red rubies on the green covered bushes, the rabbits still run and the grasshoppers whirr. Time has stood still on the blue, hazy hills.

August 21, 1941

There is something about canning that makes one have a miserly spirit. Not one bean or peach is wasted but hurried into glass. No matter how many pickles swim in vinegar on our shelves, more are added as long as the cucumbers last. Instead of sitting in a dark room like King Midas with our laps and hands full of gold, we stand by our pantry shelves and fairly gloat over the rows of creamy corn, the jars of peas and beans, the brown fried chickens and the jewels of our heart, the jams, preserves and jellies. Instead of turning our loved ones into molten gold, like Midas and his daughter, these treasures of the garden and field will bring the pulsing life into their bodies this winter.

How different was the winter supply that my grandmother put up. I can just see the sacks of dried corn and smell the sacks of dried peaches in the old attic on the farm. Then there was a five-gallon jar of preserves we children called "shoe soles," because they could be dipped out of their thick, spicy sweet juice and eaten like a piece of candy. Dried beans and peas, also dried pumpkin, well I started to say punkin, and I wish I had, because it has always been plain punkin to me, not pumpkin like the speller said. There were quaint cream-colored crock jars filled with sweets of all kinds and sealed with a rind of red sealing wax. Strings of red peppers hung by the side of strings of green dried okra. A flour sack of sun-jerked beef and antelope rattled when moved. There were a few bluish glass jars, usually having a rubber made from an old felt hat. Nevertheless, Grandmother's table was well supplied with good things to eat. Somehow I cannot see that one generation is smarter than the other. Each makes the best use of the materials at hand.

I do not want to forget the turnips and cashaws walled around with sorghum bundles to keep out the cold and frost, nor the pounds of yellow butter each stamped with a sheaf of wheat and wrapped in a clean white cloth and placed in a barrel of brine for the winter supply when no one would think of milking a cow. Ah, my dear readers, going to Grandpa's and Grandma's house was one of the happiest times of children's lives and remains all the days one of the happiest memories.

Somehow I cannot leave the attic, so will just rummage around some more and see what I have forgotten to tell. There were the china dolls with red, red cheeks and black, black hair. There were the old clothes one could dress up in and play "ladies." Gunny sacks full to bursting with peanuts and popcorn. Garden and flower seed rolled in newspaper. A pallet bed for extra use. No, you would not find discarded furniture and many trunks filled with relics, for Grandpa Jones was a pioneer, and pioneers do not have room to take anything that dire necessity does not call for.

October 23, 1941

I have always longed for red velvet curtains. This has been a symbol of the greatest luxury. Always in the novels I once read (sometimes paperbacks) the beautiful woman pulled back the red velvet curtains and gazed at the glittering stars or she tapped a silver bell and a soft-footed servant pulled together the hangings of the thick, rich material and set a small table with lustrous and shining china. It seems like now, as the rain falls and the bad news of the war pours in over the radio and the daily paper, if I could pull the soft folds of red velvet over the windows of my soul, the bad could be shut out. But it is my power to pull the red velvet curtains that hide the past and sit in the beautiful room of happy memory and live again some bright days of the long ago.

I am again a little girl with long plaits of hair. I lie on the rag carpet at my great-grandmother's home in Weatherford. The fire burns bright on the hearth of the big fireplace, making pictures that delight a child as she listens to the talk of the grown folks. The Civil War is not far behind, the talk still is on battles, retreats and hard times during the war. I shudder as the talk turns to Indians, still such a tragic memory in the hearts of Parker County people. I slide closer to my mother's chair and touch her skirts. They laugh and tell about the time my grandmother got an Indian scare and took her children down in an old dry well and stayed so long. And how Tom Franklin ran so hard, whipping himself with a whip as if riding a horse, when his brother, Felix, scared him so. Grandma Hunter tells of how embarrassed she was when the preacher caught her drinking coffee from the coffee pot, a favorite way with her during the day.

The folks draw their rawhide-bottomed chairs closer to the dying fire, the smell of clean straw under the rag carpet blends with that of the wood smoke as another log is put on the dying fire. The talk grows dim, sounds like the murmur of the little stream that passes by our little house in Weatherford, where the tall water oaks spread their leafy boughs. It grows louder as I awake at the talk of mad dogs. I rise up and ask my mother if there are any mad dogs around. At her assurance, I slip down on the good carpet by the fire again, close by the table made of rope and broomsticks that holds the big Bible with all the family names, deaths, marriages and births. I doze and wake. Now the rustle of starched petticoats as the women arise to go to bed, the sweet voice of my mother calling me as she stoops and draws me in her arms to carry me to the fat featherbed. Oh would you put the curtain of yesterday back, or would you sleep on in the soft featherbed at your grandmother's house?

January 15, 1942

Sheltered from the raging blue northers of winter and cooled by soft summer winds that ripple the water of White River, the old Rock House, built long ago with native stone, sat in dignity under tall pecan trees that Uncle Hank Smith planted so that in his old age he could sit in their shade and smoke his pipe, Aunt Hank by his side, both remembering the time when they were the first settlers and kept the post office and the weather bureau, frying the buffalo and antelope meat for the weary nesters moving west and stopping for a night. Now great-grandchildren pick up the pecans under the tall trees, and tourists look with interest at this pioneer home that has become a historic landmark of Crosby County. . . .

A gleam of bronze on a low, gray marble shaft catches the eye of the passing motorist. Some look immediately back to the road, never giving it another thought; some slow down and try to read the words at a swift glance, then speed up, wondering for a second what the shaft commemorates; others stop and read carefully every word carved in memory of the Quakers who came to Crosby County and settled the first colony, Estacado. The Quakers have gone, but in the memory of some today there was a time when the soft thee and thou of peaceful men could be heard as they set out box elder and bois d'arc trees and moved cottonwoods from the canyon to shade their homes on summer days and fling a yellow flag to the blue autumn sky. They tell of gray-clad women, stepping across the grassy street to borrow a cup of flour as an excuse to talk awhile, or hang sober-colored clothing on a barbed wire fence to dry. The old two-story hotel still stands, its once white clapboards grayed with time. The panes of glass that once turned the setting sun

into fire have fallen in splinters on the ground; the green shutters have slammed off in many a hard wind. But once men sat around the long, well-laden table in the dining room and bowed their heads while the owner said Grace. Cowboys with frozen slickers creaking like tarpaper found food and shelter. Women stiff and tired from a journey of hundreds of miles from the east, unpacked Rising Star and Sunburst quilts to show to the friendly Quaker women. The Quakers have gone, long many years, but here and there a lone bois d'arc tree stands, a living memorial to the hardy friends who settled the first town in Crosby County.

April 2, 1942

I had only been married a few months and was coming back on the train from a visit to my parents at Hereford. I heard two men talking who were sitting in the seat just ahead of mine. One pointed to a new home on the unsettled prairie and said, "I wonder how anyone could live away out on this lonely prairie like that. Nothing but a tiny house and barbed wire lot?" I smiled to myself, for every clack of the spinning train wheels was taking me

Uncle Hank and Aunt Hank Smith, ca. 1888. *Left to right:* Robert Burns
Smith, George Smith, Annie Josephine Smith, Hank C. Smith, Elizabeth
Boyle Smith, Mary Magdelene Smith, and Leila E. Smith. Photograph cour-
tesy of Crosby County Pioneer Memorial Museum, Crosbyton, Texas, 0496.

nearer to a home like that. I could
have told these city men why folks
could live like that and be happy.

There were only two unpapered
rooms in my new home that my
husband had built from new pine
when we married for the "duration,"
but there was a lovely picture hanging on the splintery walls and some
books in a paper-covered box. The
plain table was covered with a linen
cloth hemstitched and embroidered
with my own hands. The secondhand chairs rested us when we were
tired, and the cookstove baked good
biscuits and fried and boiled good
food. When I got home there would
be a loving welcome from my husband, and he would take me to the
garden just a few weeks from sod,
where clear, life-giving water would
be running down by the side of pale
green lettuce and the pink of forming radishes. We would look at the
new baby white-faced calves whose
hair was being curled by their mothers' rough tongue; there were newly
hatched chickens to feed the cold

cornbread to. Fidy and Callie, the mules in the barbed wire lot, were to be seen. Baby killdees would jerk their fuzzy heads and chee-chee, while fluttering mothers played a broken wing. Brown limbs were in a straight row, a young orchard in the making, the field was plowed ready for the planting.

Lonely? No! God was in the new home on the prairie, there were things to be fed and work to do.

Ranching was lucrative in the 1870s and early 1880s, drawing considerable investment from the eastern United States and overseas, especially from England and Scotland. Many Texas cowboys received their pay envelopes from British owners. But the ranching industry began to decline after 1887, when drought and hard winters killed millions of cattle and demand for beef in the industrializing East diminished. By the early twentieth century many ranch owners decided their land was more valuable than the cattle grazing on it, and they began to subdivide their ranches into small 160- or 320-acre units for farm families. Sometimes they hired hands to plow up sod to entice purchasers; sometimes they sold the land "raw." In 1901, with an influx of agricultural settlers, the enormous XIT began to liquidate its landholdings, in large and small parcels, to both farmers and speculators who then resold to farmers. The sale proceeded slowly, but by 1950 the XIT was in the hands of thousands of small operators.

Julian Bassett, a Chicago businessman, owned the C. B. Livestock Company and was the largest landholder in Crosby County, operating the ninety-thousand-acre Bar-N-Bar Ranch. Between 1906 and 1910 the company broke sod on ten thousand acres and began to subdivide the ranch. The breakup of ranches finally opened the Texas high plains to farm families, and population grew rapidly in small towns between 1900 and 1935.

April 9, 1942

The rhubarb is coming on and it makes me think of a little eager-eyed girl dressed in a white cross-barrel lawn dress held at the waist by a narrow sash of blue ribbon, a kindly old gentleman warning not to get printer's ink on the pretty dress, for it would not wash out. And a sweet, juicy rhubarb pie for din-

Bassett Land Company sales office, Crosbyton, Texas, 1911. Photograph courtesy of Crosby County Pioneer Memorial Museum,
Crosbyton, Texas, 0102.

Breaking sod on a ten-thousand-acre portion of C. B. Livestock Company land, January 20, 1912. Photograph courtesy of Crosby County
Pioneer Memorial Museum, Crosbyton, Texas, 0030.

ner, for we were spending the day at the home of the *Crosby County News*, edited by Judge Murray at Emma. The smell of the black ink on the steel type, the aroma of the baking pie, the fragrance of the opening yellow roses at the door, the old leather bindings on the many books, the friendly people, the hospitable home. How it comes back to me sweet and clear as the blue sky like a china bowl that was over the green of the West. The sound of pleasant conversation, the rattling of the press as the handle turned out the news.

July 2, 1942

It was summer: hot, and water everywhere. John Witt and Jeff Spikes had sold the General Merchandise at Emma. John Witt was moving his family to Hereford. From the piano to the old-fashioned trunk with the locks of hair, Mother's wedding dress and the badge Father wore in a prohibition rally, and little sister Frances's pink dress she no longer needed, as she was left sleeping in the rock-walled plot of Jones graves near Weatherford. The wagons slushed through mud and water; millions of hopping frogs, tails just shed and legs grown on,

popped under the steel tires—miles of frogs and miles of water and mud. A cloud of mosquitoes accompanied the wagon train, joined at every lake by hordes of more, almost veiling the travelers and causing incessant motion of horses' tails and slapping hands. One day was spent in camp, Mother combing our long braids while Father went one way to hunt the escaped horses and the other men in the party went another. Camping at night, keeping up a smudge of cowchip fires, eyes smarting and throats burning.

The summer of 1905 was wet. Big chunks of mud gathered on the rolling wheels, slung off only for more to collect. The little children fretted with the stings and the heat. Mother was sad, for she was leaving her people behind. Old ties were broken; what would the new ones be? We children were excited and happy about the new home. We would live in a town where big puffing engines drew mysterious people in shiny cars to distant places. There would be a drugstore where ice cream could be bought in the summer time. And there would be church, not in a schoolhouse, but in real church houses. . . .

Again I long to walk the streets of Hereford, sit in the Baptist church and remember the faces I once saw there, or go past the drugstore and look in its wonderful windows, or go to meet a train, never allowed then, only to meet or say goodbye to someone. Sweet dreams of a lovely town and kind hospitality.

March 25, 1943

I remember the story of the Quakers living in Estacado that cold, windy spring so long ago. The winter had been hard, the frail tents not too warm, the endurance of the plain people almost to the breaking point. The spring they had so longed for as they battled the winter brought no relief; in fact an extra hard wind blew down some tents and scattered the Quakers' few belongings across the bare land. Aunt Hank Smith related that some of the things reached the canyon and found lodging there. But the Quakers, though they did not stay long in an unfriendly climate, left much to make lighter the burdens of the incoming "gentiles." They left a story of endurance and of kindness. The perfume of the flowers they raised in the summer has sweetened the lives of many. They set out trees that still stand, built such a strong house that time with its many winters and springs of high winds has not destroyed. They left lessons of hope and courage, and they softened the harsh ways of the cow country with their gentleness.

The focus of settlement in Crosby County shifted from place to place in the nineteenth and twentieth centuries as the economy changed. The first county seat was at Estacado, a short-lived community of Quaker immigrants from the Midwest who established a town of over four hundred people in 1879. There was a considerable amount of animosity between the Quakers and the ranchers and cowboys in the area, but the Quakers could mobilize more voters and prevailed in county elections. But by 1898 the last Quaker family had left Estacado, driven away by drought, grasshoppers, range fires, and crop failure, and the town ceased to exist. Emma, center of a community of small ranchers and farmers who immigrated from further east in Texas in the 1880s and 1890s, became the second county seat. The recent immigrants' new numerical superiority allowed Emma to wrest the county seat away from the declining Quaker community in 1891 by a narrow vote of 109 for Emma to 103 for Estacado. County officials dismantled the grand, three-year-old courthouse building in Estacado and reassembled it in Emma, even straightening and reusing the same nails.

In 1909 the Pecos and Northern Railroad extended southward from Amarillo to Plainview and down to Lubbock, some thirty miles west of Emma. To make its extensive landholdings more attractive to small farmers, Julian Bassett's C. B. Livestock Company founded the new town of Crosbyton on the edge of the Llano Estacado, overlooking the eroded plains to the east. The company financed an extension of the railroad line from Lubbock to its new town, where the first locomotive arrived in 1911. The railroad meant everything to a commercial farming economy, and the rail line bypassed Emma, the county seat, by five miles. Bassett couldn't make money by bringing his railroad to an existing town, but by creating new towns along the line he could sell commercial and residential lots at a considerable profit. Three new towns sprang up along the tracks: Lorenzo, Ralls, and Crosbyton. Most residents of Emma abandoned that town to move north to the rail line, where they created Ralls, which competed with the C. B. Company's Crosbyton for supremacy. Others in Emma moved to Crosbyton. Business owners even moved their buildings across the prairie to the new community. Emma became a ghost town.

Crosbyton stole the county records that Emma's citizens had intended to transfer to Ralls, and a county election in 1910 established Crosbyton as the new county seat, which role it maintains, although the rivalry between Ralls and Crosbyton lasted for decades. When the irrigation revolution shifted the county's economic center again after the 1940s, Ralls was better positioned over the Ogallala Aquifer than Crosbyton and took sweet revenge on its neighbor as bank deposits, population, and business flowed uphill toward money, water, and Ralls.

June 24, 1943

This particular time wheat harvest takes the most prominent place. The cotton and feed crop have to wait; it makes one think of a new baby getting all the attention while the older child has to wait. Many harvests have come and gone since I moved my rocking chair, silk embroidered centerpiece and set of plated silver to the new house that looked like a hunk of yellow cheese in the mild spring sun. I said harvests when for those years I should have said harvest time. . . . Then the big old engine with wheels the size of water

A passenger train arrives at the station, Lorenzo, Texas, ca. 1911. Note
the poles in the photograph; with the railroad line came telegraph
service. Photograph courtesy of Southwest Collection, Texas Tech
University, Lubbock, SWCPC 291 E6 #18.

tanks puffed from one wheat field to
another, haughty and proud, belch-
ing smoke and cinders, making a
noise like a train, hungry for sheaves
of wheat, tossing the straw to one
side in huge stacks while sweating
men fed endless bundles brought by
loaded wagons from the field.

Oh that was a busy, happy time.
Dinner was put on early in huge
pots, while pies cooled and cakes
looked like great white drifts of
snow. Homemade lightbread and
fresh hot biscuits, potato salad

with its smell of onions and spicy
vinegar, chickens browning in hot
grease, cold slices of ham, red beans
no end. My, how I love to think
about it now. The first men to the
house, washing up, joking and hur-
rahing one another; the table made
as long as possible was surrounded
by hungry men whose greatest
compliments were that they ate with
such relish. Tableful after tableful
ate and hurriedly left, till there was
time for the women and children
to sit down and eat at leisure.

Somehow every traveler found where the threshing was that day and stopped to join the crowd, not to work but to get a good dinner, and would you have blamed them?

In the far distant future I can see some college professors digging up parts of one of those old Rumley threshers, a wheel buried here and parts there, and when it is all put together it would take its place in museums with dinosaurs and big lizards.

Threshers were enormous pieces of farm equipment used in the wheat harvest to separate grain from waste straw. When the knee-high wheat was ripe, farmers cut the slender stems near ground level, then bundled the cut wheat into sheaves—cone-shaped stacks that needed several days or more to dry in the field. Rain during harvest time could severely damage the wheat crop. Farmers arranged with a threshing crew to bring a thresher to the farm for a few days. The thresher crew, the farm family, and, often, temporary hired hands all worked to load bundles of dried wheat into the coal-powered machine that roared and bellowed black smoke as it separated valuable grain from the wheat straw. The thresher blew waste out one end and a stream of wheat grains out the other. Farm laborers filled burlap or canvas bags with wheat, loaded them into wagons, and hauled them to the nearest grain elevator along the railroad tracks. At the elevator farmers sold their year's harvest to middlemen who stored it in tall silos or shipped it immediately in rail cars to flour mills and urban markets in the East. Without the railroad farmers would have been unable to sell their grain.

Harvest time required intense work and very long days from everyone on the farm, including men and boys who cut and stacked grain and operated the thresher; women and girls who cooked three meals a day for dozens of famished workers, then cleaned up after them; and draft animals who pulled implements and hauled wagons back and forth from field to elevator.

Technology continues to change. Threshers were a technological innovation that replaced older, more labor-intensive methods. Farmers used to thresh, or flail, wheat by hand, whipping it to break the grain free from the chaff. Threshing machines reduced the effort and time of the harvest but were more expensive than most farmers could afford. Instead, custom threshing crews moved from farm to farm at harvest time. Farmers rented the machines and their operators for a few days, often paying in a percentage of the wheat threshed. Machines and crews traveled from county to county as the harvest progressed. The wheat harvest began in late June in the Texas Panhandle, around the Fourth of July in Kansas, and later in the summer on the northern plains. Thresher crews and itinerant hired laborers moved northward during the summer, following the harvest, taking advantage of short-term demand for extra labor. The system worked well for small farmers, too. They had access to the technology and extra work that they needed for only a few weeks of the year without the high capital investment of buying a bulky machine or hiring farm hands year-round.

The heyday of the thresher was between 1870 and 1930. By the middle of the twentieth century a new technological innovation, the combine, made wheat harvest faster and easier yet. The new harvester combined the jobs of cutting, bundling, and threshing into a single, quick operation. By the 1950s itinerant thresher crews were a thing of the past, but some people continued to operate custom combining services for farmers who did not want to invest in their own machinery.

September 2, 1943

Time was, when to sing ballads was the style and most everyone knew from one to a dozen or more, and they were good and long, most of them sad and tragic. Uncle George could sing the ones I liked as well as the ones Aunt Mirt sang when we begged real hard. We all gathered 'round and became very quiet, and soon the sad strains of the "Silver Dagger" enchanted us with its romance and terrible ending, "Let parents all take warning that lovers here should never part." Then there was the one that began, "Brave Sons of Columbia, There's a story I'll relate, Of what happened here of late in the Indian State of a hero that none can excel." Thus going on in a long line of breathtaking excitement. Uncle George could sing of "Young Charlotta," who lived in the mountains and froze to death while her sweetheart was carrying her to a dance in a sleigh because she was too proud and haughty to have a blanket wrapped 'round her silken-clad shoulders.

We all liked in particular the one where the girl, "Cut off her hair and she dressed in men's clothes," fooling her own father and getting a boat to go after her lover. If we begged long enough and made good promises which we too often forgot next day, Aunt Mirt would sing on and on. "Hangman, Hang the Rope" had lots and lots of good verses, and it was such a thrill for the sweetheart to save the unhung man after all his kin and friends had denied him help. Even on a hot night we shivered when Father sang of the little girl who stood in her bare feet in the snow at a rich man's door, while the rich man lay on a marble couch and dreamed of his silver and gold, then tears would come as he sang of the orphan girl dying on the night her father was bringing her a new mother. What a place the old ballads held in the making of America and especially in the frontiers where folks were often lonely!

October 22, 1943

We have been looking at pictures of various schools I attended at Emma. I look at myself as if looking at a stranger and wonder what filled my mind at that particular moment. The first one, my first school, the younger children were toeing a rope on the ground. I am looking down, probably scared that teacher would not like it if my bare toes did not actually just touch the line. I pick out each face in the group, wonder where some are now. Teachers stand at the ends, taking time from the group to look to the photographer just in time to get the picture. In another picture I am growing up, probably worried about algebra and thinking some about boys, I suppose. Wondering if the boy I liked best had my name written in his book, or perhaps my initials, N. W., carved on his desk. Then the last picture, I do not find myself with the grown girls with the high pompadours, the high stiff collars and the beribboned black hair. I was some ten miles out in the country teaching school. . . .

It brings to me the night we put on plays at the schoolhouse or the night at the courthouse when I was the famed Joan of Arc and burned by enemies at the stake. While I looked heavenward a woman fainted and had to be carried out, much to my disappointment in not seeing that fine effect. Then the same night I was the wife of a drunkard in *Ten Nights in a Barroom,* and if you did not think my husband, Walter Davies, was realistic in his delirium tremens, you do not know O. N. Watts, who coached him in this scene.

Emma, Texas, school, 1895–96. Marcus Phillips, principal; Kincher Carter, assistant. Nellie is unidentified in this picture but would have been seven years old. Photograph courtesy of Southwest Collection, Texas Tech University, Lubbock, SWCPC 291 E1 #6.

February 4, 1944

Since we first put up our cookstove and iron beds in our new two-room home . . . we have turned no one away that would stay. I am not saying this as bragging, only remembering, and glad we did not forget the hospitality the West had taught us. There were the fruit tree men and long the roses bloom 'round our door and red apples and yellow peaches hung from well-laden trees, better and more beautiful than the pictures in the black book we selected them from. There was the boy tramp that waited until we went to bed to get us up. Fixed him some supper and a pallet on the kitchen floor. Men running for office stayed the night or at least made it here for the noon meal. Cowmen buying cattle or looking for strays propped their boots on the hearth of the kitchen stove. There was the man and woman with seven little boys whose car stopped a half a mile away and they came to stay all night;

needless to say there were pallets all over the floor. Three men in a buggy from Floydada got us up one warm summer night for a bit of supper and a place for the night.

July 14, 1944

Once upon a time, as all good stories should start, and when I was a child, an awful long time ago it seems today, Mother decided she would go out to visit her sister who lived some six or seven miles from Emma. Old Leta was brought in from the prairies, hitched to the topless buggy and Mother and children all got in, followed in another buggy by Ernest Witt, her sister's son. His topless, worn-out buggy was pulled, reluctantly, by a lazy old burro. We made the first mile to the sandhill, as it was called, pretty well, but Leta was not pleased with her part in the parade. She longed to be out on the prairies eating her beloved loco-weed, which made her kind of wild and skittish, to say the least. The buggy rattled, Mother got alarmed, and stopped to wait for Ernest. She put all of us out in the buggy with him and started on west down the road at a pretty fair clip. Leta did not like the shaves, the rattling nor the pulling on her mouth. She decided to run away from it all and took

off down the lakeside at a gallop. Mother stayed with her, and 'round the lake they both went, the buggy almost coming to pieces like the one hoss shay. Mother headed her back to the road where we were inching along and got Leta stopped but not calmed down. Sweat was pouring from her skinny sides, and her eyes were wild. She trembled in every joint as if she would fall right there and then. Somehow Mother and Ernest got her unharnessed, and away Leta went, swinging her head from side to side as she hunted up another bite of loco.

November 3, 1944

We have sorghum molasses on our table, fresh from the mill in East Texas. And is it good? Well, yes. It makes me think of the year I taught school at LaBarque. Grandma Jones fixed our school dinner, not lunch. She put in a can of black-eyed peas seasoned with a hunk of salt pork and a can of sorghum molasses made by Uncle Jim Witt. In this she put some butter, and we knew as we stirred the butter in the rich syrup that all the butter she churned that winter was reserved for the school children. . . . All of us gathered around the full bucket, sopping the sorghum and enjoying the peas with a complement of red tomatoes and hot pepper. Soda biscuit in the early fall and late spring when there was milk, but sourdough biscuits in the cold of the winter. Sometimes there were slices of cake, or wedges of pie, but always something good. The children must have the best.

June 1, 1945

Grandpa's chair was the best one in the house, or so we children thought, and now I know why it was the best. We only got to sit in it while he was away from it, and the minute he came in he pointed a long, bony finger at us, and did we "get." The back was high, and a bunch of flowers, softly blurred by Grandpa's gray head, had the same pretty, bright colors that were in the big clock that Grandpa wound every night as he rose from his last smoke in the chair. The cushion was pieced of gay woolen scraps, feather-stitched together with bright silk thread, and the cushion was tied to the back of the slick-bottomed chair. In the winter the chair was drawn in front of the long, black wood heater where Grandpa could reach over and put in another stick of mesquite wood. In the summer it was near the open door, where Grandpa could look over the waving prairie grass and watch for the boys to come by from a ranch or a herd being driven by. He could see the antelope race across when scared by the cowboys; he could see the tall poplar trees near the tank gently sway with the breeze. He would smoke and sleep and perhaps dream of the time when his life was active and full, of the rigors of the Civil War, the taming of the frontier in Red River County, of the Indians when he moved farther west to Parker. And now he was the one to sit and watch the life in the new, new West go by.

June 8, 1945

Nothing was so fascinating when a child as watching Dr. Carter measure out the medicine he was to leave. All we children crowded around him, and I wonder if we did not jog his elbow occasionally as we tiptoed to see. He took out his pocket knife, cut white paper in small pieces, then reached in his medicine case and took out a small bottle and drew out the tight cork. Then he measured the medicine with the point of his knife onto the papers, folding each one so that the powder would stay in, and gave instructions for its use.

September 7, 1945

This Monday morning I would like to be a little schoolgirl with long braids hanging down my gingham-covered back and to see the flash of the brand new tin dipper as it clinks against the side of the shiny new water bucket as it sits in the place of the old rusty, leaky one of the year before. I would even like to feel the burning of the squeaky new shoes on my sunburned feet, feel the new-ness of the long, red pencil in my hands as I write on the first white page of the pretty pictured tablet. I would like to see the sweet faces of Lena and Rena, of Esther and Maude and Kate. To see the clean blouses and scrubbed hands of Russell and Stanley and Milton. Would like to hear the peal of the bell as it rings out that school days are beginning, the squeak of the slate pencil as a boy tries to attract attention. Of black hair on the head of Mr. Glass and to see the glitter of Mrs. Glass's watch pinned on the front of her silk shirtwaist. I am homesick for the feel of fingers running around the carved names on my desk, thrill at the sight of three initials in my book that stand for "you-know-who," as I glance to the boys' side of the room where the owner of the initials sits, meeting my glance with a timid smile. Yes, I would like to be starting to school again.

July 18, 1947

In the cowboy lingo of my childhood days, we had lick for breakfast. For the benefit of the ones who do not know, or think any kind of syrup is lick, we affirm as one who knows that lick is only the one sweet made by boiling sugar and water together till it somewhat thickens. And it needs to be herded up from the plate with hot soda biscuits. Lightbread is not much good, and by all means do not try a piece of toast!

August 27, 1948

We might take time to put our feet under the long table in the old Witt Hotel in Emma. Yes, there are feet underneath with boots and spurs. Those yellow shoes are worn by the drummer from Amarillo and are polished like a top. Yes, the district judge has a bunion, and his shoes are cut a little at the sides. You will also see a pair or so of brogans; takes heavy shoes to follow a sod plow. Father's feet are small and his shoes are neat and polished. Big feet and small feet, boots and shoes and

The Witt Hotel and wagon yard at Emma, Texas, established in 1892 by John and Margaret Witt and later sold to brother George Witt and wife Fannie. Photograph courtesy of Southwest Collection, Texas Tech University, Lubbock, SWCPC 291 E1 #2.

maybe a pair of dancing slippers on a young man ready for the dance at night in the courthouse. Some boots will have mud from Yellow House Canyon, others from Mount Blanco. All along the table are plates and case knives and forks.

Mother and Aunt Mirt have cooked the dinner, and it is a good one, too. Black-eyed peas with a fat piece of pork, string beans cooked till sweet and tender. Dishes of okra and onions and red ripe tomatoes. It is the season for vegetables, and not shipped in ones as at other times.

No light bread on this table, but plates heaped high with good soda biscuits, brown and tender and hot enough to melt butter. There is a good steak, brown and crisp with bowls of gravy, creamed corn, pickles and plum butter and grape jam. Everyone eats all he wants, the feet under the table shuffle, and hands are busy. Coffee and buttermilk, big glasses of fresh well water, no ice in summer this side of Amarillo. Then when it seems that nothing more could be desired than a cool, shady place to lie down, the pie comes on.

This day it is made of good canned California peaches with crusts that melt like butter in hot bread, sweet and syrupy, just cool enough from the oven to eat. My, my, let's pay our quarter and get out before we bust.

November 23, 1950

'Long about this time of the year I love to take from my treasure room of happy memories the good times we had at Emma from Thanksgiving on until Christmas. In fact, my whole life at Emma was a happy one. Beef and antelope, prairie chickens, quail and fried chicken tasted good, but oh, those pork sausages Mrs. Reagan placed on the checked tablecloth at the Thanksgiving Day dinner at the schoolhouse! A rarity on the Plains at that time, for not many hogs rooted the mud and grunted satisfaction for their feed at that time.

Pork was a staple of the diet in eastern and central Texas and throughout the south but was rare on the Texas high plains. Southern settlers wanted to bring their traditional diets with them when they moved, but it was not always possible. In this case corn was the crux of the problem. Nearly all Southern farmers grew corn. It formed the basis of traditional Southern foods such as corn bread, corn pone, and grits. More importantly, corn was a feed crop for livestock. Corn provided the fuel for draft horses and mules, and it fattened hogs for pork. When farmers moved west to ever drier climates, they found that thirsty corn crops often failed during hot, dry western summers. Without reliable corn fields, hog raising faltered, and pork became a rare treat at mealtime. Farmers also grew sorghum, a sweet, cornlike plant that they used to make syrup. By the 1920s, as Texas farmers adapted to their new environment, sorghum began to replace corn as a staple feed crop for livestock. Sorghum had nutritional value similar to that of corn but was much more drought-hardy. By the 1940s a typical West Texas farm grew cotton and some wheat as cash crops, plus sorghum for livestock feed. When Spikes refers to the "feed," she is talking about corn, or, more likely, sorghum for the animals.

August 14, 1952

Mr. Spikes, Joe Ellis and myself were honored guests at the Parrish reunion in Ralls at the home of Delmar and Eula Parrish. . . . All the family were so congenial and so happy to be together. They are an honor to the father and the mother who brought them up, the father and mother who were pioneers of the plains and who so fearlessly and so bravely met the responsibilities and the disappointments of a new country. And there was lots of fun, too, as the brothers and sisters talked, fourteen of them, only one absent. They recalled the old pranks they played, the fun they had. We talked with Bonnie and learned [the origin of the lakes] formed in this prairie land. . . . "We had come to a flat land. So," Bonnie laughed, "we needed water. So some of us boys started out digging the lakes. We carried the water from the canyon in gallon syrup buckets. Jeff Spikes, Delmar, and some others helped." But I told Bonnie some years they must have been too lazy to carry water in gallon buckets to fill the lakes, for I saw them dry and cracked open.

I knew that Uncle Hank Smith and Uncle Charlie Hawes had the honor of digging the Blanco Canyon. I even talked with a woman who carried drinking water to them, but it was the first time I had ever known who was responsible for the many beautiful lakes we found on the plains. Now you who live far away from this magic land on the plains may just think this is another tall tale from Texas. But when you come here and see how the farmers have filled up many of these smaller lakes and drained others to make crops of cotton, and have found the water in deep underground rivers instead of having to carry it from the canyon in gallon buckets, as did the first settlers, you may well see and believe even the tallest of the tales of West Texas.

March 24, 1961

In my father's store at Emma was candy. How many times a day we children went in behind the counter and reached in a candy bucket or chose higher priced candies from the showcase, I have no idea, but in my father's old account books I find this item ever' so often: J. M. Witt, to candy, 40c. Some other equally interesting things I find that tell tales of those days. [ca. 2]-26-1900 W. W. Watts 2 cans peaches 40c, 6 cans sardines $1.00, 2 cans beans 25c, 2 cans tomatoes 25c. This tells that W. W. Watts, owner of the Z-L

Ranch, was in Emma on this date from his ranch in the southeast part of the country.

Now Major Watts lived in Kentucky and only visited his ranch, but this time he must have stayed some time, for I find on 6-11-1900 he bought five bushels of millet seed. The major was tall and broad—a military man, weighing about 180 pounds. He received his title, major, in the Civil War. He owned about one-fourth of Crosby County. His land came near the town section of Emma and extended into Garza County. The ranch house, a two-room house with two other rooms running back making a T, was situated just under the caprock about half a mile away. There were corrals and sheds and a draw ran in front of the house. Many of his ranch hands were from Kentucky, and I find their names, as well as the other hands, on these old daybooks. Christmas 1901 finds several in Emma for celebration. E. J. Powell bought a jumping jack— E. J. Moore 1 lb. candy. . . . Green Igo buying groceries and W. B. Millions and Steve Bates buying their dinner of salmon and crackers. Pink Parrish buying a saddle. Bruce Mitchell and A. K. Lackey and the name of Tom Burleson brings back memories of his early death.

Cowboys in Emma for a day. Usu-ally two or three at a time. I, a little girl eating candy and listening to the cowboys telling of their work. In the spring they told how the cook called them early, then they would drink a cup of coffee, hot and black, then saddle their broncos and ride the range. "I went down to the Salt Fork the other day," one said, "and I found an old cow bogged down in quicksand. The old critter was weak and when she made feeble struggles, that sand would tighten around her feet. She was sunk to her belly. The sand was cold, boys. I tell you, but I pulled off my boots and socks and tromped her out." I could see him patiently tramping one foot then another till she was free. Another cowboy told about finding a yearling that was killed the night before by a hungry loafer. "That ole loafer was still a eatin' on that pore yearlin' but when he saw me coming he beat it. I shot a couple of times but he was too far away to hit him." Common talk about everyday things.

Little did I dream that in later days, cowboys would be pictured with such thrills. "We had a peck of fun the other day with an old nester from the Plains who was getting a jag of mesquite wood, but when we found he had a sick wife and a passel of children we stopped our joking and helped him get wood even if 'twas against orders to let people get wood." They told of poor cows being bogged down in slimy mud along the creek. Two cowboys would rope them and pull them out. "I am glad it has come warm weather. I have had to break ice every morning up and down the creek so as the cows could get water and I am plumb sick of pulling their carcasses out of the mud," one complained. They talked of the blizzard we had had that winter, of cattle dead in piles along the drift fence. The storm drifted the cattle south—no time to eat—tired, hungry and cold they lay down when the drift fence was reached, and died.

But other things they talked about—the dances at various ranches—were forgotten for a time with cows bogged in mud and ice to break and long, cold nights herding in drizzled rain. The pretty girls at the dances, the good midnight suppers where they feasted on pies and cakes, and the music the fiddlers made still rang in their ears. One cowboy told of the wild plums and grapes that were in bloom and that

their sweetness filled the canyon. "You should have seen that tenderfoot when Green Igo put him on old Dick Turpin. That boy never got on him till he was throwed," laughed a tall cowboy who had been talking. I wonder where the Wild West writers get as much fighting and killing among the cowboys? Why, the cowboys I knew were hard-working, and on most ranches a fight meant the loss of a job, and as jobs were scarce no one liked to lose his. Cowboys buying presents at Christmas—other times buying overalls, candy, tobacco and wax. Sometimes cologne and bay rum.

The Z-L Ranch is no more. Its broad acres of green land are now turned with the plow. Homes and schoolhouses now stand where the cattle used to roam. Where cowboys used to run cattle now cars run faster than any cow pony. Airplanes fly over the hills where only the eagle and other winged birds could fly in those days. But many a man today looks back and wishes in his heart he was again on a good cow pony and ridin' for the Z-Ls.

The material dated March 24, 1961, is the last known piece that Nellie Witt Spikes authored for the newspaper. The latest column under the title "As a Farm Woman Thinks" that I have been able to locate is dated July 15, 1960. The March 24, 1961, piece appeared in the *Ralls Banner* as a standard article attributed to "Willie Witt Spikes," although Nellie is clearly the author. At the end of her career she came back to her father's mercantile daybooks, the same material used almost three decades earlier in the columns at the beginning of this chapter.

Cowboys at headquarters, Half-Circle-S Ranch, southeastern Crosby County, ca. 1905. Photograph courtesy of Southwest Collection, Texas Tech University, Lubbock, SWCPC 291 E5 #12.

Small Town Life

Farmers were not isolated on their farmsteads on the southern plains. Rural life relied on the services of small towns, and this may be one of the greatest changes between the early twentieth and the early twenty-first centuries. In Spikes's articles small towns such as Ralls, Floydada, Crosbyton, and the now extinct Emma leap to life. On market Saturday we see farmers selling produce, families shopping on bustling main streets, people pausing to socialize with friends. Towns now moribund teemed with life and commercial activity. Spikes described the vibrancy and energy of those small towns, the carefully planted flower gardens, the new houses and commercial buildings under construction. They appear in her columns as places of realized progress and of considerable future potential. These stories make clear the social and economic connections between small rural villages and the dispersed farms around them.

As automobiles made transportation faster, easier, and cheaper in the late twentieth century, many small towns in the Great Plains declined. People left rural villages to move to Lubbock, Dallas, and cities farther afield where jobs and economic opportunities beckoned. Even those who remained in small towns began to shop in larger cities, driving to Lubbock for weekly grocery trips, to Dallas for Christmas presents. Local merchants suffered and went out of business as consumers abandoned Main Street. By the turn of the twenty-first century few small towns, other than county seats, held their own, and many had ceased to serve any social or economic function.

These cycles of growth, prosperity, decline, and disappearance were not new. In the nineteenth century towns favored with railroad connections prospered, while those bypassed by the tracks withered and died. Spikes's girlhood home, Emma, which she described vividly as a thriving, up-and-coming town, is now a ghost town, recalled only in memoirs such as these. Towns come and go on the plains, shifting with the economic winds, sustaining families and then passing away when no longer needed. The selections below capture life in the small towns of rural West Texas in the early twentieth century, many of which have since fallen on hard times. Today Emma exists only as a historical marker by the road, a few withering buildings, and a cemetery; but in Spikes's memory it comes alive with settlers anticipating a prosperous future.

July 8, 1937

The wheat harvest is over; the combines are at rest till another year. Farm people sleep once more at night. In memory only we shall live again the thrilling days of the wonderful harvest. As I go about my usual duties, once more, I think over the days of rush and hurry. A day in a nearby town, in the height of the harvest. Trucks pouring liquid gold into waiting [railroad] cars and elevators, women coming in with bundles of soiled clothing. Grain from overall pockets choking the drain pipes of the washing machines. Tired, sleepy truck drivers, hurriedly drinking cups of strong black coffee, eating platters of ham and eggs. Oil trucks hurrying life-giving oil and gas to the combines.

Garage men servicing trucks and cars. Farmers in sweaty blue shirts and overalls hurrying in and out of implement stores. Birds were flying down from telephone posts and greedily eating the staff of life. . . . Cars were dodging chickens, turkeys and even shoats that were picking up grain scattered in the highways.

In all this hustle and bustle, a Negro was asleep on a shady porch of a store. Relaxed, caring not whether the wheat was saved or not, he lay sprawled in an easy chair. I live again the night we were kept awake by one of our trucks being stuck on a grade across the lake. Another night, one of the combine men had to be carried to a doctor at two o'clock. The hours of anxiety when we feared something would happen to the wheat and the relaxation that followed when it was saved. Humor and tragedy, work, hard work, sleepless nights, shall we ever forget? A young man, working at a busy elevator one night said, at the close of the harvest, "I am going to sleep till six o'clock in the morning, even if it makes me have bed sores." . . .

We have music night and day. Not one cent does it cost, not even a button to turn on nor off. A mockingbird sings at night. Thrills and calls, high notes and soft, sweet notes flood the night with soft melody.

Daytime, the little boy from town, who is helping me this summer, sings. Cowboy melodies, school songs, gay and sober, fall from his lips as easy as does the mockingbird's song. A sweet, clear voice he has. We milk to tunes like, "Frog Went A-courtin'," "Jingle Bells," and such. A farm needs a boy. The farm dog needs company; the pony needs a rider; the tank needs a boy to swim and splash in its cool waters. It has been many years since my boy was at home. My little helper this summer runs my errands, keeps me amused. May I have some part in helping him be an upright, useful citizen.

October 14, 1937

Petersburg was a busy place last Saturday as we waited for the clerks to get to us. We watched the people buying their groceries, clothing and other needs. A nice looking Mexican family was buying clothing. How the fond little brown-eyed mother stroked the warm brown jacket her grown son was trying on! The proud papa and the round-eyed baby looked on. Aren't Mexican children good in company? You never hear them crying. Isn't it nice to think people will be fed and warm this winter from our beautiful harvest? Perhaps we, as individuals, will not get as much as we wish from our crops, but we rejoice that many will share in the returns of the harvest.

November 11, 1937

Floydada was a busy place Saturday, and to me a place of unusual interest. I like to watch the people buying nice warm clothing—new shoes and boots—warm blankets—new stoves and good things to eat. I saw two young Indian boys, their straight black hair brushed back and oiled, wearing clothes like the well-dressed man of today wears. I thought what a short time it had been since their forefathers had camped where so many people were trading and the young men were in war paints with feathers in their hair. A car loaded with trunks bore an Arkansas license. The canning kitchen was a busy place and I had a nice visit with the lady in charge, Mrs. Taylor.

"Got a ketch in my gitalong." "What is the price of turkeys and when does the market open?" "I think boots are nice for school girls don't you?" "Yes we have out twenty bales." "Have you seen the oil derrick?" Snatches of conversation on the street. . . . It looked good seeing the people buying fruit, yellow pears and bananas, red apples, and golden oranges. I remember when I was a child, fruit was only to be had around Christmas, then it was lemons, oranges and apples. Bananas were almost unknown. Once when I went with my father to the Dallas Fair I bought two dozen bananas. As I remember now, I ate them all, but surely I did not.

I remember Floydada when I went to town, a young woman then. Before cold weather, the country women would go to town. New hats for the women, new hats for the men. One nice dress (a Sunday dress then), yards of gingham, and percale, red flannel for underwear, a bolt of bleached domestic for petticoats and other unmentionable garments. Buttons, pins, needles, ribbon—nothing must be forgotten, there would not be another trip before Christmas. And whisper to the lady clerks about the corsets. Yards and yards of outing, cotton flannel, by the bolt. One woman spent a hundred dollars at one time for winter clothing, and it was the talk of the county. Maybe Ma would have enough money to get a set of dishes. Perhaps Pa would have enough to get him a new pair of pants. His old coat would do. Times change, but we are glad that we can remember the days that were.

The severe economic distress between 1929 and 1933 prompted the creation of New Deal federal farm programs that transformed farm finances and have been the organizing force in American agriculture ever since. When government farm program checks began arriving in 1933, many farmers spent the money on consumer goods, from clothing and food to new cars and tractors. The opening of Washington's cash tap came as a pleasant shock to the people of the Great Plains. To farmers it was "manna from a clear sky." Farmers, merchants, and politicians welcomed the money wholeheartedly, with little hesitation about federal influence or control. In the spring of 1933 Congress created the Agricultural Adjustment Administration (AAA) weeks after Southern farmers had planted one of the biggest cotton crops ever, even as crop prices dropped into the basement. The already serious glut of cotton was sure to increase. Secretary of Agriculture Henry A. Wallace acted quickly, taking the extraordinary step of asking farmers to plow up part of the cotton they had just planted. This cut against the conservative grain, yet in Crosby County, Texas, and in farming communities across the South farmers lined up at courthouses to sign up for the plan. In mid-July, 1933, farmers waited in line all afternoon and evening at Crosbyton on the last day to enroll in the cotton program. They exhausted all of the available application forms and waited for more. When the deadline passed, 1,494 cotton farmers, nearly 100 percent, had enrolled. Federal administrators had initially hoped Crosby County farmers would plow up thirty-five thousand acres of young cotton plants. By early August they had destroyed fifty-six thousand acres under the program.

Farmers earned quick returns for their cooperation. In three months farmers enrolled, plowed up their crops, certified their compliance, and picked up checks from the county agent. The first batch of cotton checks—worth $180,000—arrived in the county at the end of September 1933. By October $406,000 had come into the county, with more expected. At the end of the year the cotton program had netted Crosby County $800,000. The program for wheat, a minor crop in the county, brought in another $31,000, and the corn-hog program $108,000. To farmers who had faced overproduction and dropping prices throughout the 1920s, followed by the national collapse into four years of depression and now the worst drought and dust storms in decades, this indeed was manna from a clear, hot, and very dry sky. And it was not simply a one-time emergency measure, although it was initially designed so. The government cash tap remained open year after year. The commodities programs continued to put money into farmers' pockets. In 1940, eight years into the programs, Crosby County earned $717,000 from the federal farm programs, with nearly 100 percent participation.

Car dealers benefited from the farm program money. As early as July 1933, Crosby County dealerships began increasing their inventory. A week after farmers signed cotton contracts, locking them into the program, the newspaper reported, "Many new cars are now seen on the streets of Crosbyton and dealers are expecting a greater business in a short time." By the end of August the Ford and Chevrolet dealers had empty lots, selling cars as soon as they arrived. Car sales continued high through the fall and winter, and the business boom extended to many merchants in Crosbyton and Ralls, with people "buying freely of most everything."

December 23, 1937

The Mexicans have gone. Gone to where there is warm sunshine and the beauty of summer. They have quit pulling bolls of cotton to gather golden oranges from trees. An hour's notice and their belongings are packed, ready to go where there is work. Happy and friendly were my friends and I miss them. But next year when our fields are white with cotton again, they have promised to be back.

January 20, 1938

The sale as I saw it: A clear, cold day. Cars with trailers and more cars with trailers. Unusually crowded with eager faced men and here and there, a woman. Two big pots of coffee, the fragrance mingling with the scent of burning pine; the candy man, with sweet candies, golden oranges, red apples. Two auctioneers, standing on a wagon, the men crowding close, bidding on this horse collar or that set of harness. The man with the butcher knives, "Yes ma'am, I made them myself; they are made of the very best metal." The whinnying of horses, wondering what the curious crowd of people meant. The bawling of cows, separated from their calves and waiting to go to the green wheat fields. Good-natured people, jostling and crowding to get to the sandwiches and to buy a good home-made country pie, sold by the ladies of the neighborhood. The shouts of

Last bale of cotton, Christmas, 1923. Photograph courtesy of Southwest Collection, Texas Tech University, Lubbock, SWCPC 322 E1 #175.

little children, too young to be in
school. The music of a radio. The
whirr of an aeroplane, sailing over
our heads like a huge hawk. Frightened white leghorn hens in a coop.
Little pigs squealing and grunting.
Friends meeting friends, people
making new acquaintances.

But the men interested me most.
Men enjoying the sale as a woman
enjoys shopping in town. The men,
big men, little men, farmers dressed
in blue denim with brown jackets
and corduroy caps. I could not tell
my own husband until I looked him

in the face, there were so many
dressed like him. Men from town
dressed in overcoats and hats. I like
a sale. Don't you?

October 27, 1938

The first cold norther hits Floydada.
I was in town. These are some of the
things I saw. Two well-dressed men
running with several joints of new,
black stovepipe in each hand. Their
dignity was thrown to the cold north
wind, as it were, for the time being.
Two dozen or so pigeons sitting

on the south side of a barn, hover-
ing downy feathers over their cold
feet. Women snipping off red roses,
dahlias to save beautiful bouquets
from the frost. A grown Negro boy
school-hopping across the street
to keep himself warm (where ever
have I seen anyone school-hop?).
Cars with oil barrels on the front
bumpers. Cars with trailers holding
barrels of oil. Sacks of coal on the
running boards. A Negro putting
joints of rusty stovepipe together.
The town smelled of apples, of moth
balls, burning cotton bolls, smoke
from gins, flakes of cotton settling
down, making one think of snow. My
clothing was half and half. Winter coat, white shoes, light hose, a
summer hat. Been thinking I would
get some new winter things but just
kept putting it off getting them. Old
men buying long-handled underwear. Young men wishing it was still
stylish. Little boys bareheaded but
wearing heavy mackinaws. Chili in
Spanish display on the counters.
Bolts of outing and stacks of blankets where organdie and thin sheets
have lain so long. Trees wearing
suits of gold and pale yellow. White
petunias looking like ghost flowers
in the cold. I like to go to Floydada.

November 24, 1938

The little city of Lubbock looked
very busy last Saturday. Where once
the cowboy ran his fast pony after
the bawling steers, now college boys
run with a football. Where the herd
lay bedded and sleeping under the
stars now many boys and girls are
sleeping under the dormitory roofs.
Where the loafer wolf howled, the
sirens of the fire wagons and ambu-
lances shriek and moan. Where the
shy antelope drank from the canyon
springs, a beautiful park invites
the merry crowds to stop and play.
Where the prairie grass lay long and
green, now are beautiful lawns, and
where the catclaw and mesquite
reached out long, lacy fingers, tall
trees and evergreens, planted by the
hand of man, now cast dark shade
over the passerby. Where once the
wildflowers bloomed grow flowers
of many hues. These are some of
the changes we have seen. And who
knows what we shall see yet? I like
to go to the big towns, but I like best
to trade, as we once said, instead
of shop, in the little towns. There
in the big places we are not known;
our few bills look so small as we
see the heaps of things; we are hard
to please after we see hundreds of
dresses, hats and shoes; the clerks
do not know us, are not interested

in our troubles and pleasures, but in the little town it is different: our few bills do not look so hopeless; we are pleased in selecting a dress, a hat, some shoes; the clerks know us, ask about our husband and the new baby. We get sympathy and help with our purchases. Hurrah for the little towns, may they never die!

December 15, 1938

Don't suppose there is any use to tell you about the fire sale day last week. All of you were there that lived within fifteen or twenty miles. I saw so many people I knew, I asked if the dates on the old settler's reunion had been changed. We pushed and elbowed, but with what a friendly spirit. Men sat in cars and held babies while mothers shopped. Around and around cars drove hunting a place to park so they would still be in town. Like a holiday, it was, football boys, men carrying baby buggies, blankets, dolls, colored people enjoying the day.

January 26, 1939

I was in a little town not so far distant last Saturday afternoon, and it was a busy, entertaining place. A row of cars on either side of the one street, two rows in the center with just enough room on either side to get through. Merchants were going in a run, filling orders of groceries, testing cream, counting out eggs and measuring off yards of goods. The druggist sold ice cream, cough medicine and gave almanacs and calendars. A sweet old grandmother sat in a warm car and watched the crowd; fat babies in other cars, safe and warm while their mothers did their shopping. Old men sat on benches, talked of crops and tractors and the government; women talked with neighbor women of chickens and babies and quilts and gardens; young girls with lovely curls and pretty dresses talked to young men, but their talk was not of crops nor gardens.

A modern wheat tractor with cab and radio strutted up and down the street. A colored man drove a tractor pulling two empty wagons and looked like he felt like a million. A sign on the street, "Shoat for sale." A load of cedar posts needing buyers. The bumpers on cars were filled with laying mash and stock salt. People got in cars, so crowded with bundles and sacks there was no room to put one's feet. Little boys ran here and there, set firecrackers under the feet of older people and laughed when they jumped; little girls held ice cream cones and sticks of candy, careful not to get any on their nice dresses. I came away reluctantly, for the crowd had only begun to leave, and there was not any telling what old friends one would meet.

March 9, 1939

This is the first time I have ever been in Floydada early Sunday morning. As I go to the cafe for bacon and coffee, everything looks so queer, used as I am to seeing everything so busy. The barber chairs sit in a row, prim and white as if in their Sunday garb. The dresses and shoes in the windows do not beckon as they do on weekdays. The fruits and vegetables look more like decorations than for consumption. The storekeepers and clerks have all left for a brief holiday. As I walk along the deserted streets this thought comes to me: What if the Last Day had come and by some miracle I was the only one left? Of what use would all these things in the nice little town be to me when the inhabitants and all my friends had gone?

March 21, 1940

Friday we went to Petersburg to see a tractor demonstration. As we left home all the world around us was shades of brown under the blue bowl of the sky, with here and there a moving tractor lending a spot of green or of red as it quilted the brown earth into curves of parallel lines. Brown tree trunks rose from brown soil. Our road ran by a green wheatfield, where red, white-faced cows grazed on the tender blades of the wheat. Then we saw the town of Petersburg. The wavering mirage blurred the pinks, the greens, the whites and the blues into a mile of Dresden ribbon. Old Mother Earth seemed to have pinned the ribbon on her brown dress as if expecting company. When we entered the town, the mirage had faded and the streets looked like a flower show was being held, but the flowers were gay reds and intense greens and flaunting orange of tractors, and instead of women talking of posies, men talked of tractors, of power lifts and dual wheels.

How very thankful we should be, I thought, to live in a land where men could take a holiday and talk of machinery to raise food for a nation, of cattle and even talk about the high officials if they chose, instead of speaking of guns and poison gas and afraid to even whisper a thought to anyone about how their country was ruled. A few women stood in line with the men and reached in for delicious sandwiches, sugary doughnuts and a cup of good hot coffee. We applauded at the first picture show when men and boys boxed and fought and kicked one another, watched with interest men and boys doing hard work with ease by the use of modern machinery. But it was decidedly a man's day, and we women felt like men must do at a women's quilting party.

April 25, 1940

It was my happy privilege to be in Floydada last Monday when the cleanup parade passed around the square with music by the band, boys and girls following with their teachers, armed with brooms, mops and hoes and rakes. Oh, for the time to come, we pray, when nations of the earth will throw down their guns, used to kill one another, and take up the brooms and mops to clean out dirt and disease, take up books to wipe out ignorance, use martial music to fight the things that are evil and right the wrongs of their own people. Let us not pray for another armistice, which only means a brief cessation of fighting, but let our prayers and our conversation to always be for "peace"! May we wipe the word "armistice" from our calendars and put in the word "peace day." Let

us never be content to substitute one word for another that does not mean the real thing!

April 10, 1941

April turned a blue bowl over the plains last Friday, scattered a few soft, white clouds across its calm surface, warmed a light wind and turned a sunshiny smile on the crowd at the fat stock show in Floydada. It was a scene full of color. Sleek calves and cows looked with large eyes at the curious, smiling people, hogs grunted in the shade of boards on their pens. Hogs are always contented, I find, when they have something to eat and shade and water. You can move them anywhere you please and they are at home with the above requirements. Not so with many animals. Did you ever try to make a cow drink out of a strange trough? A&M graduates walked among the farmers and the 4-H boys. Women and girls took a keen interest in the judging and the ribbons tied on the winners. A tragedy. A boy of about eight or ten came to his mother with chewing gum all over his clean shirt. No amount of scraping seemed to dislodge the sticky stuff, so he went on all stuck up and enjoyed the day nevertheless. Two young lads took time off to see who was the better man. Fists flew for a little while. The bawling of the cattle, the grunting of the hogs and the bleating of the sheep with the calls of the soda pop boys made country sounds in town.

May 15, 1941

We went to the dairy show at Plainview last Thursday and dutifully went around and looked at all the stock, exclaimed at the size of the Durhams, patted the little Jersey calf but had a better time watching a cow get a bath and being groomed for the judging ring. She had so much enjoyment out of the cold water being squirted on her, and stock show cattle seem to have so much pride in being exhibited.

In the Plainview park there were eight hundred of Uncle Sam's boys, some spreading their cots and others cooking dinner and some polishing up on old ugly trucks for the parade that afternoon. As the boys paraded down main street, one looking like his brother, near, and he like the next, people stood in a silence that was too deep for tears, along the path of the marching boys and trucks filled with their guns. Not a cheer, that may have to come later, God forbid, if the boys need to be spurred on to meet the

enemy. America does not want war. They want a world free from wars and causes of wars. Oh, if this year of training is all the boys will have to do, men and women whispered to themselves as the sun-tanned boys passed before their tear-filled eyes. It will not hurt them but perhaps help, but Oh, not to be sent on to war, not that, we pray.

July 23, 1942

Well I must get dinner ready for the men in the field. Would you like to put on this bonnet and go with me? First we will get the chicken. Look how wary that young rooster is of crumbled bread and the wire hidden behind my back. Just a jiffy and he will be dressed and cooling. It will not take long to pick some string beans; better get a few cucumbers and onions, and three or four beets, we like them buttered. After the beans are strung and on cooking, we will go to the smokehouse for a hunk of bacon to boil with the beans. Next, to the potato patch, where some small potatoes can be gotten. They are pretty easy to scrape while the skin is so tender. You may beat this bowl of cream for butter; I will make a peach cobbler. Syrup sweetens peaches now as well as it did for our grandmothers. It is so nice to have milk and butter in the refrigerator instead of the well. Yes, we have walked a good piece, several blocks if we were in town. Meals are so scattered this time of the year, but how nice it is to pick your own.

While you are watching the boiling pot I will try to tell about the fine city of Petersburg, a place where I have gone since a store and office were kept in a dugout. This is a busy, friendly town. The golden grain from a field of wheat pours into the tall elevators and waiting boxcars, fleecy cotton rolls out in the bound bales from puffing gins. Clacking chickens with yellow legs tied together are shut in coops, rich cream stands on scales, crates of brown and white eggs, squealing porkers fat from maize crops, make a picture of plenty. A baker rushes golden loaves of tender white bread to the stores where clerks are putting groceries from their shelves into large paper bags. Sun tanning, overall-clad farmers stand around and visit. Children rush here and there with ice cream, candy and bananas. Farm women laugh and talk with one another, glad of a chance to rest and see friends. If you want a real good time and to see rural America at her best, go to Petersburg some Saturday afternoon.

July 1, 1943

The cool of the night was still on the leaves of the trees that shaded the pleasant homes in Idalou as my husband and I went through taking a load of hogs to market one day last week. The good red land with its growing crops of many shades of green marched right up to the town. The wheat was spun gold, waiting the harvest. I thought of the old fairy tale of the poor girl that married the king and whose father told the king that the girl could spin straw into gold. Right before my eyes I had seen the miracle of gold being made from straw; gold that would buy clothes and fuel and food; gold that would buy bombs for our boys overseas. I saw the gins that would pull soft, fleecy cotton from burs, cloth for many uses, feed for cattle and hogs. Churches stood pointing the way to heaven; schools were open for children to learn a better way. I watched a sow going down a row of sudan, followed by a bunch of grunting pigs; a boy, very proud of his new boots, rolled a worn-out tire around; men were opening up their stores, I heard the click of their keys and the tramping of feet as they entered the dim interior, smelling of ripe pineapple and golden oranges. I saw women hoeing in their garden;

I wished I could stop and visit in the tree-shaded, flower-bordered homes. I would like to see the pictures of the boys in service, hear bits of letters, see the friendly smiles and hear the pleasant voices of new acquaintances. But the road led on, and I had only time to pass through and wish I could get acquainted with the Idalou folks.

March 3, 1944

Seen at Cone, the old store building of the Bartley family, being loaded on trucks to be hauled away. The old store . . . has long stood facing the road, once a muddy street in rainy times. The old store has weathered many a high, cold wind, steamed in the heat of summer suns, sheltered many a man and woman in its coal stove—warmed insides, in its cool and shade on the front porch in lazy warm afternoons. Many a stick has been whittled, many a conversation taken place there, but the wind swept the whittlings away as time has carried away the talk. Many a sign was tacked to the front advertising this and that—only the tacks still stay, the cards as well as most of the things they told of are no more. Once there were horses and mules stomping flies outside the store building, their owners waiting for

the mail that was brought there in the open buggy by a frail woman, Mrs. Ramsuer. Folks waiting for groceries, visiting then as is the group that is now standing in front of the store.

July 21, 1944

I find I am still thinking of going to Petersburg the other day. Wilda, the baby, and I went with Mr. Spikes after repairs, and as we had nothing much to do sat in front of a store on a long wooden bench that has done duty there for many years and watched the people come and go. Invisible links went out from that place that day to boys in foreign lands we knew. As merchants rolled potatoes and onions in a hard-to-get brown paper sack, they were thinking of their boy far away that had stood behind the same counter. We knew that the barber, now clicking his shears over more gray heads than brown, was remembering boys who once sat with the cloth under their own unsheared heads. Type clinked into place as Mr. Suits printed the latest news about these same boys. We saw farmers of middle age hurry into repair stores, taking the place of a fighting boy who once so proudly rode the new red tractor. We knew many bonds lay secure in the big brick bank vault, placed there by trembling hands against the day when son and daughter would come home. The many churches stood, a place of prayer for the absent; mothers passed by, letters clasped in their work-worn hands, letters from overseas and letters to far places. "I have a boy in England," I would say, and there was a bond between a stranger and myself, now strangers no longer but friends. Hearts would

be opened to me, a picture shown and pride, even through tears, in a son who was giving his all to his country he so longed to see again. Yes, I felt unafraid and undaunted as I watched the people in this fine little town go about the business of carrying on, for I know all over this land of ours thousands and thousands of little towns were doing the same, helping the big towns keep on keeping on.

Local newspapers were an important part of small town life through the first half of the twentieth century. Every new town in the plains needed one, and it was not unusual for towns numbering in the hundreds to host two or even three competing papers. Many towns in other plains states had both Democratic and Republican newspapers, but in Texas after the Civil War there were few Republicans to be found. Newspapers were small operations, with circulations of a few thousand, that rarely spread beyond the county boundaries. Papers came out weekly, often on Thursday or Friday, and consisted of only eight to twelve pages. Advertising occupied much of that space, and there was a lot of boilerplate national and international news taken wholesale from distant news services. Still, local news is what sold papers, and these publications provide a rich source of information for historians interested in local events. The papers covered county and town politics, social and cultural events, farming developments, weather, and gossip of all kinds.

Another important component of local journalism was boosterism. Newspaper publishers relied for their income primarily on advertisers, meaning that their interests aligned closely with the business community. Town businessmen, and therefore their newspaper colleagues, wanted rapid population growth. Farmers, who were often land speculators on the side, wanted population growth, too. Newspapers bragged about the thriving businesses, the emerging opportunities, the fine weather and attractive landscape, the educational institutions and churches that made their town appealing to potential immigrants. The rhetoric drifted from mere description to exaggeration to downright lies. Small-town newspapers had two audiences: regional residents on farms and in town and distant immigrants who might consider moving there. While local newspapers are an invaluable source of information about rural places, it is important to read them with a grain of salt, remembering that publishers accentuated the positive and often simply ignored the negative.

Crosby County had a typical newspaper history. The first paper, the *Crosby County News*, opened in the Quaker village of Estacado in 1886 when John Murray brought a printing press from Hardeman County. As there were only three businesses in Estacado, Murray recruited advertising from Amarillo, 140 miles to the north, and Colorado City, 125 miles south. There were no other towns of their size in the Texas high plains. Murray sometimes could publish only a half-sheet issue when the shipment of paper failed to appear. And he initially did not run any national or international news because it was already six weeks old by the time it arrived. In 1912 Murray remembered that "the *Crosby County News* was not only the pioneer paper but the pioneer booster as well. Several hundred copies of each issue would be printed, giving glowing descriptions of the country, and these would be mailed to all parts of the United States." But in the unique context of West Texas, not everyone appreciated the boosterism. Ranchers did not want small farmers moving in to compete with them for access to the grassland, and the Quakers had hoped the region would be settled primarily by those of their own faith. Both groups pressured him, and Murray responded by abandoning Estacado in favor of Emma, whose promoters lured him with a free town lot and house. In 1890 he moved his printing press to Emma, giving it new legitimacy as a viable county seat. The *Crosby County News* continued publishing from Emma until 1911, when the next political upheaval shifted the county seat to Crosbyton. The newspaper followed, where it merged with a new upstart, the *Crosbyton Review,* and continued under the latter name.

Nellie Witt Spikes provided columns for four different small-town newspapers during her journalistic career: the *Crosbyton Review,* the *Ralls Banner,* the *Lorenzo Tribune,* and the *Floyd County Hesperian* across the county line in Floydada. It was editor Harold Steen, of the *Hesperian,* who gave Spikes her first writing assignment, asking her to fill in for a young columnist who quit suddenly. Eventually the other three papers picked up the column, and for many years identical columns ran in two or three different newspapers each week.

April 6, 1945

Last Thursday Mr. Spikes took some stock to Lubbock, so Wilda, Margaret Nell, and I went along to do some shopping and some visiting. We got up early, hurried the work, and reached Lubbock about twelve, but we like to have never found the end of the long line of cars with trailers and pickups all on the same business as ours, to sell stock. Cows still with the taste of green wheat in their mouths switched and bawled as the cars stood still waiting for the one at the unloading end to get out of the way. Four blocks long was the line, and we at one end, only for a few seconds, until others came and got behind. The outside bidder began on us. Soon there was a little auction going on, with my husband shaking his head at every bid, till at last convinced, they turned and hopped another car behind. We pulled up some fifty feet, then settled back to wait again and again.

Wilda and the baby could not stand it any longer; they decided to walk on to the Commission House. Airplanes circled overhead; puffing engines belched out black smoke in the air and rattled long trails of cars behind. The man in the car with the small trailer ahead of us never was there when the time came to pull up. He visited back and forth as did many others. Once as he stopped at our car, he said, "I am not in a hurry, jest peears like I am." One man called to another: "Bet you're out of snuff or you wouldn't be whistling." I longed for the book *Young'un* I was so interested in and had left at home. There was not a single thing in the car to read. . . . The white caliche dirt picked up by every vehicle settled on us and made the new green leaves on the trees look as if children had used mother's powder on them. We got hungry but dared not lose our place. Mr. Spikes got tired and visited up and down the line. When I didn't pull up quickly enough someone behind was always ready to call out, "Move up there, Sister," which anyway I was glad to do. At last the big gate swung open, and believe it or not we were next.

August 3, 1945

One of my earliest remembrances is living in Parker County near Weatherford in a small house on the nursery. I went to town with my father, John Witt, in a small cart pulled with one horse. I liked to hear the clop-clop of the horse's hoofs on the cobbled streets. The bushel baskets of blackberries and dewberries and raspberries behind the seat where we rode so proudly, it seemed to me, shining like jewels in the summer sun. The baskets of red and yellow peaches smelling like heaven, the long, green, cool Parker County melons, wasn't that a nice place for a little girl with long pigtails and ruffled sunbonnet to be riding? And how the tin quart cup glistened in the sun as Father measured out the shiny jewels to the waiting women! How patiently the old horse stood switching off flies! And then as Father took up the reins we clopped, clopped to another house and to the stores till at last the baskets were all empty and we turned and went back to the lovely nursery where all these good things grew in profusion.

November 2, 1945

The other afternoon the store at Farmer was a busy place as Fletcher Stark unloaded his pickup after a trip to market. It made me think of the times Mr. Spikes would be gone to town all day in the wagon and the children and I watched with keen interest everything he had brought home. Always the sack of candy was the first, and as the children and I enjoyed the sweets, we looked at everything and wanted to know the details of the day's trip. It also reminded Mrs. Tomlinson of child-

hood days when her father would go on a long trip to market. "We could not all have shoes at one time," she laughed, "And one time when pa came in my brother said he had just as well try on his shoes to see if they fit, and pa informed him that he did not bring him any shoes that time." Fletcher did not have much room to work as we all crowded around, and how we gasped when we saw the Hershey bars. And hunted our nickels!

May 27, 1949

Announcer for KAMQ, Amarillo, Texas: "Well, here is a card from Petersburg, Texas. Where in the world is Petersburg, anyway?" Well, Mr. Announcer, your education on West Texas has been sadly neglected. This growing town started way back when the big white mail hacks carried mail and passengers to and from Amarillo. No need for radios then when little Spanish mules were so swift on foot and Buddy Coke Fullingim, Chad Gott, Bud English and Mr. Reagan kept the nesters' feet dancing with cowboy-spurred boots to their fine fiddle tunes. A Mr. Peter dug in and started a store. The post office was called Petersburg. A fine beginning from a hole in the ground. Other settlers liked the location. Still do I, for that matter. If you want to see business transacted in a hurry, just drop in the town someday. No, there is not a dugout to drop into, but up-to-date stores, fine residences, churches, and consolidated schools. No, I do not live in this little city, but if I turn fourteen corners I am in the town, which is some ten miles toward where northers and blizzards clear off. Cars with four county licenses stand at the curbs, and if a high wind were to blow the town away it would not be far to Floyd, Crosby or Lubbock counties.

You guessed it; it is in Hale. There are several oil wells pumping away not far on two sides of the town, but there is no more to-do over them than there is over windmills. Petersburg stretches across the land like a mile of Dresden ribbon, green, white, pink, yellow, blue; water gushes from big wells down rows of cotton, wheat and hegari. If you ask the people who live there they will tell you it is the greatest town in West Texas—maybe the whole world. Many of its sons have traveled around the world, in many cities and towns and lands. Who could be better judges? Mr. Announcer, my education has been neglected as to the names of radio announcers as close by as Amarillo. I do not know

yours. If you will dedicate a number to me, all will be happy.

July 8, 1949

Fair, fat and forty: Fair with beautiful homes, green trees and flowering plants; fat with rich farmlands, oil wells, cattle and dairy products; and forty years old on the second day of July, the little city of Abernathy put the big pot in the little one and pulled off a celebration that the children who rode the swings, ate the ice cream and begged fathers, mothers and grandparents for more money will tell to their own grandchildren in the years to come. Mr. Spikes and I sat under the shady trees, out of our own environment and knowing none of the people shaking hands and greeting one another with laughter sometimes mixed with tears of joy. We sat there enjoying every minute. "I used to come to this part of the country and see hundreds of cattle rounded up," Mr. Spikes remembered, "But now I see they have gotten to rounding up the people."

Overheard as group after group formed, changing, and forming again and again: "I know your face, I am trying to place you." . . . "My operation was an unusual one." (A young woman could not shake the memory and was boring, perhaps, an unwilling listener.) "Hope we all will be here another forty years" (this with regret and a laugh and a sigh). . . . "Oh, He's a great-granddad now." . . . "Yes, she was in my class." . . . "I used to live here and still love it." . . . "Now don't you slip off (a mother to a young son); I will never in this world find you." . . . "We could ride a horse by the time we could walk." . . . "Meet my friends, Mr." . . . "He has as many oil wells as he has teeth." . . . Overhead the sun shone hot, the sky was clear, cars roared down the highway, many tired people passing through smiled as they saw the crowd having a glorious time; . . . mothers held babies, and the babies soon got hot, sticky and sleepy; . . . love and affection held sway as friends, long parted, met. . . . Surprise on many faces, but none showed the sorrow that might be hiding under the smiles. Abernathy was celebratin' and life was still sweet and good. . . .

I could not do justice to the parade. Maybe most of you will see the pictures in the papers. . . . It was well planned and traffic stopped to let the parade go by. . . . But I think the thing that most interested me was the hands of the older people who sat or stood there by the cov-

ered wagon registering and talking of other days. I saw old, work-worn hands that once held bridle reins, plow reins over teams of mules in the field and down the long freight roads, now holding canes or trembling with age. . . . Hands wrinkled that once carried buckets of water from mills not too close by. . . . Hands that once were brown and smooth poking cow chips in bachelor stoves, or feeding the small bunch of cattle in the sleet and snow when the husband was gone. Now this day of July the second, 1949, these hands folded in laps or given in greeting of old friends.

I looked in the eyes that once saw herds of antelope running like the wind. Eyes that saw drouths burn up their crops, eyes that could see in the past more clearly than they named the stores across the streets. . . . I saw shoulders bent with putting them to the wheels of making a mighty empire of the Plains, shoulders that once were straight and strong. . . . Hats off to these grand men and women who have made such sections as Abernathy strong, fruitful and enterprising. Now these men and women are looking with pride on the second and third generations to carry on . . . and with such a background, they will!

August 5, 1949

Maybe it is time to . . . look around the sleepy town to those hot summer days, forty-six years ago. The wind stirred the windmill and cold water ran into the big overhead tank with a cooling sound. . . . Cowboy watered his tired, thirsty horse at the trough on the north side. A freight wagon creaked and rattled into town, the driver worn out from the long trip to and from the railroad at Canyon City. . . . The breeze ruffled the cottonwood leaves at the Martin home. . . . The scent of sweetish-sour canyon plums came on the air from several homes. . . . A few men sat on the worn porch in front of the store and whittled small sticks into curly whittlings. No smoke from rushing trains mingled with the smoke from cow chip fires in the frame dwellings. . . . Children scream and laugh and shout from their play, but for the most part you can hear the sound of locusts and the chirping of the mud dauber birds under the eaves of the courthouse.

Only a few short years Emma played a leading role in Crosby County, from 1891 to 1908 or '10. But she lives on in the memory of the ones who knew and loved her. The scent of blossoming wild plums and yellow roses at the Murray orchard, the exquisite perfume of honeysuckle and roses from the Martin home, the magic perfume of waxy white locust blossoms in the moonlight of the courtyard—these live on. The sound of running water in barrels, the click of a key as the merchant locks up his stock of goods to go home, the sound of a galloping horse, the rattling of wagons and buggies, the singing of Will Reagan bringing in the mail, the dancing fiddle tunes from the big courtroom; oh, those are not forgotten. The sight of long lances as the boys ran the tournaments at picnics, the big frosted cakes and chess pies and the smoke from the roasting barbecue. No, we do not forget. But as you read this your memories will blot out these I am recording and yours will come clear and sweet and take their place and we shall all be happier for the days that once were.

October 7, 1949

The autumns at Emma were so very quiet compared to the ones now. School started around the first of September, and children were not bothered about it stopping for them to pick cotton, for cotton was something one's father and mother told about having to pick back in East Texas or pictured in the big geogra-

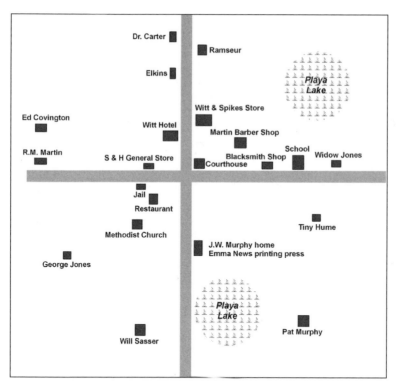

Old Emma in 1900, drawn by Geoff Cunfer after a sketch map prepared by Nellie Witt Spikes for Ralls Scout Post 333, ca. 1970. This intersection is about five miles south of Ralls near the intersection of State Highway 207 and County Road 182. Original sketch held at Ralls Historical Museum, Ralls, Texas, adapted with permission.

phy book. Father would put knives on a sled and cut the small sorghum crop. The ranch hands would be in town for a day eating sardines and crackers with plenty of pepper sauce as they sat on the scarred counters in the stores. They would buy a slicker, maybe a red or blue bandana to keep the dust from going down their backs or to keep lips from chapping. A blue shirt and blue overalls, and they would be ready to go up-trail for the fall drives. Men stood around the quiet town and talked of the coming election, which would make the town anything but quiet for a few days with the shooting of anvils and the loud calls of victory by the winning ones. No clicking of running machinery as now, no filling the towns to overflowing on Saturdays. Men would go to the brakes and bring back loads of mesquite wood for the winter when the cow chips would be damp and smoky or covered up with snow.

Freighters would pull out for Amarillo, but their creaking wagons would only be a spot on the long, empty freight road and would disturb only a few as they passed on. No buzzing above in the heavens greater than the whizzing wings of the bull-bat. Quiet, so very quiet, it seems to me looking back. So much time. Not pulled from one thing to another before the first was fully done. No radios running at full blast, only the soft music from the piano at Dr. Carter's. Or the running of cool water in the big tank in the courtyard. The click of a key in the lock at the store, the soft beating of hoofs of the cowboy's horse leaving town.

Autumn at Emma. The leaves on the locust and cottonwood trees turning yellow as the sunshine. No startling reds and blazing orange as in the timber. Green summer grasses now a pale brown. Mrs. R. N. Martin's chrysanthemums white as snow, yellow as soft gold. Pale blue skies, a vast bowl turned over a flat world. Tonight I am homesick, homesick for another autumn at Emma.

March 17, 1950

All of a sudden we took the notion to move to town and for the past month have been so busy that this space has

been neglected, but I hope you have not forgotten me. It was with mixed feeling of the joy of a new home mixed with the sorrow of leaving the old that we saw our few household possessions loaded on the trucks. Few, did I say? Well, it seemed so many that we wondered if we would get them all in the new home. The dresser that I heralded with pride when my husband loaded it from the wagon long ago. . . . It was going back to Floydada from whence it came. I could only bring three bookcases, so I weeded out many books and stored them in the attic. But the boys thought they would never get all the boxes and boxes of books loaded and unloaded. Forty-three years of collecting. The first night we spent in our new home our things looked so strange in the new surroundings. I went from table to chair to realize the change. . . . Everyone is so good and kind to us. Paul and John took out a day to get us moved. I slipped in some buckets and boxes of rocks, but the large ones I left. I suppose as I go to the farm I will bring a few with me from time to time.

March 31, 1950

When asked just why we moved to Floydada, we would say there are many reasons. We could not find a

White Auto and Ralls Pharmacy, Ralls, Texas, mid- to late 1950s.
Photograph courtesy of Southwest Collection, Texas Tech University,
Lubbock, SWCPC 291 E8.

suitable place in Ralls at the same time we made our decision. We have lived between Ralls and Floydada for forty-three years, or at least Floydada was here then. It seemed we were as much at home in one place as another. It is only a few minutes' drive from all our children and friends in Crosby County. . . . We are very pleased with our nice little home and the pleasant neighbors near us. It may be like moving old, rooted plants for us to move, but if we have plenty of friends to call, time to read and to write, garden a little and raise plenty of flowers, we will take deep roots and, like the plants, take a new growth. One reason that might have been hidden deep in my heart is the love of the canyons in this country. When we go south to visit there is always the canyon to cross, giving inspiration and help and comfort as it has done through the years.

April 7, 1950

Lifetime habits are hard to break. For some forty years we ate our supper on the farm after everything else was finished. Now we are in town with nothing special to do, we wait till after dark for supper. Just does not seem right otherwise. I am glad for Lon Davis's windmill. I like to look at one and know which direction the wind is from. I would not like to live where I could not see a windmill.

October 26, 1951

The cotton fields look like mattresses ready for the covering. The white gold of the Plains has everything and everyone in motion, and our towns take on the color of a foreign land. In Ralls last Saturday I stood on the upstairs porch of my son's hospital and leaned over the rail and looked and looked, listened and thrilled at the sight. Cars and trucks and pickups of every color, dresses and sweaters and scarves of our latest population added every color of the rainbow, blues and reds, greens and purples, yellows of every shade, greens, all turning and blending in the bright sunshine of a perfect day. Spanish tunes came gaily from stands, the bystanders cutting a few dance steps to the music, more and more families unloaded from the parked trucks, and papa and mama, grandpa and grandma and children like stairsteps added to the crowd, which was happy and good-humored. The black-eyed children did not cry and beg, they laughed but hid in their

mother's skirts at the approach of admiring "strangers," for many are so very pretty. The dogs were having a feast as they got the scraps from any dropped ice cream cones or hamburgers. Grocer boys carried huge sacks and boxes of groceries to the trucks, merchants sweated in their hurry to get to the "waiter." Passers-by dodged wispy cotton candy on long sticks, ice cream drips and banana peels. It seemed as I watched that Ralls was like a bright-colored merry-go-round with music, and everybody having a grand time.

October 13, 1952

Last Saturday afternoon as we looked and marveled at the huge crowds which swept down the streets of Ralls, like a river of moving color, we thought of other falls in other years of our being in Ralls on a Saturday afternoon. We recalled empty store buildings that looked so tragic and forlorn. We remembered some hundred people or so, standing and holding some tickets to get the twenty-five or so dollar prize money. We from the country never bought electric light bulbs, for we never had any electricity. We either stopped on the way to town or home to work on our car, fix a flat or to lend some tire patching to another

Top: Corner of Watts and Main Street in Ralls, Texas, May 1, 1928.
Photograph courtesy of Crosby County Pioneer Memorial Museum,
Crosbyton, Texas, 2181.
Bottom: Main Street, Ralls, Texas, mid- to late 1950s. Photograph
courtesy of Crosby County Pioneer Memorial Museum, Crosbyton,
Texas, 0322.

in need. We had a little money in our purses which was gotten the hard way, milking cows in an open wire lot on cold mornings, chickens raised in the cellar in an old cranky incubator, from eggs and maybe a bushel of turnips or black-eyed peas. No, I am not complaining: I was just a-thinking as I watched the buying crowds, standing thick in the stores handing out twenty- and one-hundred-dollar bills like children with no care for the handful of nick- els and pennies. We saw the once-empty store buildings piled to the top with groceries and dresses and all kinds of dry goods. We saw the farmers in cars whose tires would not go flat for being worn as thin as a jacket elbow, buying electric supplies along with other wonder-ful modern comforts. We saw boys hauling big supplies of groceries to trucks, laughing children with toys which once were only for Christmas.

Drought and Dust Storms

Rainfall in the Great Plains varies dramatically from year to year. Positioned at the center of the continent, far from any ocean, and shielded to the west by the high Rocky Mountains, little rain comes to the Llano Estacado. High temperatures and long summers mean that potential evaporation exceeds average rainfall. Crosby County averaged nineteen inches of rain per year between 1895 and 1993. But averages mean little; variability is the key to understanding rainfall on the grassland. Luckily for farmers, most of the region's rain falls during the growing season. In general, a wheat crop needs about twenty inches of rain to succeed. Thirstier crops like corn, sorghum, and cotton need even more. Thus, Crosby County is marginal for dryland farming.

The big conversion from ranchland to cropland happened after 1905, when thirty-three inches of rain fell. Serious

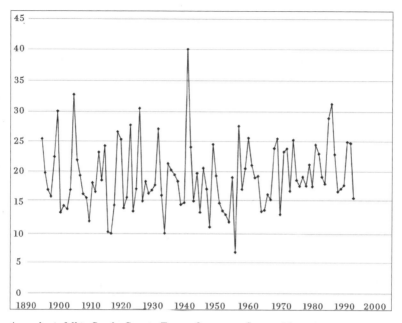

Annual rainfall in Crosby County, Texas, 1895–1993. Source: Myron
P. Gutmann, "Great Plains Population and Environment Data," On-
Line Extraction System, Ann Arbor: University of Michigan, 2005.
Drawn by Geoff Cunfer.

droughts occurred in 1916 and
1917, again in 1934 during the Dust
Bowl, and in 1956, when the county
received only seven inches of rain.
Most of the 1930s were at or a little
below average, with exceptions in
1932 (twenty-seven inches) and
1934 (ten inches). The rainiest year
on record was 1941, which exceeded
forty inches and brought a close
to the drought, dust storms, and
depression of the 1930s.

When most people think of dust
storms, they think of the 1930s. But
blowing dust was not a newcomer to
the southern plains in that decade,
and it did not cease with the onset
of World War II. Droughts and dust
storms are a routine part of life on
the Llano Estacado, and they have
been for millennia. Despite the
national media attention to the
Dust Bowl, Nellie Witt Spikes took
the "dirty thirties" in stride. She
described the discomfort of blowing dust and the worries of farmers
facing extended dry periods. Her
articles placed these events in a
broad context. Dust storms did not
happen only in the 1930s but off and

on throughout the twentieth century. She described them and their impact on people's lives without the hyperbole often present in Dust Bowl memoirs.

July 29, 1937

We need rain. Rain to make feed for our stock. Rain to make the fleecy white cotton that we need to exchange for warm clothing, the good hot fires, the medical care and the few simple luxuries that farm people have. We have worked, got our crop clean and have done all we can. We hope and pray that our labor shall be rewarded by a bounteous harvest. When the leaves of a plant begin to wilt and turn brown it seems that I can hear the plants begging for water, almost human in their suffering.

August 5, 1937

There is no water for the garden. It hurts to watch the garden and flower beds burn. We still hope for rain.

January 20, 1938

Yesterday, Old Mother Nature gave us warning that she still had wind stored away even if she hasn't used much of it in the last few months. Warned us that she could turn the wind loose and fill our eyes and houses with dust and dirt. Gray sticky dust from Kansas, red dirt from Colorado and just common West Texas soil.

April 21, 1938

What do you think of wheat? This is the question of the hour. Many and varied are the answers. Time alone can only tell what these plains will do. Never one year can be judged by another. If variety is the spice of life, then we do not need to find a new road to the spice lands.

May 12, 1938

In some ways this has been a pleasant weekend; in other ways it has been quite depressing. The cold wind has blown. May is too late for cold weather. The sand has blown in my house and in my hair. My hands are rough. My face is chapped. The young chickens get cold every time I put them out. In and out, out and in I have carried these incubator chickens. Sometimes I regret that we have improved (?) on mother hen. She at least furnished a feather-lined brooder for her babies. You don't have to worry about the lamp burning everything up.

I went to a quilting at the home of Mrs. W. W. Smith and had a delightful time with friends both old and

new. As our shining needles followed the lines of the soft yellow and
orchid quilt, we laughed and joked.
Told of our chickens and gardens,
our husbands and children, while
we knew that our wheat was dying
for lack of rain, that the land was too
dry for row crop planting; no one
murmured or complained. Farm
women have learned patience and
resignation to droughts and weather
conditions we cannot help.

May 19, 1938

The sound of the voices of the young
orators at the graduating exer-
cises and the yelling of voices at the
baseball games fill our ears these
days. The picnic crowds spread their
baskets of dinner and fight flies and
ants as of yore. The bullbat makes
the funny sound as of milk falling in
a tin bucket. We wear a wool dress
one day and a thin dress the next.
Clouds rise dark and angry, lightning flashes, thunder rolls, and the
sandstorm descends on us in full
fury. This is as much spring as plains
people expect. "Give me one or two
sandstorms, a heavy fog and a few
dews and I'll make a crop," an old-
timer tells us. My husband was fussing about the dry weather. "Looks
like I won't be able to plant a seed of
cotton this year." But, I remind him,
that is the same thing he has said for

years and years at this time of year,
and planting time has always come.

June 16, 1938

We look out over the place this
morning and as the grass and crops
need rain so badly it looks like a
great drought is on. But reports
from many sections indicate there
has been too much rain. We see so
little of anything at a time. We judge
the whole world by our own selves.
Our own needs look so much larger
than the needs of our neighbors.

August 25, 1938

Cousin Olga has gone, and we miss
her. I laughed at her East Texas way
of setting out buckets and pans to
catch rainwater. The first night, the
buckets and pans blew away and
were covered with sand. But the
next afternoon she had better luck.
As she decided to go away the next
morning, the rainwater was wasted.
It is so seldom I have rainwater I
never think to use it.

January 12, 1939

The good rain has washed away the
doubts and fears the drouth was
causing. Has put new hope in our

lives. The old saying is that one sparrow does not make a summer. We realize that one rain does not make a crop, but where one swallow comes, others will follow, and more moisture will likely follow this.

January 19, 1939

Was there ever such a rain and such lovely weather? Maybe so, but we forget, and say there never was. Anyway, the farmers' faces have straightened up like wilted crops after a good rain.

February 2, 1939

The wild west wind has begun to bluster and blow. We tell each other we are not going to stay in such a country where nothing can be kept clean and our hands, faces and clothes are gritty. But after a while the wind will quiet down as a bronc horse does, and we forget our wild threats.

March 2, 1939

As many sandstorms as I have seen, I wonder if I could describe one so that ones who have never seen one would understand. This morn-ing there was a light wind from the southwest. I hurried to get out some clothes to dry. There was a sand-filled sky in the west, but I thought it would not get here for some thirty or forty minutes. The clothes froze and were left on the line. In about five minutes I looked out, and the wall of sand was here. The frozen clothes were hurriedly gotten in and spread on chairs. The bright sun was soon obscured. The high wind picked up more loose dirt from the fields and the roads. As a heavy fog hides the neighbors' houses from our view, so the sandstorm hides them. At times we can not see the barn. Clouds of fine sand hurry overhead, the doors and windows rattle and knock as if a thousand people were in a hurry to get in. The fine sand finds the keyholes, the tiny cracks round the doors and windows, settles on our furniture, covers the floors, so that when we walk we leave footprints.

"That wind!" says my husband, "no one can work out in that wind," so the farm work comes to a stop. The cold wind gets higher as the day advances, the sun looks like it does through a smoked glass. We resign ourselves to another bad day. How can anyone think when the sound of shrieking wind is in their ears and dirt is covering everything? Not a neighbor's house in view, trees look like gray ghosts, sand piles in on the flower bed where it will have to be moved out with spades, Russian thistles race across the pasture looking like huge bushel baskets, as my Tennessee friend says. Cows, sheep and horses stand in the lots, dirty water streaming from their eyes. Our hands are doughy and dry, we hate to touch anything. We get electric shocks from the tie-off on the windmill and the wire fences. Our faces look weird in the yellowish light. The day grows darker, we need a light to sew by, or to read, if we can settle down to it. Our eyes, though, are watching the moving world outside, and we are longing for the wind to cease.

On the southern plains dust storms can happen at any time of the year, but there is certainly a dust storm season. Spring is the time for blowing sand in West Texas, the Texas and Oklahoma Panhandles, eastern New Mexico and Colorado, and western Kansas. In most years March is the dustiest month, followed by April and February. There are few dust storms in the summer and winter, though they sometimes occur then, and a smaller peak in the fall. But longtime residents know to brace for blowing dirt in February, just when the weather begins to warm up. As early as 1885 the Salina, Kansas, newspaper commented: "When the March winds commenced raising dust Monday, the average citizen calmly smiled and whispered 'so natural.'"

Spring is dust season because of a combination of climate, vegetation, and soil characteristics. Wind erosion happens when high winds sweep over dry, bare soils. Soil moisture is crucial, and the ground is often driest in early spring, following typically dry winters. Spring is also the windiest season of the year in a very windy region. The combination of strong winds and dry soils means that the climatic conditions are often ideal for dust storms between February and April. Plants resist soil erosion, slowing wind velocities at ground level and holding soil together with strong roots. Even though summer can be both dry and windy, it is less dusty because growing plants, whether native prairie grasses or crops of cotton and sorghum, resist erosion. But in early spring few plants have begun to grow, and there is little vegetation to hold soils in place. When the weather first warms, when spring winds rise, dust clouds often rise with them on the southern high plains.

"Heavy black clouds of dust rising over the Texas panhandle," March
1936. Photograph by Arthur Rothstein. Library of Congress, Prints
and Photographs Division, FSA-OWI Collection, LC-USZ62-125986.

March 9, 1939

As we look into the deep cobalt blue sky, we forget the sand of yesterday. The air feels so clean and cool we wonder how it is. Miss Laura Hamner, of Amarillo, in her teenage column in the *Amarillo News,* says of the sandstorms: "Remember it takes stamina to make the best of life, be what it may. Some folks cannot take it, others can. Some fuss and stew, others are philosophical, and do not worry. Make your choice on what you intend to be and practice on the Panhandle weather." Still quoting Miss Hamner, she says, "As you go strolling through clouds of dust this spring see if you can not feel this. Good old sandstorm, you are making me strong and able to bear things. You are testing my character and I am showing you that I can whip you. You tried to whip my father and grandfather in this country but they would not give up to you. Neither will I, good old sandstorms."

"Dust Storm, Amarillo, Texas," April 1936. Photograph by Arthur Rothstein. Library of Congress, Prints and Photographs Division, FSA-OWI Collection, LC-USZ62-131180.

May 25, 1939

Yesterday I was dismayed, the garden was wilted and the flowers hung low with thirst. The west wind scorched with its hot breath, grey fuzzy cottonseed lay in their dry beds, not enough moisture to spring into shiny green leaves on the surface. "There is no use," I nearly told myself, "One had better quit." But a friend, former neighbor Mrs. Earl Norman, came from her home near Lockney, drove many miles to see me. What hot west wind could scorch and blight a friendship like that? And there was a cactus blooming on the rock fence, placed there in March without water or soil. How could this be? Then I realized that the cactus stored up moisture and food so that under any conditions they can open soft pink and yellow satin and gay red blooms to delight the beholder. I wondered if I had stored up in good times enough faith and hope and love to meet life when conditions were bad. Thus I got two lessons, and my courage returned.

In June 1935 Rexford Tugwell, a member of President Franklin Roosevelt's "brain trust," appointed Roy Stryker to create a Historical Section within the new Resettlement Administration (RA). The RA was a New Deal reform agency within the Department of Agriculture. Two years later the RA became the Farm Security Administration (FSA), but the Historical Section continued the work of documenting the Great Depression in photographs.

Stryker quickly assembled a talented team of photographers and began dispatching them around the nation to capture images of Americans struggling with the nation's worst economic collapse. Standout photographers included Dorothea Lange, Arthur Rothstein, Russell Lee, and Marion Post Wolcott. The project had three overlapping missions. The photographers had aesthetic ambitions: they wanted to create important photographic art. Stryker had historical ambitions: he perceived that his nation was in the midst of a great historical event—the Great Depression, the Dust Bowl, and the dramatic re-creation of national politics represented by the New Deal—and he wanted to document those events for posterity. FSA bureaucrats had political ambitions: they wanted to generate propaganda that would cast New Deal social, political, and land use reforms in a positive light and build popular political support for Roosevelt's initiatives.

The FSA Historical Section was remarkably successful in all three endeavors. Members of Stryker's team were some of the greatest American photographers of the twentieth century. The tens of thousands of images they created are rich historical sources and appear routinely in history textbooks. The public generally accepts that the New Deal effectively dealt with the 1930s crisis.

Roy Stryker instructed FSA photographers in the field to write captions for their images from day to day. Photographers developed their pictures, numbered them, and wrote captions for the best images. They then packaged up prints, negatives, and captions and mailed them to Washington, where Stryker and his office staff cataloged, stored, and published the photographs.

In May 1939 FSA photographer Russell Lee visited Crosby County and produced a series of photographs on a farm near Ralls. Consider the power of captions to interpret photographic images. The captions Lee wrote for these pictures not only describe the scene, but also interpret its political meaning. It is clear that Lee was interested in exposing social inequality on this large farm. There is also a subtext that is critical of new technology—tractors—as a contributor to the concentration of wealth.

"Day laborer at wheel of tractor on a large farm near Ralls, Texas," May 1939. Photograph by Russell Lee. Library of Congress, Prints and Photographs Division, FSA-OWI Collection, LC-USF33-012231-M3.

"Home of owner of 4900 acre farm near Ralls, Texas," May 1939. Photograph by Russell Lee. Library of Congress, Prints and Photographs Division, FSA-OWI Collection, LC-USF34-033354-D.

"Tractor farming on 4900 acre ranch near Ralls, Texas," May 1939. Photograph by Russell Lee. Library of Congress, Prints and Photographs Division, FSA-OWI Collection, LC-USF34-033333-D.

"Day laborer drinking from a desert water bag, large farm near Ralls, Texas," May 1939. Photograph by Russell Lee. Library of Congress, Prints and Photographs Division, FSA-OWI Collection, LC-USF34-012219-M3.

"Homes of day laborers on large farm near Ralls, Texas. There are 4,900 acres in this farm. Nine tractors are used." May 1939. Photograph by Russell Lee. Library of Congress, Prints and Photographs Division, FSA-OWI Collection, LC-USF34-033317-D.

Over 160,000 FSA images are available at the Library of Congress Prints and Photographs Division. They are freely available to the public, and library staff have digitized them all so that patrons can download archival quality images from the Internet. To view FSA images taken throughout the United States, visit the Library of Congress's American Memory website: http://memory.loc.gov/ammem/fsahtml/.

July 6, 1939

Somehow it seems too bad not to want it to rain for a while. So long we have gazed in the heavens and prayed for the refreshing showers. But the weeds have started with the cotton and the maize and we need dry weather to kill them before our crops are choked out. Everybody is at work on the farm. Mother prepares meals while husband and children are in the field. Tractors roar up and down the rows, sweating horses switch flies and pull the cultivator and the slide. Sharp hoes gleam in the sunshine. The rain made my flowers grow. New shiny leaves have replaced the scorched ones. Gay flowers are opening: sweet peas, gaillardias, red and pink zinnias and sky blue forget-me-nots. Flowers for the house, for the church, and to give to friends.

October 12, 1939

As I write a soft rain is falling, washing the dust off the leaves of the dingy trees, soaking down to water roots starved for moisture. Yellow grains of wheat lying in dry, loose soil will drink, and swell, and grow; will make the brown earth green, bring hope of another crop to us, who have to patiently await Mother Nature's own good time for a harvest. It has long been said that it could wait 15 years to rain here or rain in 15 minutes. Yesterday we were surprised that we did not even have the 15 minutes to gather in a line of clothes, put up the car, and get a wagon of cotton from the field, not to mention forgetting to shut doors or a hen with tiny chicks.

February 8, 1940

Each drop of the recent rain glittered and shone in the eyes of the farmers like brand new dimes from the mint of the heavens. And we hope this fall they will be real dimes that will bring us comfort and supply our many needs.

February 29, 1940

Things are about normal on the farm again, all but the muddy feed lot. Bundles have to be carried out in the pasture so a dry place can be had to feed the hungry stock. The snow has melted enough for us to see our washtubs and the wash against the white snow. Most of the rock fence on the east is uncovered now. "For once," said Cub Parrish last Sunday, "I was glad to see the sandstorm yesterday."

August 29, 1940

Things about the farm do not look so well just now. We have had no rain. The row crop, after standing so long awaiting rain to make it grow, has about given up the battle. The pasture is brown. The garden is still good, but the turkeys have started to eat up the Kentucky Wonder beans planted to run on the fence that encloses the garden. I read somewhere the other day that a turkey knew two things: Where he is going and how to get there. There is still time for rain to make winter wheat for pasture. We cling to this hope.

Great Plains farmers grow two major types of wheat: spring wheat and winter wheat. Farmers on the northern plains, from the Canadian prairies south to the Dakotas and Montana, plant spring wheat after the snow melts. It grows through the summer for harvest in the fall. Among other uses, spring wheat is especially good for pasta noodles.

On the central and southern plains, where winters are more mild, from Nebraska southward to Texas, farmers grow winter wheat. They plant wheat in the fall; it emerges and grows a few inches high before the first freeze, greening autumn fields even after native grasses have yellowed and dried. When winter sets in, the wheat goes dormant but does not die. After the first spring thaws, the wheat plants come back to life and grow vigorously into early summer for harvest in June and July. Farmers with winter wheat sometimes pasture their livestock on it in the fall when dried native grasses are less nutritious. They get some benefit for their cattle without injuring next year's wheat crop.

September 19, 1940

Although the lightning flashed and thunder deafened our ears, we were still left in the dark streak as a rain crossed south of us Saturday night. We should change the old maxim, "Save up for a rainy day" to "Save up on a rainy day for a dry year." . . . All the men are getting agitated over whether to or whether to not put in a big well for irrigation. The dried-out farmer looks with bulging eyes on his brother farmer's fine crop that has had water to irrigate with. The fragrant fields of alfalfa, rivaling those of the famous Roswell Valley, bring a longing to his soul as he thinks of his stock without feed. The golden rich heads of maize, the creamy white of hegari call to him in a language he well knows, a language of well-fed stock. He thinks of the streams of water under his own dry farm and longs to bring it to his fields. A new era seems to be coming to the plains. An era of crops every year, of full barns and feed lots, of farmers getting over dry-weather blues.

Access to the water stockpiled in the Ogallala Aquifer required four key technological developments: a high-volume pump, a low-cost engine to power the pump, an inexpensive energy source, and deep well drilling technologies. Lacking any one of these, large-scale irrigation could not happen. Between 1890 and 1920 each of the pieces fell into place. A centrifugal pump delivered lift, internal combustion engines adapted from automobiles after the turn of the century provided power, gasoline served as cheap energy, and drilling rigs could now bore deep into the earth. By 1905 an irrigation well could water fifty acres of cropland, ten times a windmill's production, but the cost was prohibitive. In 1920 a turnkey job on an irrigation well cost six thousand dollars, far beyond the means of most farmers.

Irrigators on the Llano Estacado tapped the Ogallala Aquifer for the first time in 1908. But farmers had little money to risk on wells and pumps, little experience operating and maintaining gasoline engines, and plenty of conservative hesitation to innovate. Low crop prices through the 1920s and early 1930s meant irrigation was unlikely to be cost effective. The modern irrigation revolution on the southern plains only began in the late 1930s. By then the cost of a turnkey irrigation job had fallen to about two thousand dollars. Desperation in the face of depression, drought, and dust storms was partially responsible for the transformation. By the mid-1930s most farmers owned automobiles, and many had tractors, so internal combustion was less intimidating.

In small towns on the southern plains business owners feared depopulation of their trade areas, with disastrous consequences for commerce. Businessmen in Plainview, just northwest of Ralls, in Swisher County, and in Floydada promoted irrigation as an alternative to farm abandonment in the 1930s. The Floydada Chamber of Commerce offered subsidies for installation of irrigation wells, and Artie Baker, a banker in Lockney, offered credit to small farmers who wanted to make a try at irrigation. The business community was prepared to gamble along with the farmers who comprised its customer base. A final and possibly decisive factor was the creation of annual subsidies from New Deal farm programs. A regular cash payment from Uncle Sam provided farmers with money to invest in wells, a minimum, predictable yearly income, and guaranteed base prices for crops, something farming had never before achieved.

In 1920 farmers irrigated only 7,027 acres of land on the Llano Estacado; by 1930 the irrigated area was 18,010 acres. Every Texas county over the aquifer reported some irrigation, but none watered as much as 2 percent of its total area. The real growth began in the late 1930s, so by 1940 West Texans irrigated over 200,000 acres, mostly in a core of seven counties. Between 1930 and 1940 the number of wells in the area rose toward three thousand, and the volume of water pumped annually approached 200,000 acre-feet. (An acre-foot is the volume of water sufficient to cover one acre of land one foot deep: 325,851 gallons.)

During the 1940s and 1950s the Texas high plains became full-fledged irrigated farm country. Irrigated land jumped from 0.2 million acres in 1940 to 2.9 million acres in 1950 to 4.3 million acres in 1959. In 1950 Lubbock and Hale County farmers irrigated more than 50 percent of the entire surface area of those counties, and six other Llano Estacado counties, including Crosby, irrigated over 25 percent of their area. The number of wells on the southern plains skyrocketed from five thousand in 1947 to over twenty-five thousand in 1955. But the most important number was the volume of water pumped, which ballooned from just under 0.5 million acre-feet per year in 1945 to over 5 million acre-feet ten years later. By then high plains farmers were pumping out more than 1.6 trillion gallons of water every year, and growth was exponential.

February 20, 1941

A West Texas sandstorm with all the trimmings is on. We only sigh as sand covers our pretty curtains, piles up under the doors and windows. We turn the radio on, only to hear maniacal shrieks. Turn it off and wish that mail would come. Russian thistles pile in the gates and under clotheslines and on back porches, their favorite haunts. They stick our fingers with fine briers as we try to push them out of the doorways. Scared looking gray clouds come over and it is dark; we turn on the electric lights; the wind has blown out a fuse. Our hands get sewing dirty, we lay it aside. We look at one another; why, we must all have the yaller janders, we are so yellow and ghastly looking. We fix a little lunch, have to wash out the dishes we use before we eat. Dirt makes patterns in the sink and bathtub. We forget to cover the separator. It will have to be washed before it is used. The whistling wind never ceases. Small pebbles and dirt hit our faces if we dare venture outside. Passing cars creep along with lights dimmed from the sand.

Why don't we leave? Well, stranger, we all plan to have our minds fully made up by the time the wind ceases. But the next day we sweep the dirt up into shovels, dust off the enlarged pictures of Pa and Ma, put the beds out to sun, listen to the radio while we work. When all is done, the house clean, the fresh-smelling quilts brought in, a pot of red beans simmering on the stove and fresh-ironed clothes hung up, somehow we forget our resolve made while the sandstorm raged. The plains has days so promising. Days of mellow sunshine and cool, soft winds. A wonderful year is just ahead of you, she murmurs in our willing ears. Just stay, silver slanting rains will sweep over the prairie, blades of maize will look like cool, clear water as they wave; cotton will bloom and turn to fields of snow. Don't leave me, she urges, you could never forget the good, clear water in such never-failing abundance, nights in the summer you will not turn over and over, sleepless from the heat. "I promise you," the plains plays over and over on her mighty stringed instrument—the wind.

May 15, 1941

Rain every few days does not seem to agree with the average West Texan. He tries not to complain at something he has prayed for so many dry years, but the fact remains, if he would be truly honest, he would say he wanted some dry weather just now. Always with apprehension we watch the thunderhead clouds that form in the north this time of year. In the past they have meant storms, hail and wind and beating rains. Friday was no exception to this rule. At noon Friday thunderheads loomed up in the north, making rapidly after dinner. The hail sign began to form in the top edges of the dark cloud, little puffy clouds like small sacks of different shapes and sizes. Lightning tore the black cloud with silver veins. The wind changed to the north. The storm was on. Rain began falling, blotting out the world. Then pop pop came the hail. Would it quit in a few minutes, or would it last till everything was a mass of torn leaves and beaten down wheat? The cloud pressed on; we were safe from this storm. But we were touched because we knew someone had their hopes torn to shreds by the cutting hailstones. The farmer lives dangerously near to losing everything he has worked for most all of the time.

Drought may cut the growing crop short, hail and wind ruin it in a few minutes, insects may blight, devour, rust and smut. But the farmer always has another year.

May 22, 1941

Wife, give me a piece of bread and butter and I will go out and see how much it has rained. Wife, give me another piece of bread and butter and I will go out and see how much my wheat has grown. I know this sounds like a jack-and-the-beanstalk story, but really the old giant, drouth, who has ruled several years, has been laid under tons of water, and the farmer looks forward to climbing to the top of his wheat and bringing back golden dollars from the grain to his patient, waiting wife.

May 29, 1941

The seeds I planted just before the last rain, or young flood, are buried and the ground as smooth as a board. This country never does anything by the halves. Whole hog or none. Sandstorms come by assorted dozens and drouths drag for months and years. We live for years hoping for rain, and then when the heavens pour out buckets and barrels of

water on us, we start hoping for dry weather again.

November 13, 1941

A whole week of sunshine! What a news item here in the west that is supposed to be so sunny and usually is, rather too sunny many seasons. Something to remember and date back to. Yes, that was the year it rained and rained. "I remember because we stuck in the mud and was late at Mary's wedding." So slip the memoranda of this year's too-much rainfall in with that of 1934's too little; perhaps they will help balance the lean and the fat of life.

March 19, 1942

Yesterday, Sunday, was such a warm, pleasant day. A few peach blossoms slipped out of the green covering, the willow limbs sprouted a fuzzy green. I began to hunt poetry of spring to quote in this column. For example, "When brooks are laughing, and winds are whispering," when all of a sudden there was such a blustering outside we thought of bombings as the electric lights blacked out. "Is it raining?" my husband asked. "No, indeed," I answered as the house filled with sand as if a giant blower had turned on inside the house. "Just another sandstorm with all the trimmings," and I closed my book of poetry and went to bed to dread another house-cleaning.

April 2, 1942

"Every day I see new evidence of spring in the air," the young lady trilled over the radio. A sandstorm was on. I looked outside. I, too, saw evidences of spring in the air. The tender willow leaves, whipped from the tree, bits of crushed pink silk of peach blossoms flying like wounded butterflies from the tree, tiny rosettes whirled from the spirea, sand-covered lilac leaves fluttered and sailed away. Yes, spring was in the air and moving swiftly past the house.

June 18, 1942

Grasshoppers, poison, weeds, flats, more grasshoppers, more poison, more weeds, more flats. A small war is being waged on the farm over this year's crop. Hail and wind and some drought, then flooding rain, washing deep soil over tiny seed, never to see the sun. Replanting and hoping again, weary but unwhipped, the farmer carries on, knowing that not until fall will he know just where he lost and where he gained.

May 8, 1943

Emerson says, "The rain comes when the wind calls." All last week a hot, scorching wind called. It sucked the moisture from the listed beds in the fields as though they were sponges. It burnt our faces, tender from the winter's stay in the house; dirt was whipped in the houses and sifted over everything; chickens sat in the shade with open mouths. It was extra warm weather for the first of May, but this morning all the dryness has gone; the rain came when the wind called. All night I heard it whispering as it fell softly from the eaves above my window, whispering of food, food in plenty for the boys at war, for the starving when they can be fed, and for the cows to have plenty of green grass, and for all the living things on the farm to be fed. The lake mirrors the clouds, which are only ragged gray tatters this morning; the chickens look white as snow in their warm, dry coops; the cows which shivered in the drizzling rain yesterday are sunning themselves on the wet, warm ground; we find work long neglected in the house. Thank you, Dear Father, for the rain that comes when the wind calls.

August 26, 1943

Still no rain, yet each night the clouds hang low across the distant horizon and the lightning licks out long silver tongues and the thunder growls like angry dogs, then all disappear and the stars shine forth in beauty and splendor as if trying to make amends for the heavens that give no rain. Wilda and I sleep outside these warm nights and watch for the rain that somehow fails to come. At times our eyes are almost blinded by the quick flashing of a falling star that leaves a trail of fire behind its mad flight into oblivion. We see Job's Coffin, count over and over the seven brilliant stars in the Big Dipper, figure out designs here and there of our own pleasing, wonder about the Milky Way, taking a vacation in our own yard but up among the stars . . . traveling on beams of light . . . resting our tired bodies and minds with the glories of the night, the sunned bed, the cool winds of the night, the reassurance that all will be right again, truly, "The Heavens declare the glory of God and the firmament sheweth His handiwork."

September 2, 1943

Time: late Sunday afternoon—weather: still dry, and we are still telling visitors from far off that it is the hottest weather we ever had. . . . And what is more, we can brag about for years, "Why this is not hot weather, remember back in '43 when one day was so nigh alike, for over a month you could not have told one day from another if they had been shaken up in an old hat." We will bring it out on every occasion like we do the year of '34. That year is our yardstick for dry, hard times, and we measure each year with it. I thought surely this week I could tell about a rain—well, if not as big as the one Marvin McLaughlin once wanted, one so deep that a man could stand up and drink, but a rain that would at least assure moisture for growing feed and for planting wheat. There seems to be a change in the weather, however, this Monday morn as the wind is blowing and the sand comes sweeping down the road. We will have water for the garden and stock, and it will be nothing new to sweep out dust.

Okra and tomatoes are about all the vegetables the garden affords just now, not to forget the pepper. The Porter tomato is tedious to gather and can, but it makes, a fact not to be overlooked. The lawn is brown, but somehow I do not care so much about this, for in the early summer the grass was so thick and tough the lawnmower did not make much headway on it, and besides, there was too much to do to push it, anyway. The shrubs around the door have been kept alive, and that is about all. It is hot and dry outside, and we take no pleasure in looking at wilted things so will come in the house and read and listen to the radio.

February 4, 1944

A dark cloud came up last Thursday late afternoon, thundering and lightning as if it meant business, and buckets of rain soon came pouring down, making the darkened land bright with running water, catching many a farmer away from his waiting cows and chickens. Sliding tires went suddenly into the bar ditches, the owners having to lock them up and leave them until the next day. Somehow a rain always comes as a surprise to the West Texas people. The approaching cloud only seems an eye-filling, windpipe-choking windstorm, so they are never quite ready for a rain.

In West Texas "bar ditches" line every road, whether a paved highway or a remote gravel farm-to-market road. Engineers design roads to be slightly higher than the surrounding landscape so that rainwater flows quickly off the road surface. But the Llano Estacado topography is so flat that fill dirt is not readily available to raise road grades. Instead, it is necessary to bulldoze a ditch on each side to accumulate soil for a slightly higher road surface in the middle. Construction crews "borrow" soil from the new ditches to raise the road. These "borrow ditches" (slurred to "bar ditches") also serve to channel runoff after rainstorms.

March 3, 1944

The drip, drip, drip of a slow-falling, steady rain woke me from deep sleep this morning, and I remembered how the moon lay, like a silver bowl, in last night's dark blue sky, holding water in its deep curve, dark clouds at times blurring the shining silver bowl from our sight. This month was washed in with rain, and now it seems that rain will wash it from the year's calendar of months for eternity. Only one sandstorm could February manage this year, and it did not find too much sand to stir up. When I got up this morning the trees outside the window were a lovely sight, each trunk and limb hung with bright drops of water, like clear glass beads strung on brown strings. As I write, the rain has gone, a dense fog taking its place; the trees are wrapped in soft wisps of gray as night draws near. A killdeer arrived from the south early this year, has a plaintive cry as it flies by; the brown fields, with unbroken ridges from last year's crops, are soaked with the rain.

April 28, 1944

Friday night I was awakened suddenly by the sharp rumbling of thunder. In a few minutes rain was spouting down the alleys of the roof, which took on the appearance of a swift-flowing river as seen by the flashes of lightning every few seconds. How good the rain sounded! Now the restless sand would be settled, so I thought just before I dropped back to sleep. The next morning we found it did not rain much, but things looked fresh and damp. The wind arose, soon dried out the top of the ground, setting the sand loose again. In that air it hurled, joined with sand from other parts of the land. The sky became darker, sand poured through every crevice and crack, whipping off tender edges of leaves, cutting down tiny plants in the garden, on again, never to rest as long as the wind is raging. Higher and higher the wind became as the day advanced, never stopping as night came on. The sun sank in a haze of sand, and all night long the wind whipped and roared, chill as from the frozen north. This morning was no better; the wind had shifted more to the north and seemed to have renewed strength. Now after dinner as I write, the sand is still making a veil to hide the rest of the world from our view, the tender leaves on the trees are crisped and curled with black edges, our garden looks like a slate washed clean of all marks, and we long for the quiet that only the ceasing of the wind will give.

I remember another time of long-lasting winds, a time when I was small. . . . After the wind died sometime in the night or the next day, I have forgotten which, we all went the mile to Grandpa's house, which was on the edge of the shinnery. How strange everything looked: sand was heaped around the orchard fence and we walked over it, holes were scooped out here, long bars of still sand lay unruffled there.

March 30, 1945

Way back when the March winds had a hard time finding a plowed land to sweep up and to carry madly from one place to put in another, there was a day of high, high wind remembered by all the old settlers as "the day the wind blew the worst." A mile from Grandfather's place was a tiny shack set on the prairie of dry grass in the winter and green, swaying grass in the summer. On this day when the wind blew the worst my mother, with pretty red in her cheeks and faith in her heart, watched through the one window as the wind arose ever higher and higher and the sand kept her from seeing her father's home. Father was gone; Uncle Tom, to whom

the shack belonged, was gone. My brother, Lowell, and myself watched Mother's face to see if she were afraid as she sang our sister, Edna, to sleep, her soft voice so clear we did not hear the howling of the wind so plain. Her long skirt of calico with its wide ruffle swept pretty patterns on the floor as she went back and forth trying to prepare something to eat for her children.

She went to the stove only to draw back with a shock of pain as an electric spark ran up her arm. No cooking that day. She moved a heavy trunk to the west side of the room, which had only thin box walls between her and the tempest outside. The house shook, but she called us to the window to see the chickens blowing away, the wind catching under their wings and making them go fast, only to be stopped when they reached a little lake, where they sat till the next day. Not by one look or word did Mother let on that there was any danger, and we played on, but I remember the glad look on her face late that afternoon when she opened the door to let in her young brother, Eli, to keep her company and spend the night.

June 1, 1945

This day, the twentieth of May, has been a regular March sandstorm. Our feelings seem as wilted as the things in the garden. No prospect of rain is in sight, and we farm people wait and hope and wait and hope; each day takes more toll on the moisture that was left deep in the ground. Carey and Joe are in the kitchen, all the chairs in line for the train, and I found them playing and dragging around one of my bedspreads. "But Grandmother," explains Joe, "it was already dirty."

July 27, 1945

Did rain, didn't it? The water swooshed down from our steep roof and splashed on the ground right outside my window and I thought how nice it would be to stick my feet under the drip. The lightning cut like sharp knives, the thunder shook the earth, but we were happy, the rain was falling. The smell of freshly turned ground, the green grass, the new leaves on the trees, things coming up everywhere; it is spring, only the calendar is wrong.

August 3, 1945

The green world has been wonderful after looking at a brown one so long, at the summer time of year when things should be green and growing. The little green feathers of feed stand straight down the long, curved rows of the field, brave soldiers against the cold and want of winter. Whether they are too few and too late cannot be told as yet, but we hope rains will come and hurry them up higher and higher till each wears a golden plume of grain. When the beans did make, they made plenty. Beans are like that—usually make too many at once and then quit. I like the pintos for the reason they will keep on making if they have plenty of water, if you will keep the beans gathered off. We canned some and put others in the locker. The tomatoes die one at a time with wilt. They are wilt-resistant variety, but they stood so long without sufficient moisture, they were weakened down. The late beans and peas are up and growing.

I have to let the cement pool keep full for Joe and Carey to swim in even if the garden is skimped a little. Both boys can swim, and they scare me to death by turning somersets (perhaps this way of spelling is not found in Webster's, but you will

Two women cooling off in a windmill tank near Idalou, Texas, early 1920s. Photograph courtesy of Southwest Collection, Texas Tech University, Lubbock, SWCPC 322 #23.

recognize the word) in the water as they dive from the bank. The wind is blowing this lovely summer Monday morning, and the windmill keeps a clear stream running in the overhead tank with a splash that makes music to my soul. Water, running water, fresh, cool and plentiful, maybe that is the reason folks stayed with the plains and keep on staying regardless of the sandstorms and drouths.

September 28, 1945

Monday morning, September 24, 1945, finds us with no rain and the southwest wind still filling her big cheeks and blowing sand down the dirt roads and into the house. Last night we watched the bright flashes that cut the eastern horizon in two and almost felt envy of the fortunate ones whom we supposed were getting the blessings of rain. The windmill is fixed, but the pipes had to be pulled. Holes were found in one joint, and both valves needed replacing. Now we have plenty of water, but the garden burned up for the want of it. The other afternoon just before the darkness descended like a black cloak over the earth, it looked like rain. The cloud was coming with the blowing of thunder trumpets and the glittering of lightning swords. I hurried to the garden, grabbed a hoe, which was dull as my mind is this morning, feverishly cut the weeds and grass from a section of ground, raked them to one side, and just as the last light was fading I sowed turnips and mustard. Aching and sweaty and tired I came in and waited for the rain to fall on my newly planted plot. The cloud sprinkled stingily then passed on; another hope gone, a spot of ground dry as ever.

August 22, 1947

No rain as yet, but we recall all the old sayings we can to bolster up our morale. My sign of rain is when the morning lake on the north of the house looks very near and the farthest hillside looks unusually steep. Uncle Tom Franklin liked to see the sky filled with "rain seed." "Yes, Nell, it will rain 'fore night." Some like to see a giant thunderhead far to the southwest before sunrise, others, the sun to rise from behind a

bank. The windmill pipe sweats, we hope for rain. It gets very hot, maybe rain. The wind blows and blows, perhaps it will bring up a cloud. No sign of rain, whatsoever, many believe is the best sign. What is your best sign? Of course it has failed along with all the rest. . . .

April 9, 1948

All signs pointed the other morning to a high wind. I made all the trips outside that I had to make, went to the shack and got some feed sacks to wash and bleach (don't see why feed companies have to letter all over both sides of a sack) and prepared for a good sandstorm.

With a shriek the wind rose ever high and higher, pushing the sand as if it were in its way. The big weeping willow north side of the house did not weep that day. The long, slender whips, with blossoms and green leaves, stood straight out and tried to leave the tree. The silk-white blossoms sifted in every crack and crevice; lay deep in bar ditches and hid the sun. Not much a housewife can do while the storm lasts, only to walk from room to room, muttering, "Why did I ever come to West Texas?" But by the time next day she gets the sand out, she is usually good and angry, or that night has to shake out all the covers before anyone can sleep. But by the time the house is all clean, the washing and ironing done, everyone's hair washed, the weather repents and brings such a lovely day we are all encouraged to stay and hope that such a day of sand will not come again for some time.

April 30, 1948

This is the time of year when folks scan the heavens and almanacs for signs of rain till their eyes are sore. Yesterday a cloud came from the west on wings of dust and scattered a few drops. Most of them fell on Mr. Spikes and me as we hurriedly made our way into the house from the garage. This morning I heard the weatherman at English Field, Amarillo, say that there was some rain fell from the clouds yesterday, but most of it was taken up by the dry atmosphere. Brother Hayes says this is a new alibi on the rain situation.

February 18, 1949

Seems as if folks are just as happy to see dry roads, sunshine and warmer weather as they were to see much-needed moisture. We excuse this by saying we want to get back to work, but West Texas people do not like to stay in mud for any length of time. When I was a child my idea of a perfect town of Emma in which I lived was for streets and roads around to be made of wide planks. I did not like the mud, and there was not a sidewalk in the little town, so I take very kindly to paved streets and roads.

March 24, 1950

It is time to get out in the yard and set some roses and other plants, but the wind blows so much we will wait for better weather. . . . The weatherman just said more sand this afternoon. Maybe the floor did not need sweeping, anyway.

March 31, 1950

This soil is high in price when it is for sale, but what comes in our houses is free.

April 20, 1951

The West Wind filled his cheeks with strong wind and started the dust to rolling last week. When he got tired, he turned the job over to North Wind, and he cracked his heels and dug up more and more sand and turned on the cold freezing unit. Mortals bowed their heads and tried to be philosophical about it, but the old-timer who has lived through scores of such days was about as aggravated as the person who was feeling the winds for the first spring.

May 18, 1951

This is a hard spring to get annuals up. The wind blows the moisture off so quickly the tiny seed just under the top of the ground cannot germinate. Zinnias, though, are up; they come so easily one does not have to bother about them. Carrots have been very trying, but to my surprise okra, which is a hot-weather plant, has come up well. So many are horrified to see water running from fields; looks to them it is an utter waste. But on our farm, dry years when our neighbor was watering his cotton land, which sloped at the ends, the water ran under the culvert, fanned out across a bit of our pasture and on to the lake, making green grass and water for the stock, and for this reason I had so much more for my garden. When the lake was dry there was another spot of green grazing for the cattle. So when you see water running away, many times it is to the advantage of a lake pasture and for stock water, which is no small item when the years are dry.

February 22, 1952

There is a nervous tension about a sandstormy day that keeps one going from window to window, looking out at trees bending and swaying as if in some kind of a dance. The air is thick between you and your neighbor like an old-time thick, brown veil women and girls used to wear. The screens knock on the windows, doors rattle, everything makes one kind of jumpy. Hands feel gritty though often washed; hair is rough and blowsy if you step out of doors for anything. Spring comes hard to the Plains Country, with a big Blowout, one might say. Spring comes to some parts of the world stepping softly and sweetly as a bridal march. But to our own small spot of the great world, spring is more like a battle of the elements, trying to see if high winds, clouds of dust and dryness of the earth can outdo the patience of humans who have dared settle the Estacado Desert, as it was known in the early geographies.

The following description of a typical dust storm comes from the book Nellie Witt Spikes coauthored with Temple Ann Ellis, *Through the Years: A History of Crosby County, Texas*, in 1952. It is from a chapter entitled "Disasters."

Sandstorms have many and varied ways of approach. The housewife on the Plains learned to foretell their coming, and to prepare herself and her belongings to meet it in force. Sandstorms are always preceded by a cloud, which more often than not rises in the west or northwest. Sometimes the clouds will lay over in that direction for hours, occasionally spending themselves before they reach Crosby County.

However, when the cloud comes up in a hurry, the cloud boils like a seething volcano. Some parts of the cloud look black, other parts red to light tan, sometimes with streaks of brown and red, according to the different kinds of soil they pick up as they pass. When clouds like these appeared, it was time to get started, for all too soon something was going to happen, and that in a hurry. If the housekeeper was alone, she doubled time. Things like washtubs, chicken coops and little chickens themselves had to be put indoors. Nothing was left out that would roll. Likely the wind had struck by the time the outside job was done. She hurried, if possible, more than ever. She closed, locked and propped the door with a chair, put a heavy rug over the crack in the door, stuffed rags and papers in her windows and waited breathlessly for the worst. Usually her wait was short-lived. Presently the house quivered, then settled itself for the siege that was to follow. The door started rattling, the window screens banging as she covered her nice bedspread with a sheet. She turned to peep out the window; she could not see the familiar windmill that always caught her eyes the first thing. She saw an old hen, her wings caught extended by the wind as she blew across the yard; her prized red rooster was coming on behind also propelled by the wind. A tub she didn't have time to locate rattled out of hiding and rolled across the field; well she knew it wouldn't stop until a fence or other obstruction got in its way.

Turning from the dust-obscured window she threw a light cover over the face of her sleeping child to keep out the dust. The woman, accustomed to these nerve-racking phenomena, had herself completely under control until she put some fuel on the fire. In the early days when cowchips were burned, the suction of the wind in the stovepipe has been known to draw burning particles of chips from the stove. Reaching for water with which to extinguish the fire, she beheld streaks of electricity meeting her hand. It was more than the stoutest heart could endure alone; she either paced the floor, hands clasped praying, or fell across the bed as she cried her tired heart out. It wasn't over yet; the wind raged on for hours until her courage returned, since the house still stood, and her child was all right, she calmly sat and awaited the end of the storm.

If the little woman were an old-timer, she knew that the sandstorm would stop in its own good time. If she happened to be a newcomer, she knew she was leaving the darned country for sure.

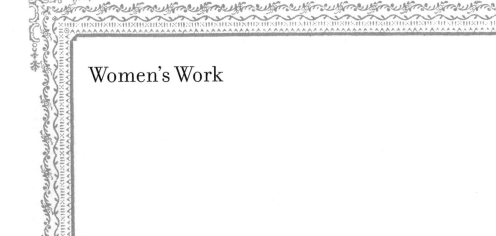

Women's Work

Spikes entitled her column "As a Farm Woman Thinks," bringing an explicitly gendered perspective to her writing. Before World War II rural labor was organized through the family, with understood categories of "women's work" and "men's work." In general, women were responsible for subsistence activities that contributed directly to feeding, housing, and clothing the family, plus child rearing. Men were typically responsible for the field work that generated cash income for the family, usually from crops and livestock. Thus, women were responsible for family gardens, for chickens and their eggs, and for a milk cow or two. Men were responsible for the cotton and feed crops, the work horses, and the beef cattle. There could be ambiguity sometimes, as when a woman's barnyard chickens produced more eggs than needed for the family. Then women sometimes sold surplus eggs at market to bring in some extra cash, or "egg money," that was hers to spend. On the other hand, milk cows were a woman's responsibility when they provided milk, butter, and cheese for the family, but when a family decided to shift into the dairy business with many milk cows, the animals moved into the men's realm. Children provided a considerable amount of farm labor, usually following a gendered path. Girls helped their mothers in the kitchen, garden, and farmyard. Boys learned to plow, plant, and harvest with their fathers in the fields. In practice, of course, life was not always so clear cut. Spikes occasionally notes when labor crossed gender lines. When it was too rainy to work in the fields, Jeff helped Nellie with her housework, washing dishes or canning food. Likewise, during the urgency of harvest women regularly helped in the fields. But even as they did so, they were aware that these activities were out of the ordinary, a temporary aberration.

We hear little in Spikes's columns about men's work on the farm—plowing, planting, cultivating, harvesting, and marketing cash crops. Those subjects appear from time to time as asides in some columns,

but central to these articles were the daily activities of rural women. Those routine activities included an enormous amount of work. We hear about making a garden and tending it through hot, dry summers, then about the immense effort of canning the produce of that garden in the fall, of preserving hundreds of jars of vegetables and fruit each year. Spikes described the challenges of caring for children and churning butter at the same time, butchering hogs in the depths of winter, and a myriad of other tasks.

Many of these stories describe her own work, but she also addressed that of other women: her mother, who cooked for dozens of visitors at her parents' hotel in the 1890s; neighbors who sewed and quilted to satisfy everyday needs and artistic impulses; friends who took pride in their carefully planted flower gardens. What emerges from this collection of columns is a sense of how women constructed and sustained their families, raised children, grew and processed food, and kept homes clean and comfortable. Although Spikes lamented the hard work necessary to support a family from one year to the next, she also took pride in doing it well.

May 13, 1937

"It costs so much to live in town. You farmers have your living," wails the city woman. The farmer's family rises when the first pink glow lights the eastern sky. Sleepy eyes are rubbed as the milk pails are taken down. The milking has to be done. Then at night it has to be done again. In the winter your hands and feet freeze while you sit there milking, milking, an eternity it seems. Summertime if you milk before sundown, the flies make the cows kick. If you wait till the flies go to bed, mosquitoes take the opportunity to bite your feet and ankles. Milk has to be separated, the washing of the milk things is endless. Twice a day, Sunday always included, milking time comes. Yes, the farmer has his milk and butter.

Hogs have to be fed. Cold mornings, hot mornings, evenings when you are dead tired and want to go places the greedy things want to eat. Shade they want in the summer, shelter in the winter, the hard day of butchering and putting up the products. Yes the farmer has his meat.

Chickens like to eat also; when the storm cloud advances swiftly with its hail and lightning the farm wife is shooing the contrary old hens with their silly chickens into shelter. Hot days, when your feet are swollen, biddie wants water and more feed. The numberless trips up cellar steps, down cellar steps, to see that the incubator has not left the nest. When the snow is deep on the ground, when your feet sink deep in slimy mud, these chickens need water and feed to eat. Yes, the farmer has his eggs and chickens.

Of course the garden is ready with its supply of fresh, crisp, vegetables, but what about the warfare that the farm woman has waged against insects that chew, and insects that suck? Against the weeds that grow so gaily and nothing but a sharp hoe will stop them? The hail comes and beats the tender young things in the ground. Ditches have to be made to carry the life-giving water to the thirsty roots, then Mr. Sun comes out and cooks the top of the ground to adobe, and it takes some work to break it. Then the hot work of canning. Yes, the farmer has his vegetables. One of the nicest things that has come to the farmer is that ice is being delivered to the country. Just as soon as you quit taking ice from the weather man, ice is brought to your door and put in your icebox.

June 10, 1937

"Eleven o'clock," exclaims the city wife, as she reaches for the

Mrs. J. M. (Nora) Sherred holding Alice McArthur and tending chickens, Tell, Texas, 1918. Photograph courtesy of Crosby County Pioneer Memorial Museum, Crosbyton, Texas, 0410.

telephone. "I must hurry, my husband will be here at twelve." "Can you bring some groceries right up?" she asks her grocer. "Then please send me one can English peas, loaf of bread, two pounds new potatoes, one pound butter, one head lettuce, bunch of radishes, one can lard, one box strawberries, one box prepared shortcakes, one pint whipping cream, one dressed chicken." The woman gets her order. Dinner is started. The telephone rings. The baby runs into the street, has to be brought back, is given some toys, but when Mr. Husband gets in, there is a dinner fit for the Gods on the table. Words of appreciation bring a glow to the face of Mrs. City-wife.

"Nine o'clock says Mrs. Country-wife. I must begin my preparation for dinner." She hurries to the chicken yard, catches a fat fryer, off comes his head. The eyes of the chicken look reproachfully at the woman as the head lies separated from the body. "It is too bad," sighs the woman, as she

A family meal, Plainview, Texas, 1940s. Note that there is a place at
the table for each of the men and children but not for the two women,
who serve while everyone else eats. Photograph courtesy of Southwest
Collection, Texas Tech University, Lubbock, SWCPC 222 E16.

thinks of the many times she has
fed and cared for the chickens. They
are more like pets. The chicken
is dressed, put in a pan of cool
salted water. Mrs. C then goes to the
garden, hoes a row of beans—then
gathers her vegetables for dinner.
New potatoes are dug, how easy the
tender jacket comes off with scraping. Tender lettuce, crisp radishes
are gathered and washed. A basket of
English peas. What a nice sound is
made as the peas rub together in the
basket. The fat little peas jump from
the hull as the skilled fingers break

their prisons open. The woman
thinks of the hard work, most of it
done in the heat of the day after the
morning work was done and before
the chores of the evening began. The
men have been too busy in the field
to help with the garden. The strawberries, what a pleasure to gather
them. The cows are up for water, are
turned in. What a long time it takes
them to fill their water tanks. An old
hen and her chickens are scratching
up a flower bed. The woman flaps
her apron and shoos at them. An old
turkey hen with her twenty babies

have to be driven off to where they can catch bugs.

Ten-thirty, eleven. Time to get the dinner on. The oil tank is filled. Easier than bringing in coal and kindling. The lard bucket is empty— a trip to the cellar for more. The woman remembers the cold day the lard was rendered. A bucket of fresh water has to be carried from the well. "Running water in the house," laughs the woman, but I do the running—after it." Butter has to be churned. Easier though than the old churn and dash method. Thick separated cream is soon golden butter, when beaten with an egg beater. The shortcake dough is made, cooked, the luscious shortcake is a mound of snow covered with red berries. A pan of brown biscuit, another of cornbread (the cornbread is mainly for supper). The chicken fries a golden brown. Peas and potatoes lie in their blanket of white sauce. The men are washing up for dinner. Long hours they have worked. Dinner is eaten with such keen relish; the woman needs no other praise.

June 24, 1937

Nine o'clock Monday morning, not a word written. Dinner to be cooked for six men. Breakfast dishes unwashed. After breakfast and the milking done, there were chickens to be taken off. Then my husband sent me to a neighbor's to find a truck to haul grain. Combining is just beginning. Pie crusts are in the oven, and I am jumping up every minute to stir the cream filling. Did I put everything in? Let me check up: 2/3 cup sugar, 4 tablespoons flour, 2 cups milk, 3 egg yolks, vanilla flavoring. (A narrow escape, someone had put the furniture polish in the cabinet, I thought to look at the label just in time). Yes, I doubled the receipt for two pies. Mercy, I forgot to put the raisins in the cream filling before I poured it in the crusts. Never mind, I will cut up some bananas on the top of the pies. Will the meringue be fine or will it be leathery? A few minutes will tell. How can I collect my thoughts to write?

There is to be a stork shower this afternoon. What shall I take, with no gift on hand? Fifteen miles to town. I was in three nearby towns the last of the week but no thought of the gift entered my mind. I was hunting a combine, while my husband was killing weeds. Let me think, my neighbor's cousin is visiting her. He has a nice line of toilet articles. How about a cake of pure soap—a box of dainty talcum—a soft fleecy wash rag? There is some tissue paper, (I can iron it out) and some ribbon that was on a present to me. Yes the present can be managed after all. Why didn't I write this column while I had time? The other night I started it, but I stepped outside to see if I could think better. The moonlight caught me in its soft radiance and charmed me. All else was forgotten. The tin roof of the shack was turned to a silver sheet, and I thought I was the bright little star, that I was nestled up close to the moon, looking down at her beautiful image in the silver mirror of the fish pool. Moonlight on my rock fence. It almost took my breath. It might have been easier to move to a country where there were rocks to build a fence. For a year, I have been building this fence. A rock from the canyon—broken cement from the towns, a few feet at a time. Hard work it has been but how I am repaid. Time only adds to its beauty. The flowers bloom brighter from behind the shelter of the rock fence. My fence is not finished. I shall build it as I can.

While I stood in the moonlight a cool breeze fanned my face. A mockingbird loosed a string of silver notes, tossed them to the moon. The moonlight played through the ash trees, made black lace on the lawn. The scent of fresh-cut grass mingled with that from the four-o'clocks that were holding their red and white cups to be filled with dew—but the pie—oh, it is just ready to be taken from the oven. The meringue holds its shape. Tiny gold beads cover the brown surface. It is almost time for the mail carrier, this must be mailed. I must not disappoint Mr. Steen. He needs this to fill the space, even if no one reads it. Next week I must have this ready earlier. Perhaps I should begin this afternoon. But there is the family reunion next Sunday. House cleaning, the lawn to be mowed, garden plowed. I did want to make my new dress. There will be two men to board all week. Glad this is not club week. I fear next Monday morning will find me frantically trying to write this column and get it mailed on time.

July 22, 1937

Collecting elephants is my hobby. Oh, no, not "really real," as children say. China and brass and plaster of paris elephants march on my shelves. No, I am not a Republican. The reason is, perhaps, my grandfathers way back yon' hitched the old mule to their democratic wagons. Sometimes our family has ridden in the lead of the parade, sometimes they have followed the crowd that rode on the huge elephant, whose rich trappings far outshone the old cotton lines, the hay-stuffed collar and chain traces of the mule. Some years we have had to whip and plead with the old mule that was stubborn, balky and turned out at the end of the row too soon. Some of us would fall off and run catch up with the elephant and get on for a ride. So I guess I will jog along behind the old mule, as I think he is the farmers' friend, even if he does have many faults. It does not take as much food to make him go as it does the elephant, and he has pulled the farmer out of many places. Now I have gone and written about politics, just because I wanted to tell about my collection of elephants. But I like to live in a country where those who like the mule best and those who like to ride the elephant live peacefully side by side and work together for the good of the nation.

October 14, 1937

The other night we were awakened by the flashing of zigzag lightning and thunder and a swish of rain on our windows. "Nothing out that can hurt," I was calmly saying to myself, when my husband sprang out of bed, saying, "We must get that load of wheat out of the weather," so we put our raincoats on over our night clothes and hurried out to the rescue of the wheat. The horses were gone, the car called into duty. I drove while my husband and little boy pushed on the heavy loaded wagon. I missed the entrance as the car slipped to the left. We were stuck, there in the rain and the night. We got the car in the shed and pulled the wagon in, and in two hours and twenty minutes we were back in bed, the stars shining and the rain over.

Some say there is monotony on the farm. Wonder if they ever tried to drive an old contrary sow and her bunch of squealing pigs into shelter? Or on a dark night tried to put a bunch of foolish sheep and baby lambs into the barn before the dashing rains strike? Sometimes I think country people would appreciate a little monotony. I have never done any planting of farm crops or the cultivating, outside of hoeing, but in years past my help was given in gathering crops. Many an acre of feed I have cut with the row binder. I know the joy of leaving fine bundles of feed tightly bound in windrows behind the moving binder, and I know the aggravations of trying to cut the short, dry feed. The choking of the binder, the piles of unbound feed. Somehow I could never get any cotton in my sack, perhaps it was because I never had any to practice on when I was growing up, but I could cut and throw maize pretty fast.

Mexican field hands weighing cotton while a farm woman keeps
accounts, near Crosbyton, Texas, ca. 1950. Photograph courtesy
of Southwest Collection, Texas Tech University, Lubbock,
SWCPC 291 E4.

November 18, 1937

What a task it is to me to count off
the cotton weights. Saturday there
was a week's row of figures. Twenty
thousand pounds of cotton. I never
saw so many eights and nines and
sevens. I would count—seven and
nine are sixteen—wonder if my
lightbread is up?—and eight is
twenty-four—wish the Mexican
boy would not count his figures out
loud—viente-e-quatro—no, I am
counting in American. Wish the
weights would end in five. But isn't

it nice to be here—cotton money to
give hardworking people? Money
buys warm clothes and nourishing
food. Someone has said he never
found anyone but that he could
learn something from that person.
I am learning from the Mexicans—
learning how to make delicious hot
tamales, to be content, to thank
graciously with a smile. "Madame,"
the kindly old senora calls me. It
brings visions of the Spanish court,
the black lace mantillas held in
place by tall carved combs, of a lover
sitting under a barred window in

Old Mexico, playing the guitar and singing love songs to the beautiful senorita in the room above.

April 21, 1938

Wash day is no longer a blue day. It is nice to dress up, come to town and wash. I visited with Mr. and Mrs. Olson who were at one tub near. (I wonder if I am giving away Mr. Olson helping wash), at another was pretty Mrs. Guy Jackson. New thoughts, clean clothes, rested women. Life does change. The old days were good to me. The new are still better.

June 9, 1938

I thought I would do my household work early this morning and write my column and some letters, but alas for good intentions. I left the dishwater to heat, fed and watered the chickens, drove off some turkeys that the hens had left, then I decided to set a little grass in the bare spot on the lawn. I dug and worked, got my feet muddy and wet, hauled a wheelbarrow of dirt to fill in the low places. When I got to the house the oil was out of the stove, the water cold and the dishes hard to wash. It is eleven o'clock and the writing has only begun. Perhaps I will get the

letters mailed after all. The light-bread is almost ready to be made into rolls and dinner to be cooked.

June 16, 1938

It is hard to stay in the house and wash dishes and hear the teakettle sing when just outside the trumpet-vine is flaunting orange trumpets to the blue sky and the mockingbird is pouring out his heart in the top of the ash tree. It is very uninteresting to sweep and mop hard floors when there is a soft carpet of green grass on the lawn and a good seat in the shade of a tree inviting you to leave unpleasant duties. As I hurry after a bucket of water a whiff of petunias fragrant and sweet is on the air. A killdeer flies up from the water trough where he has come for a drink of water and a bath. He calls kill-dee-dee-dee as he leaves. I leave my work to take a look at the garden. The beans are growing but need water. Black-eyed peas must be planted. There are some weeds that I failed to get. Tomatoes are not doing so well. The sweet corn given by the experiment station is growing. It is a cross with June corn, and the husk is supposed to be tough enough to discourage Mr. Worm, his wife, and numerous children from trying to cut through to the tender corn they like so well. And while I am out I will feed the little ducks. They are so cute, nine in all. They do not heed their mother's warning but run to me and eat the egg greedily. The white first then the yellow. Even ducks are "choosy," I see. I hope the old Muscovy mother does not bring them in the yard to paddle down my irrigation ditches. But the work inside must be finished and this column written in time for the mail.

September 1, 1938

No wonder the girls are thrilled over the cowboy. Cowboys make pretty fair husbands. In cow camps the one who complained of the cooking soon learned the cook would not stand for it. The cowboys' wives hardly ever hear anything said about the cooking. The cowboy worked long and hard hours in the heat and the cold and the rain. Whenever he got an hour off he was asleep under the chuckwagon. Now when work is done and his wife wants to go places, he is usually asleep in his chair. The cowboy learned to wait on himself and be as little trouble as possible. My good husband is still the cowboy at heart even if he plows the land where he once punched cattle. . . .

Do you of my age remember the ironing days of old? Mother's and

sister's ruffled, tucked lace petticoats hanging with Dad's white shirts on the back of a cane-bottomed chair in a sunny doorway. Little sister's lace-trimmed white aprons and her plain gingham ones—little brother's shirt with the horseshoes and anchors, the mother hubbard dresses and the fancy wrappers. Higher and higher the pile grew. Baby's long dresses and petticoats, trimmed with lace and embroidery. How the smell of freshly ironed clothes fills me with a longing to be a child once more.

September 22, 1938

One day Autumn heats us with summer heat, but the next she gives us a taste of frost and cold. Everyone is in a hurry, so much to do. Crops to be gathered, saved from the winds and the sometimes early freezes. While we milk in the cold, early mornings, we see lights in the windows of our neighbors. We know mothers are there making biscuits and frying meat and eggs. Husbands and sons have to be gotten off to the fields, children have to have lunches made ready. As the sun comes up we hear the rattle of the maize wagons, the hum of the binder, the swishing noise of the cotton sacks dragged over hard ground. The gins whistle and pour out black smoke. The school bus roars on its way to the towns carrying eager boys and girls wanting to learn how to make the most of their lives. I stay in the house and cook and sweep, but once I joined the harvesters. I know the aching back and sore muscles from slapping the slow horses or trying to knock off a hungry horsefly. And when the feed was short and had to be knocked off the carrier with a stick, or the binder choked up and had to be cleaned out, stalk by stalk, and how bad it was to look back and see twine strung out for several hundred yards. The blooms from the feed went down my neck, careless weeds stung my legs, the children, left at the end of the row, sometimes used the grease to grease their legs and their clothes and poured out the drinking water. How I disliked to oil the binder, especially the holes that had to be cleaned out with a wire. But as the last rows were cut and dumped into the long windrows, I delighted to look back and knew the joy of finishing and having the joy of knowing I was help to my husband.

October 6, 1938

It is five o'clock Monday morning. Already the farm work has started. Mr. Spikes has had to help with the milking so I have an extra hour before time for breakfast. Today is my twin girls' birthday and as usual I am looking back, seeing two tiny babies and a little boy almost two years old. A bewildered young mother, far from her mother. Neighbors scarce and a mile or more away. No telephone, no doctor near. But youth accepts whatever comes and goes ahead blithely. I did not know my limitations then, as I do now.

October 20, 1938

I will have to crowd writing this week in between washing dishes, seeing after the new grandson, cooking dinner and helping my husband trailing after cotton wagons. Yes we have a new boss at our house. Though tiny and helpless, we are his willing workers. The daily routine of work has been changed. Everything must wait until the baby has attention. Born in the same house where his own mother was born, in the same month, October, the same day, Sunday, but the sixteenth day of the month instead of the third as hers was. If I fill this space too much with news of the baby, I know the mothers will think it is all right and I hope the rest of you will excuse me.

February 16, 1939

The fever of flower gardening has struck me again. Seed catalogs are everywhere and are studied like schoolbooks. In our minds the flowers bloom as perfectly as they do in the pictures. I want a weeping willow tree; my daughter said to start a limb, but I do not have the patience that once I had. I want a big tree to set out and make a shade this summer. It will grow where the water from the sink runs out. It is time to make frame gardens. I have never tried to make one but intend to this year. Nothing is better than to go to the garden with salt and a cold biscuit and eat tender radishes, pungent mustard and green lettuce leaves.

October 12, 1939

Mrs. Dean and I attended the Authors and Composers Club, which met in the Hilton last Tuesday night. My rough, sunburned hands seemed so conspicuous. Wonder why women do not wear gloves instead of carry them? But on the walls of the mezzanine floor was a picture that held my eye. The picture of a brown-faced Mexican woman, sitting quietly holding her hands in her lap. Although the hands were

still you could see them at work making beautiful drawn work, so tedious and difficult, washing and ironing clothes, carrying wood to make tortillas and the frijoles, nursing the sick, fixing the dead for burial. Hands that are work-worn and scarred, broken fingernails, hands that have always borne heavy burdens! Still only for the strokes of the artist's brush which caught the beauty and made them immemorial on canvas.

February 1, 1940

Hog killing is over on this farm for another year. It is a hard task, but there is nothing that pays better dividends. Sausage, backbone, and spare ribs; lard white as snow, crackling bread, and liver sausage; the promise of baked and fried country ham, or bacon fried crisp; and there is no soap better than homemade lye soap. The first time I ever had to help with putting up the meat was when I was first married. Four days we were on the road to our home here. We got to Fred Spikes's at night. The weather had been very much like it has been here of late. I was tired, a bit homesick for the home I had just left. The next morning was cold. I was handed a knife and told to go to work on the

Woman at cauldron beneath windmill, Parmer County, Texas, ca. 1930. Photograph courtesy of Southwest Collection, Texas Tech University, Lubbock, SWCPC 341 E1 #33.

mountain of meat in the wagon bed. Not only had Fred killed six hogs of his own, but our own three, also. I did not know what to do, but I watched the others; not for nothing would I let them think Jeff had married a silly little girl from the town who did not know how to work on the farm she was now going to. My feet were cold, my hands numb and sore from the knife. Nauseated and tired I kept on the long, long day, being teased adding to my discomfort. Two days we worked with that meat and lard.

Many, many times in the years that have gone so swiftly since then have I helped with the hog killing. How hard it was to scald in a barrel! At the beginning of a cold spell, the neighbors would decide to kill hogs. The colder and more disagreeable it was, the better it suited. The women cooked dinner, while the men scraped the hogs, little boys (somehow they never went to school on those days, too cold, perhaps) got in the way, broiled pieces of meat over the coals, begged for a pipestem or burnt out a piece of grapevine for a hollow stem to blow up the bladders.

The men's beards and mustaches were icicles, their feet wet and cold. Then next day the lard had to be cooked in the black pot outside, the mother going back and forth from the house where her little ones were to the pot of cooking fat. We smelled lard till we thought we never would like meat again. Twenty or thirty gallons was not too big a supply. The first time I ever bought lard, I apologized to the merchant. A farmer was not much who could not raise his own meat and lard.

September 5, 1940

Every fruit jar I can find is being filled with something to eat. The pantry shelves begin to take on rainbow colors. Orange of pumpkin, yellow of plums, green of beans and pickles, purple of grapes. Jellies make the pinks, the reds and the purplish blues. Moving the garden from its place in the sun to a dark place in the cellar gives pleasure to many women. And in the winter to the whole family.

December 19, 1940

This is a time of mysterious doings. When you enter a room, things are hurriedly hidden, knobby packages are piled on the spare bed, women are crocheting and knitting red and blue and white yarns and soft cottons. Bedspreads, rugs, sweaters and hoods take form from their flashing steel needles. Lustrous satin, and rustling taffeta are turned into pajamas and petticoats as if by magic. Soft, fluffy wool bats are being covered with satin rayon, yellow as the harvest moon and the October sun. Rows of quilting in swirls and flowers adorn the warm comfort. Mothers are making doll dresses, stylish as the dresses of her young daughter, herself. Fathers are whittling bedsteads and wooden soldiers. Good fellows are mending and painting toys. Artificial snow gleams in the rays of the sun in every room, bows or ribbon are being tied round tissue-covered packages. The smell of cedar and spruce mingles with the smell of candy, cooling in the large platter. Spice cookies keep company with rich fruit cakes in the pantry. The cracking of nuts, the laughter of happy children make pleasant sounds. Christmas cards are being addressed, hurried trips to town are made to get the gift for Aunt May or Cousin George that one had almost forgotten.

May 1, 1941

There is one old-fashioned object
that I never read of poets singing
about or deploring their passing.
There is the old-fashioned churn.
You skimmed the milk, washed up
dozens of clabbered buckets and
jars. Put on dinner, got the baby to
sleep, reaching under a hiding place
for that thrilling tale of the "Hidden
Hand" or "Tempest and Sunshine,"
and started to read and churn. The
milk was too cold; it foamed and ran
over. You quit reading at a thrilling
place, wiped up the milk, and put
the churn on the back of the kitchen
range, trying to churn and to read as
you stood first on one foot then on
the other. The cream got too hot. You
ran your finger up the churn dash
and found this out. Cool water has
to be poured in, a hurried trip to the
water barrel, or rather it was to have
been hurried. You discover the old
hen has made a dinner table for her
brood in your sprouting tomato and
cabbage beds. By the time you run
her out the baby has waked up and
you sigh as you put the book away
and take the baby in your free hand
while the butter slowly gathers. Well
we like buttermilk, or used to, but
as we quickly beat out the little extra
milk from thick cream, we do not
care as long as we do not have to use
the old-fashioned churn.

August 28, 1941

The catalogs are so flattering this
year to women of my age and I
should add weight. It is "Clothes
for the Gracious Lady," and "Young
like your daughter," and "Clothes
for the Larger Figure." New dress
forms made of plastic which harden
to a permanent reproduction of
your figure, so reads a line in a
new magazine. Well, this brings
back a memory somewhat funny in
our family. Years ago when I was a
great deal younger than I am now, I
decided to follow the home demonstration idea of making a dress form
so my troubles of fitting would be
over. I bought a new vest (perhaps
you younger readers should ask
someone older just what was a lady's
vest) and a roll of gummed brown
paper. The vest was stretched on
carefully, the afternoon was hot, and
my children were to make the form
on my perspiring body. Around and
around the paper was unrolled and
stuck to the vest, stiffer and more
uncomfortable it got; my feet hurt,
but no sitting down was possible
in my stiff paper form. Endless it
seemed as the children laughed and
wrapped more paper high around
the neck and over the arms, following the directions minutely.

At last the paper gave out, and
there I was, looking like a dummy

in a show window that had not been dressed. The children teased, said they would not cut it off, and did run off to the barn and back, and they were not in any hurry to get back, either. The form had to be split down the back, a rather trying thing when you did not know just how deep the sharp knife in unskilled hands might cut. I gratefully shed the locust-like form and pasted it neatly together. Now my fitting troubles were over, I consoled myself as I wearily sat down. But somehow clothes draped around my dummy form did not fit; they were all too large, and for many years the old form stood on its pedestal in the attic catching dust and making a scarecrow for the mice. No sirree, I am not letting a modern plastic form be fitted to me. My clothes can not fit if that is the only way. . . .

A large black cloud came out of the north, thundering, lighting the earth with flashes of brilliant lightning and whipping deluges of water on the growing crops. All work outside had come to a stop, but the kitchen was full of peaches, tomatoes and chicken to be canned, so the men had to help. Not because they wanted to, but they could not see any way of getting out of it.

October 16, 1941

The canning season almost came to a sudden close last Saturday when two jars of black-eyed peas suddenly blew up, scattering bits of glass, boiling water and peas all over the house from the ceiling down. What was the cause we did not know, but as the jars were lifted from the canner and placed on a table, two of the jars exploded, happily with no injuries to anyone. We were so thankful no one was burned or cut we did not mind to clean up the mess. How only two quarts of peas could plaster a whole kitchen will remain a mystery.

October 30, 1941

We had fresh lye hominy for dinner from new corn. It reminded me of the first hominy I made when I was first keeping house. My aunt told me to use soda instead of lye, and with this meager direction I started out. Into my big dishpan of hot soda water I poured a gallon of shelled corn. I wanted plenty. Imagine my dismay when the dishpan swelled too full of corn and had to be emptied into other vessels. I cooked and cooked, the corn swelled, and the contrary old husk would not get off. I put in more soda in my several pots and pans. The stuff stuck, burned and boiled over. I do not remember whether any of it was fit to eat, but I do remember cleaning up the mess.

November 20, 1941

Oh, the hurry of these sunny fall days. It seems sometimes we go around flopping like a chicken with its head cut off, but crops are being gathered, wheat land prepared for sowing. Somehow we slipped in seven bales of cotton gathered last week. I left my duties at the house undone to help haul water to the fields and cotton to the gin. We snatched what we could find to eat, a piece of hard, cold cornbread will stay hunger if needed. Wearily we went to bed at night to lay awake awhile and plan for another day. Indian wigwams appeared like magic in the field as seven shockers went down the stubble. A combine poured grain into a wagon. A good week's work, but only a beginning of the work to be done.

January 15, 1942

I have gotten up to the time of life when I do not want to take out and actually be laid on the shelf, but I'd like to kinda lean against it and just do the things I want to do. But this cannot be so. My country needs my services. . . . This is true of all the farm women around. The other day when the Home Demonstration Club met, every member planned to do extra work on the farm as well as Red Cross sewing and knitting. The women in the towns around have the same determination, and as needles fly over the hanks of khaki yarn and make stitches where stitches were never made before, they will say, knit one, purl, knit two, Pearl Harbor. . . .

When I got my new desk I felt sure that glowing words and neatly turned phrases would fairly flow from my typewriter keys. Somehow it was not any easier to put my thoughts on paper than it was when my desk was the kitchen table, where at least I could keep a part of my mind on the pie in the oven or add more water to the pot of beans. Last year I studied about taking a course in journalism. I came to the conclusion that I would only find out I did not know a thing about writing. I remember some themes I wrote for the girls when they were in college that came back from the teacher marked with a big F. As long as folks like the column the way it is, I will keep on using a large supply of the letter I, with as many adjectives as I can remember.

March 19, 1942

My daughter Wilma has a bed she is very proud of. She made the stead out of a soft pine wood and will give it a coat of clear shellac. The mattress she made out of home-grown cotton by the government standard. Her quilts were pieced from scraps of dresses lined with home-grown cotton and quilted by her own hands. The blankets are from her own sheep's wool, and she has a lovely quilted comfort.

July 9, 1942

I have just come in from the garden after a couple of hours plowing and hoeing. The ground is soft and damp and the new plow was easy to push. The garden has been all green, every shade, from the pale green of lettuce ruffles through the medium shades of beans and tomatoes to the dark color of the butterbeans. Against the reddish brown of the earth the greens look so cool. Now much color is being added. Red beets with handsome tropical-looking leaves, splashes of yellow in the cucumber vines, purple dots in the beans, onions of pearl, ruby red almost hidden among the strawberry plants and the creamy white dainty blossoms of the last-year carrots. I like to see clear, cool water running down the rows, giving life to the thirsty plants. My garden will be late, but only a few days ago the crooked necks of peas and beans were only pushing up from the ground and tomatoes will soon shade the earth. Nothing gives more pleasure to me than making a garden. It is a place to relax one's mind while the hoe reaches here and there to get a weed that would destroy the vegetables.

July 16, 1942

Thoughts while hoeing. . . . I am getting the weeds pushed back to where they will not show so plain to visitors. How tough they are. My goodness how the sun shines down, hot on my head. I will hoe in the shade of the pecan tree. Whew, how the flies bite, better to hoe out in the heat. Wish someone would establish a second front. The weeds will whip me yet. It will take a Russian winter. . . . Anyone would know that potatoes will not make in hard ground, yet that is where mine got planted. Too many other things to do. Asparagus is waving willowy plumes all round the place. Dozens and dozens of bunches coming up here and there from scattered seeds. Wish a cloud would shade the

Two women showing off their garden, a field of corn in the background, Parmer County, Texas, ca. 1920. Photograph courtesy of Southwest Collection, Texas Tech University, Lubbock, SWCPC 341 E1 #95.

sun for awhile. There go two yellow butterflies, dazzling gold, now they hover over the exquisite blue of the anchusa flower. Is the hoe dull, or is it that the weeds are getting tougher? Wish I was at a roll-top desk in an air-conditioned office, a glass of frosted drink in my hand, a secretary to write down my words as I tell farmers and their families just what they must do in this emergency (as if farmers and their families have not been meeting emergencies every day and year of their lives). Sakes alive, this is complaining and envying. This will not cut any weeds.

August 6, 1942

Our field has been gone over with a hoe, but this time I did not carry one. But I have in days past. When my children were young, we all took our hoes and went to the field. How big and impossible the weed field looked as we first started in. Down the long rows, silent at times, but as the weeds thinned, how we all talked. At the end of the row, cool water from a shaded jug gurgled down our dry throats. We would sit on the ground and rest and relax. A bit of weed made a fine pen to write in the sand; turning a bug on his back watching his feet claw wildly in the air, chewing the sweet stems of mesquite grass, anything to do or see for a few restful minutes. How cool the wind blew on our sweat-covered faces. We pulled off our bonnets and hats to get more of the precious coolness. Back to the work, down another weedy row, rest at the end, back and forth across the field, day after day. What a gratified feeling to look over the field at the end of the last row.

January 14, 1943

When I get ready to go help milk I put on a long skirt woven from our own wool and terribly stylish some ten years ago, a milk apron, a heavy coat, and warm hood. Then if it is muddy, I slip a pair of my husband's old shoes (just wasn't forehanded enough to get overshoes) and start out. I feel like I am Mrs. Five by Five, and one could not tell whether I was a-coming or a-going.

January 21, 1943

Monday morning: Whew-ee, it was cold at the barn this morning while we were milking. We were almost afraid to walk for fear of breaking

our frozen toes off. The kitchen feels good now that the pain of getting hands and feet warm too quickly has gone. Perhaps if we did not feel the bitter cold we would not appreciate the blessings of the warm room, however humble. The water pipes are frozen up, too. This may be a blessing in disguise also, to make us know the blessing of water always at hand. Anyway there are books to read, and plenty of canned food to open and heat in a jiffy; there are radio programs, clippings saved all the past year, waiting to be put in a scrapbook, and I am way behind on the stamp collection I am starting for my two grandsons. I wish I had more time to devote to stamp collecting, as it is a very interesting hobby, and now that all kinds of postmarks are on letters it is even more so.

February 4, 1943

We are especially enjoying the carrots we canned last fall. They are exceptionally sweet and tender. Cut in small cubes and canned, their golden color is one of the prettiest in the pantry lineup. Vegetables grown last year were all good and now make their appearance from the jars instead of from the garden. I find it best to get seeds of wilt-resistant vegetables. The Marglobe tomato will not fail you, or I find it so. Of course the Porter still holds first place in being entirely dependable, and it makes such nice juice. Black-seeded Simpson lettuce is good. Chicago pickling cucumber is my favorite. I cleared off my garden the other day, with the help of Joe Ellis, and I wondered why it was so hard to find room to plant all I wanted to each year, it looked such a big place now. It needs to be broke, but that is one thing the man of the house does not like to do, and it will have to wait till the last minute.

February 25, 1943

Of course, you all remember that we were rationed on flour the last war. I would make biscuits, putting half oatmeal, or half potato flour or any kind of a flour we could get. The worst possible thing happened to a 48-pound sack of flour we had just brought in for our allotment of six people for a longer period of time than it could possibly last. The sack was placed near the cabinet to be emptied later. Alas, a can of kerosene oil was near, holding a few sticks for quick kindling of the big range fire. Someone turned it over. I grabbed the precious sack of flour, but too late, a trickle ran under the sack. At once I emptied the flour, but to the last biscuit that flour tasted of kerosene. How it ruined the taste of the few cakes, eked out with corn sugar and syrup. Kerosene bread—how the taste almost makes me sick today and the children will never, never forget. But it was all we had and all we could get.

I think Hoover was pretty wise the last war, as he put the housewife in uniform. How we all made the Hoover dress and caps. A pretty blue was the color of the apron dress. It made us feel so much more important in the war program, and I am sure we felt more patriotism for the wearing of a uniform.

March 25, 1943

This is March the 22 and still cold. I have to keep running out to the shack to see about the chickens. Three hundred Buff Orpingtons belong to me, and one hundred white leghorns I am starting for Wilma. As it is so much trouble to go at night to see about them, I have moved a bed in the other room of the shack and sleep out there. The pet pig sleeps in the room with the chickens, so you see I have plenty of company. The cold wind has been howling around the shack, shaking it as a dog does a rabbit; the cold creeps in every crack and crevice but I stay warm. We are making every effort on the farm to produce as much food as we possibly can, and one has to stay on the job day and night.

May 8, 1943

This morning as I listened to the advertisement of Dr. Pierce's Golden Medical Discovery, I glanced in the bookshelves at the worn copy of that famous book by Dr. Pierce. This was the only book on diseases I owned when I was rearing my family. I think it cost me twenty-five cents and worlds of grief because every time the children stopped playing or fussing for a few minutes, I hurried to the book and began to search for symptoms. I had the children having everything from anemia to yellow jaundice. I would read, then take up the protesting child and peer in his throat for the signs of diphtheria, or search his skin for the first sign of something or other breaking out, especially scarlet fever. By the time the child was thoroughly examined and the symptoms all studied, he was either worse, more often, or well. At the end of the paragraph of terrible symptoms and the passing

out of the patient one was always warned by the book to take the Medical Discovery or see a doctor at once. I can tell you today the pages I found where my children had a terrible malady. I can still feel the numbness that gripped me and the cold feeling I had when I read and read, only to have my husband laugh at me when he came in to dinner or supper and say of course it was not diphtheria, or pneumonia or just anything I found where a child had a fever.

May 20, 1943

The farmer roars into action on the battlefront of food production this lovely May morn. Tractors chug down the contoured rows, dropping fuzzy white seed into the wet, warm ground. Wilma and I have been planting the truck patch. I had better not tell just where, for we planted out watermelon seed. If one were a dozen people this morning there would be work for all. So many, many seeds to be planted and the weeds like hair on a pup's back. Clothes need to be washed and drying in the bright sunshine, the house work can go, all but the cooking and dishwashing. Will it ever be done? The farmer puts his costly cottonseed in the ground, anxiously watches the skies as so many things can happen, hard rains, or too-drying winds, but he must go ahead, always gambling on the weather, mostly missing his best guess.

June 17, 1943

The wind sighs through the young poplar tree at the west side of the rock fence, and I remember three poplar trees whose roots were cooled in the waters of a dirt tank where cattle watered and switched at flies on a hot summer day. The willowy poplars held out their fanning leaves to the blue of a summer sky flecked with floating white clouds. Nettie and I lived in one, Omega and Edna in another, while Mary Lee and Belle perched in the third. What lovely green houses they made far enough away that we could not hear Grandmother or Aunt Mirt call us to unpleasant duties, such as washing the dishes or churning or carrying in water from the well. What gorgeous dresses we played we had on! Colors taken from Aunt Mirt's gay bed of zinnias. Purple, like a queen's robe, red as the coals of the burning mesquite roots, blue as the heaven above, pink as my mother's cheeks, white as the clouds. We were ladies, haughty and proud, as we sat or stood in the branches that swayed with the wind. Crooking our little fingers as we played drinking tea in imitation of a lady we saw once do it this very way, happiness supreme was in the magic of the trees. Grandmother's garden was below our feet on the slope of the tank where we gathered red tomatoes and nibbled at cabbage leaves and shelled green peas from a pod. Farther away was the orchard, another playhouse, or rather playhouses as many as there were trees shading the deep sand from the hot sun. Would I ever forsake the love I then had for tall poplar trees?

July 29, 1943

It is always a good time of the year, when black-eyed peas air a-bilin' in the pot with a hunk of home-cured bacon, sliced tomatoes, onions and cucumbers are taking a vinegar bath in the best pickle dish, roastin' ears melting scads of butter and okra slick as oil, oh, my, and new potatoes with their brown jackets buttered, and pepper, hot and pungent as a fire under the pot of boiling vegetables, all old friends, known to our forefathers but just as good now as then. What is the use to search out and try new dishes when these plain old methods are so good and satisfying?

August 26, 1943

Corn on the cob, off the cob, or anyway is on the tables these days. But best of all I like to make bread of the fresh corn. Use corn after it has left the roastin' ear stage till it gets almost too hard to cut off the cob and then grind in a sausage mill. To two cups of the ground corn, add two cups of sour milk, one teaspoon of salt and one of soda, then bake till brown in a greased pan. Our grandmothers grated the corn and called the bread "grated bread," but grinding is much quicker and easier.

September 16, 1943

There are so many things to do I find myself going around carrying a lazy woman's load, that is, gathering more clothes off the line than I can carry without dropping some, trying to carry too full a bucket of milk to pour into the separator, stooping to pick up tomatoes dropped from too full a hand. Yes, a lazy person tries to make one job do where more than one trip should be made.

September 23, 1943

Some women cannot resist buying hats, others fall easy prey to dishes, but let me tell you my line of least resistance is books, and a book catalog or books in a store have such appeal that I do without something else and buy some. I like to sit in an easy chair in front of my small library and choose. Would I like a bit of history? There are books about the ancient Romans and Greeks, the English peoples, the French, and the Americans. Travel? Marco Polo takes me with him or I can travel with Gulliver, or go around the world in eighty days with Verne. Emil Ludwig fascinates me with the story of the Nile, and Lin Yutang interests me with the telling about his Chinese countrymen. I can go sweeping in the clouds with Antoine Exupery, or listen to a thousand tales about Arabia. I can laugh out loud with the story of Tish and her two old maid friends, or I can weep over Uncle Tom's cabin and my heart almost breaks over Jane Eyre. Old friends and new, waiting to cheer me with beautiful poems, the thrilling old Bible stories, the hope and faith and love I find in the New Testament. Always I want to read a book again and again that I especially like; only lack of time keeps me from them. Someday maybe I can sit by the fire and read and doze and read again the books I love.

January 12, 1944

The sheet and pillow slip shortage will not bother farm women too much. They have feed sacks to make them of. Of course there are seams in the sheets, but they are never felt when one is tired. The sacks bleach out snowy white, and we are using them for many things: dresses, underwear, luncheon sets, aprons and so on. We vie with one another to find new ways and uses for the sacks.

March 3, 1944

Knowing how to use a soldering iron, learned by sealing tin cans the old way, has come in mighty handy these war times. Soon I will have new bottoms in the milk buckets of solder. A handle was put back on the tin dipper. As long as I can buy solder perhaps we can keep tin things in repair.

May 18, 1945

I had been hankering for rhubarb, visions of pies and sauce as of long ago when I raised plenty of this delicious plant—remember, we used to call it pie-plant? Judge Murray raised so much of it at Emma, and did Mrs. Murray know how to cook

it? There was where I learned to love it. We had lost all our rhubarb—the dry years got it. But now we have a plentiful supply, thanks to the kindness of Mr. McCauley of East Floydada. He was so generous giving us the long, yellow roots to set in our garden and long, green stems, streaked with deep red so we could have sauce and pies at once.

June 1, 1945

The hats today remind one somewhat of the hats when I was a girl. We are using flowers again. From hats laden with flowers and illusion we went to the other extreme and wore hats as bare of trimming as those of the men. But fashion began tacking on a gay flower here and a ribbon bow there till hats are pretty again. It was a wonderful adventure when a girl got old enough to go to the milliners and pick out a hat by herself. The pretty milliner (she was always pretty) opened boxes for us, boxes of flowers and boxes of illusion and boxes of ribbon and bright ornaments for the summer and ones of feathers, ribbons, furs and sparkling pins for the styles of the winter. How undecided we were: Would we choose a leghorn frame or have the milliner make one of braid? Would we have the underside lined with soft shirred silk? The red velvet roses with the green velvet leaves? The long encircling spray of blue and pink forget-me-nots? No, they were for children! The blue violets or the purples pansies? No, they were for grandmothers. Pink silk poppies, mossy roses. We would never have decided if the milliner had not come with suggestions. She would place the flower she knew would look the best on the type of hat selected, she looped up long bows of creamy satin ribbon to be held on with the sparkling pin, and then we went home to wait till our hat was finished and dream of how pretty we would look to certain young men.

October 5, 1945

I remember what Julia used to tell about the old underwear and socks as I sort them out. Her mother was visiting, and the woman called out to her daughter, who was bending over a tub of clothes on the shady side of the house, "Daughter, you need not wash them there socks and underwear very good. I only want them for dishrags, anyway." And that makes me think of how women used to pride themselves on the whiteness of their wash and talked about a neighbor whose clothes "looked yellow as the sun." And women vied with one another as to who could get her wash out the earliest.

February 22, 1946

The other day I was burning weed around and in my garden. Yes, I let frost get them, thinking then that it was not a bad thing to do, but I find that an old weed, growing through a wire fence, is harder to do anything with than a whole lot of green weeds. Resolution: get them while young and green. All at once as the weeds burned, came the best scent, that of onions cooking. Yes, the onions were cooking, the winter onions along the fence.

October 29, 1948

I have arthritis so bad that many things have been neglected. I usually do, however, get the windmill pipes wrapped, a job that for many years has fallen to me, and I would put it off and off, having to wrap them on a cold northery day. I was told that if one would grease the pipes first with thick grease, then wrap, less danger would come from freezing. This I tried, then used thick rolls of paper, then sacks making a thick roll around the pipes.

The windmill has long been a symbol of pioneer independence in the grass-land. The first to build windmills on the southern plains were ranchers intent on providing water for their cattle. By the early twentieth century, when the region converted from large ranches to small farms, the number of windmills increased dramatically as one farmstead after another installed them. A shallow well with a windmill freed a farmer from reliance on outsiders for water and for energy. On the true high plains there is no flowing water, aside from shallow, intermittent draws that channel rainfall runoff to canyons around the edge of the plateau. Settlers found no reliable surface water in the area. A shallow well and windmill was a prerequisite to any long-term settlement.

Once built, windmills served several purposes for farm families. Farmers sometimes piped water from the windmill into the house, where it provided water for drinking, cooking, and washing. It also served for refrigeration, as the cool underground water kept milk, cream, and butter from spoiling on hot summer days. Excess water then went to the essential livestock: work horses, milk cows, hogs, chickens, and beef cattle. Finally, any remaining water served to irrigate the garden. Windmills were important to women, as they were usually responsible for cooking, cleaning, gardening, and processing dairy products, all tasks requiring water. One pioneer commented that when stock farmers were single they usually built windmills in dispersed pastures for the benefit of their cattle, but when they married they installed windmills next to their homes for the benefit of their wives.

But windmills were limited in their ability to provide water. Wind power alone was sufficient only to lift water about thirty feet. It might run constantly, but the volume was low. A single well could provide enough water to irrigate about five acres of land or to water thirty head of cattle. This was a subsistence supply of water. One windmill could keep a family from going thirsty, support fifteen head of livestock in the barnyard, and water a 2-acre garden. It could not supply a 160-acre farm with enough water to raise a cash crop or even ensure a decent feed crop in dry years. Windmills made settlement possible on the high plains and made homes more comfortable, but they could never make farming very profitable.

March 18, 1949

I found the dahlia bulbs had kept in the garden through all the cold. I never did get around to digging them last fall. Mr. Spikes was clearing off the garden yesterday. I told him I would dig the bulbs after a while, before the garden was plowed. When I went back for them, he had cut off all the tops, and I could not tell where they were—only by raking and hunting, which was not easy to do. Eve and Adam were not the only two who had a spat in the garden.

August 19, 1949

Stain made my hands yellow as I prepared a bushel of carrots for canning. Then the blue from grapes made them a sickly green. A big blister is on my arm from touching a hot pan of jelly; another is on my right forefinger from gathering peas. Plum bushes have made deep scratches as I reached in for wild plums. By the sweat of my brow preparations for winter food have been going on. My back is sore from stooping over bean vines, my hands itch from the okra stickers. My eyes are crying from the onions and hot peppers. But glory be! The shelves are getting fuller and fuller.

October 7, 1949

All over the place vegetables and fruits have been ripening for the canning, tomatoes by the bushels, peaches falling off, but at least we made a final canning of hominy and called the season over. That very night while 25 pints of hominy cooled off in their gold-lined cans, I took the canner and sealer upstairs, hoping we would not be tempted to can another thing. But yellow pears hang heavy on the tree, and big balls of quince are beginning to turn, so we may make a few more preserves and a little more jam. Not only our pantry shelves droop in the center with heavy loads, but most every woman we meet says, "I have canned and canned this year till I am completely worn out."

March 17, 1950

Someone asked the question if I would continue my column under the heading I have always used as now we are living in the town of Floydada. Yes, the heading is still correct. How could one think otherwise than as a farm woman since the last 43 years have been spent on the farm? How could I keep from worrying when a black cloud spreads its wings over the sun and brings hail and destruction? How could I forget the dry fields, scorched by hot winds? The cooling rain that saved the crop? The long days riding the binder to save bundles before a killing frost? The hog killing? The cooking for 20 or so men at a time of harvest? The chickens that drowned in a sudden shower? The raising of turkeys? The pigs getting out and rooting up my garden and flowers? No, in my thinking I am still a farm woman and as such will continue this column.

April 28, 1950

Making a garden here for the first time makes me think of the first garden I ever made, way back in 1907. It looked so pretty and it had been hard to break up the tough clods that Jeff had plowed up. Green ribbons of lettuce and radishes. But one day when we returned home what a sight! The pigs had got in and rooted up everything. I sat down and cried, not realizing then as now that tears would not plant another garden. I smoothed out the rooted furrows, planted again. Soon more green rows were showing. A freeze the first of May and plants hung like little black rags. More tears, but more work and my lesson in gardening had begun. Mr. A. D. White always said he sold the newcomers three sets of garden seed but only one to the old-timers.

October 20, 1950

It is October, say of the nineteen-twenties. I am up before day, lighting the fire already laid in the big Majestic range, making a big pan of biscuits while the bacon fries and the coffee and eggs boil. A kettle of black-eyed peas is boiling at the back and sweet potatoes are roasting in the oven, for my dinner has to be prepared, for we are all going to the field and the children need lunch for school. After breakfast Mr. Spikes hooks up the horses to the binder and I get on the seat, wearing my big khaki divided skirt made for riding horseback. My split bonnet is pulled low over my eyes, and the children ride away on their horses to school and we start cutting the long rows of cane or kaffir, perhaps milo maize. The spiders and bugs fly all over me with the chaff from the feed. I guide the contrary horses and mules down the long rows trying hard not to miss a stalk. Up the foot comes and a big bundle falls hard to the ground near its neighbors of the rows before, Mr. Spikes following, setting them up in neat tent style. The binder breaks, and altho' the day is dry and golden, tomorrow it may rain and time is valued, but the piece has to come out that is broken and a quick trip to town to be made while the horses stamp at flies and mosquitoes and try to bite heads just out of reach.

Later in the year we will head maize, and the rows are so long, and our back breaks as we stoop to pick up heads that have fallen, and our hands have blisters from the heading knife. How we count the rows that stand headless! And how many are still to be cut! I never see a combine go down a row now that I do not give thanks that someone is not going at a slow gait cutting off a head at a time and throwing them in the wagon. But there were many compensations. Purple and yellow flowers bloomed in the grass at the ends of the row. The feed tasted like heavenly manna. A watermelon left in a shock overnight was cold and delicious. There was the feeding of grain for the horses and hogs and chickens and fodder for both cows and horses. And there is the lovely remembrance of a woman gracious and thoughtful, Mrs. Lincoln, who hooked up a horse to a buggy and driving some two miles bringing us some greens and turnips cooked as she only could cook them, so that we might have them for our noon meal.

January 12, 1951

No, I was not trying to play a Christmas trick as folks once found so entertaining. I was just wanting a pan of good old "fatty bread," as Wilma had brought some cracklings. I even used an egg, high as they were, to make a pan of bread even better. I looked inside to see if it was done and, lo and behold, it was bubbling like a pan of mush. I took it out and stirred in more and more meal wondering all the time why the meal did not seem to thicken the milk. I put it back, and soon black smoke was coming out of the oven and a smell of something awful filled the house with the black smoke. I took out the mess and had to get it off the oven floor. I shuddered as I timidly took a small bite of the stuff and was it bitter! Too much soda, I said to myself. It kind of made like lye and grease do in soap. But not till late that afternoon did the whole truth bust on me like a bomb. The Tide was near the same size box of meal, and I had used it in plenty. Now, according to the advertisers, I should have used Duz, for it does everything, and Tide, as we all learned in our first lessons, waits not for any man, neither does it make crackling bread.

Two women on mules with a binder, Parmer County, Texas, ca. 1900.
Photograph courtesy of Southwest Collection, Texas Tech University,
Lubbock, SWCPC 341 E2 #2.

January 25, 1952

The new flower catalogs brighten the days and make one want to garden. But I recall when I was a young woman with my years of gardening ahead how thrilling the new colored flower catalogs were to me. One winter I helped dehorn some cane bundles. Cold it was, too. I stood in the wagon on a big heated iron, which had lain on top of the cook-stove while I prepared breakfast and would hold some heat for hours. I lifted the long, sharp blade fastened to the side of the wagon and brought it sharply down on the bundle my husband had placed to be cut, and smack, the well-grained heads would fall in the wagon. I threw them back with a pitchfork or grain fork. I would shiver after this was done and before another bundle was ready. When we got to the long stack of heads where another load was to be put, I sat down on the sunny side and took out my flower catalog. Soon the cold wind and the discomfort of stinging grain were forgotten, and I was in a world of perpetual sum-

Woman chopping feed, probably near Lubbock, Texas, ca. 1915.
Photograph courtesy of Southwest Collection, Texas Tech University,
Lubbock, SWCPC 817 E1 #17.

mer, roses and lilies and bountiful vegetable gardens. If all the things I then selected had grown, it would have taken some acres of the farm to grow them. The sour-sweet smell of the cane, the patches of unmelted snow, the rattle of the wagons on the frozen ground, the rushing sound of many wings in the blue heavens above, the scurrying of a gray field mouse taking her young to another shelter of standing shock, the sigh of white smoke coming from the horses' noses as they caught at the heads of grain, all this comes clear and very tender and sweet to me as I look in at the red roses, the blue lilies and the white daisies which have never lost their appeal and thrill, and thank God never will.

February 15, 1952

Just take a look in every pickup you see, and in many you will find some bright-eyed youngster coming to town with his father or grandfather. I like to see them stand about as the grownups talk. They put their hands in their pockets and spit now and then as do the older men. They act so grown up. Not so with mother or grandmother; they set up a howl for the variety store or the cold drink counter. They rebel at the dry-goods store. But with the men at the hardwares, the lumberyards and the implement companies, they do not give a bit of trouble. They are men in a man's world.

August 14, 1952

This is a fine Monday morning, August 11th. The year stretches on. School days are just over the horizon and the green bolls of cotton will turn to brown and pop open in the bright fall sunshine. I always felt a sadness when this time of year came around when my children were at home. I never wanted school days to come; I wanted them to get an education, but at this time of year the wind seemed to bring a reminder that time was near, the days ahead would have to be spent in the farm home, too quietly, as the children and their many activities would not break the long hours. And when the time came for them to go to college, the nights, too, would be too quiet as well as the days. So, even today, the wind whispers warnings of approaching changes, and I remember and feel an apprehension of uneasiness as I did years ago.

Portraits

Many of Nellie Witt Spikes's articles focused on one individual, painting a textual portrait of a person and his or her life, history, and bearing. The stories come from her own family and from her neighbors who she "interviewed" over a glass of iced tea on the front porch or over a cup of coffee by the fire. We might consider these columns to be oral histories recording the lives and textures of common people who lived a century and a half ago. One can almost envision the old grandma sitting in her rocker looking back on a long life or the young man riding across the plains. There was something of the artist in Spikes. Her writing was occasionally lyrical, sometimes intensely descriptive, always romantic in its fond memories of the past and its generous portrayals of family, friends, and neighbors.

This chapter selects the best of those prose portraits that bring to life characters now forgotten in West Texas's past. One benefit of local history is its ability to focus on the lives and activities of regular people. None of Spikes's subjects became famous or well known to a broader public. Few of them are remembered by any living person today. These were common people living mundane lives. But Spikes's empathy for them reminds us of the breadth and depth of experience residing in people's stories, stories that enrich our own routine lives with the heft of human experience.

August 26, 1937

"You get your love of beauty from your little Holland Dutch grand-mother," Mother Superior at a hospital told me. My Grandmother Witt was a tiny woman, her cheeks as soft and white as a Martha Washington rose. Her dresses were black and her poor, half-blind eyes some quack doctor had ruined were always shaded with a black bonnet. Her wide skirt had a set-in pocket. In this pocket was Grandmother's tobacco and a knife. Such dainty little pieces she cut and put in her mouth. Never a stain on her chin. How Grandmother loved flowers.

After she could not attend to those in the yard, there was always a pot of sweet basil on her windowsill. Sweet basil grows in my yard. It is a sweet remembrance of yesterday, and I always give fragrant sachets of it to my friends. I think of the fragrance of a good woman's life, going on down through the years and giving off perfume to all those it touches.

August 11, 1938

My father, John Marion Witt, was born in fifteen miles of Springfield and grew to young manhood there. He often laughed and told us he went to Springfield only twice. When the Witt family moved to Texas, they stopped and camped at a little town. There was a spell-ing contest there that night and my father won a quarter. The next morning he spent a nickel for a jew's harp. The wagons started on towards Texas, but my father was not satisfied with the twenty cents in his pocket, so he walked back to the little store and bought four more jew's harps.

My father had a beautiful voice; he could put a leaf in his mouth and make music. He taught singing schools and writing schools when I was a child. How I loved to hear him whistling as he came home through the dark. He has passed on to the better world, but the memory of his sweet music makes melody in many hearts.

August 18, 1938

A car drove up the other night. What a nice surprise when my aunt, Mrs. G. D. Jones, her son G. D. and her son Rene's wife Virginia and my mother got out. Only for an hour or two were they here, but what a good time we had. Mother told about the time that her nephew Lester Jones was getting ready to go see his girl. He washed out his underwear and put them on the stove in a large stew pan to boil. Now Aunt Ella had some fruit juice on the stove in another large pan. She told one of the little girls to put sugar in the juice. Not noticing, the careless child put the sugar in the wrong pan. When Lester came to get his things he found them candied.

When my uncle George brought his bride to Emma, they lived awhile with us. I admired and loved my new aunt dearly. She had the prettiest dresses; her black hair was worn over her white forehead in a soft pompadour. She could tie ribbon in the loveliest bows and knots. I tried to sing alto because she did. No one could make prettier embroidery. My regret is that I have had to live all these years so far from her.

September 8, 1938

The baseboard was put around the walls; it made me think of the early Emma days. Mrs. Carter, the doctor's wife, had a papered room and sent to the railroad for a washboard, as it was then called. How eagerly we waited the sight of the washboard but were disappointed when it was not corrugated like the rub board. Mrs. Carter had nice things. She had a canary in a cage, a three-room house, a piano with guitar attachment. She wore a black plush dolman trimmed in braid. She was from Kentucky, could sing alto and recite poetry. Her main piece was, "They've Got a Brand-New Organ, Sue, Just Like They Said They'd Do." But Mrs. Carter was not "stuck up" over her high position in Emma. She had time to make a little girl happy. She let her "play" the piano, gave her bouquets of soft, pink roses with yellow centers and with the sweet perfume of Araby. She helped with the church work and gave musicals to entertain. How we loved and admired her! And how sad her early death made us!

October 6, 1938

Coleman and Ollie have come from Mr. Spikes's home neighborhood. They are from Spikes's Prairie, Kaufman County, to make their home on our farm. How well the colored race know how to please. Their voices are soft—their laughter pleasant and gay. They observe many small courtesies many of us would do well to take up.

November 17, 1938

Yesterday it was our good fortune to be invited to the birthday reunion held at the home of Uncle John and Uncle Lish English and in honor of their seventy-eighth birthday. The day was ideal, a pale blue sky made a canopy over the jolly crowd, soft white clouds curtained the distant horizon. The sun shone warm, its heat tempered by a soft, cool breeze. Smoke curled from the chimney, where some were warming by the mellow heat of an open fireplace; women and girls were in the kitchen, cutting rich pies and cakes, taking up tender chicken and spicy dressing, heaping up bowls of salads, opening jars of pickles. The men stood in the yard, joking and laughing, sighing for the good old days, keeping a fire under the big wash pot where the fragrance of good hot coffee teased the noses of many. Sisters and brothers, nephews and nieces, old friends, remembering old times and comparing the new, Uncle John and Uncle Lish always holding the place of honor. The long tables in the yard were finally loaded to the satisfaction of the women and the gratification of the men, young people and children. Grace was said by George Rable and the fun of the eating was on. Plates were loaded till nothing else could be piled on, rapidly emptied and then filled again. Everything had to be at least tasted. One young man was heard to say he was so full he felt like twins. Then came the picture taking. What a hard job it was to gather up the crowd, who were so full they desired nothing only to be still. Sterling Parrish made everyone laugh by telling the photographer to shake well before taking. A happy day, happy people.

These twin brothers were born and reared in Fannin County, Texas. Left there at about thirty, went to Comanche, ranched a year or two, went to Seven Rivers, New Mexico, which is now Carlsbad, ranched about five years there, then moved to Crosby County. "Yes, we went up trail to Kansas in 1872 as trail hands. Got with the herd in Caldwell

County, were two months on the road and delivered about 2,300 head of cows and steers at Ellsworth, Kansas," they told in answer to my questions. "We lost some cattle that drowned in the Wichita River that was up. No, we saw some Indians but they were going from us. The country which we went through was wild. We have lived in Crosby County forty-five years." Inseparable have been the lives of these two men, born the same day so many years ago; now they sit on the shady porch in the warm summer days, whittle with sharp knives on long pine sticks, needing no talk other than an occasional word. When the cold days come they sit by the fireplace with Uncle Lish's good wife keeping them company. Near their tree-shaded home the sun shone on the marble monuments of a little cemetery where the older ones of the English family lie sleeping. In the hearts of the crowd gathered at the peaceful home I saw love, respect, and honor for the two old men that have lived good, upright lives, have been friends and neighbors, have taken their part like men.

Just four months after this description of the English twins' seventy-eighth birthday party, Spikes noted their death in her column. John died first, followed by Lish in late March 1939. "Never were they parted long in life," wrote Nellie.

December 8, 1938

The other night the colored people from the little house sang for us. Sweet and clear as a bell is Ollie's voice as she takes the lead in the spirituals. Bo follows, then Coleman comes in with his bass, and his voice is like the deep bass twang on a guitar. Such rhythm and melody! They sing with such perfect ease and with evident pleasure.

February 2, 1939

Yesterday we went to old Emma to see my Uncle John Taylor who is in bed with a leg crushed from a fall. Uncle John has lived eighty-two years, has seen and taken part in the making of a great state. When a boy, he hunted buffalo on these plains. He tells us how they ran out of anything to eat but the buffalo meat; tells us of the awful dry years of '87 and '88. He has been a keen observer of the things he has seen and heard in his eventful life, and now that he is old, he enjoys telling them to listeners.

February 9, 1939

Did you ever think how big a part the wind plays in this country? Every time we go outdoors, we look to see where the wind is. At this time of year, if the wind is from the west when we get up, we look for a sand storm, and oft times a cold norther following. When the wind goes to the east we long for the rain, which once in a while it brings. The summer winds bring us plenty of good cold water from the busy windmills. Once upon a time the direction of the wind was told by the fans on the mills, but now just drive by and every mill will tell a different tale.

Last week the old milk house by the well was torn down from where it had stood for thirty years, to give place to an elevated tank, and a bit of early history was gone. When the little house was new and alone in the prairie sunshine like a piece of yellow cheese, it was the pride of Mrs. J. K. Millwee, for she could keep her milk and butter cool and fresh. About eight miles south of the Quaker Colony, Estacado, built by Tom McDonald for J. K. Millwee, in the year of 1891, its useful life was begun. Many a cowboy, starved for milk, drank from the creamy old crocks in the milk trough while he ate a doughnut that Mrs. Millwee gave him. Refreshed from the snack and the sight of a good, beautiful woman, the cowboy rode back to the herd, where hard riding in the dust and the heat was begun again. A little windmill wheel was built on top of the new milk house and hooked to a churn.

But the Millwee family moved from the ranch, and the little house that was no longer like yellow cheese but has turned a soft gray, like the prairie in winter, became the property of Uncle Billy Weatherby and was moved to Emma to become a home. Uncle Billy was "different." He was a Yankee soldier, had been married to a Mexican woman, "a dang good woman for a Mex. But I wanted to leave New Mexico and come to the Plains, and she wouldn't come." So Uncle Billy made him a barn from big wooden packing boxes got from Witt Spikes. This was the place where Ole Deck switched the flies in summer and bent from cold northers which shook the thin boards in winter. We never heard him sing, but Tom Jones, our young uncle, told us he saw the old man coming down the street in Emma one bitter cold day and he was singing, "It is horrible in the winter to be shattered by the blast." But we always had our doubts.

Uncle Billy wore clothes too large for him to go over the hump on his back, talked like he had hot mush in his mouth. His nose dripped, summer and winter, he called all by their given names. When questioned about his youth, people got no answer. He admitted he had been born in Maine, fought in the Civil War. Once there was a letter come for him; one of the ranch boys carried it to the ranch where he was then working, and all gathered 'round to see what effect the news would have. To their keen disappointment, the little old man with the long gray locks of hair calmly walked to the red-hot stove and gave the unopened letter to the greedy flames. Uncle Billy was our friend, and once when Father and Mother were both sick and the smallpox flag flew at our gate, for Father had a strange breaking out, the doctor demanded quiet. We children were sent to Uncle Billy's, for he had had the dreaded disease. We watched closely when the old man opened his trunk for a clean towel. We might see a picture or some memento of other

days that would give us some clue to his history, but nothing did we see.

The little one-time milk house was lined overhead and on walls with an old wagon sheet. Stovepipes, flattened out, made good baseboard for the bottom. A chuck box hung on the wall, the lid let down for a table, a cot with some suggans for a bed, a little wood stove with tiny oven for a stove. We were surprised that Uncle Billy could write. Uncle Billy made a living by hauling wood and tending to the court yard. When Ole Deck was pulling the plow in the yard, people laughed at the loud voice of the old man telling the lazy old horse to gee or to haw.

The old man finally came to his last illness. "No, there is no one to let know about me, they are all gone," he said to my husband. He left all he had to his old friend, Jeff: the little house, his big gold watch, Ole Deck and the buggy, the cot and the little stove and his well-marked Bible. And so the little house became a milk house on our place. Once more cool water flowed through milk where cream-colored crocks stood. But the cowboys were gone. They and their herd of cattle were no more on the prairies. Farmers drank the cool milk and ate the firm butter. Times changed. Ice-filled boxes cooled the milk and firmed the butter. The old house, where it seemed to me the gentle ghost of Uncle Billy lived, was in the way, not needed. We tried to move it away without tearing it down, but it had stood too long and had to come down, vanished from the prairies like the mirage, the cowboys and the herds. It makes me sad. It is like the passing of an old friend.

June 27, 1940

"Mother died suddenly. I knew you would want to hear," wrote Mrs. Will McLane of Plainview, who once lived near me. Some fifteen years it was my privilege and happiness to live near Grandma, Mrs. Betty Little. She was born August 27, 1851, in Randolph County, Alabama. Grandma had a fine figure, erect even in advanced age. Her skin was smooth and white, her gray hair held neatly in place with a tucking comb. Many times Grandma took me down memory's lane with her, as her gnarled hands pieced tiny hexagons for flower garden quilts or made strong steel knitting needles make delicate white lace. One day she showed me a new dress she had made, "every stitch by her own hand." Tears gathered in my eyes as I looked on the white dress of gleaming satin ribbon and collar of filmy

lace. Grandma smiled and said, "I made my wedding dress, why not my burial robe? I have had my day." Then she told me about her wedding day, as she pushed up her chair to mine and said, "This old chair won't meach," an old-time expression meaning move, with one in it.

"We lived in the settlement near a big road called Jackson's trace. It was on Meetin' Day, and the time of day was early candlelight. There were two young couples to hold candles to read license by. Ma was afraid of lamp oil and bought some sperm candles for the occasion. On the long pine table was the wedding supper. Ma gave a woman fifty cents to make two butter burrs. Never heard of butter burrs?" Grandma's blue eyes twinkled, "They took a mound of butter and with a spoon made it look like pine burrs. They were very pretty and stylish. Cakes and fruit also were on the table." Grandma paused, busy with her thoughts of that happy day so long ago in the past. She remembered that it was the second of November when she, Betty Ingram, put her hand in that of Jim Little and vowed before all the guests standing there from the clearings about in that little home in the settlements that she would be true and a good wife, till death do us part. These vows she kept. Even after Jim Little was in his grave she was loyal and true.

As Grandma talked on, I could see her a little girl, playing under tall trees with dolls made of pine burrs, or going after blackberries in the corners of the stake and rider fence, carrying many, many buckets of water from the spring of cold, clear water on the side of the hill. "Yes, I have spun thread and made cloth as the soldiers passed near on the big road. Never saw a Yankee till I was past grown and a Southern woman married one. During the war the fiddlers was all gone and the young people would play all night. Yes I have spun thread and made cloth. Have filled quills, put them in the sheckle, I have spun twelve cuts a day." Queer terms to use about work, I thought, as Grandma went on.

"My father was buried in a winding sheet. What were they like? You want to know? Well, they were big squares like a sheet. Mother made the material for Pa's. The roll of thread from which it was spun was so fine it would go through a gold ring. The body was laid in the winding sheet. The side folded over the breast, the bottom over the feet, and the top down over the face. Mother made sister Becky promise that not a black thread should be put about me when I die."

But other things we talked of as Grandma meached her chair closer to the light. We laughed about the man that had so much beard he could not kiss his wife. She told about the old dead stump near the spring branch where an old duck sat on her eggs until they hatched. "I watched that old duck bring the little ones, one at a time in her bill and put them on the water." She laughed at the funny memory.

"Once after the young folks had played all night, I was ironing. Yes, we had big ironings of Sunday clothes. Petticoats tucked from top to bottom with fullness gathered at the top. As I was telling, I was ironing and dropped the iron rags. I stooped down for them and went sound to sleep. No, I did not like to wear mother hubbards. I made wroppers with tight lining. A funny thing was a man was hoeing in a field with a bunch of other men and women. A woman took the lead. The man said, 'I am a-goin' to git ahead of that mother hubbard if I have to chop the last stalk of cotton.'"

I did not get to go to Big Spring where Grandma was laid to rest. I like to remember her as I saw her coming down the road for a day's visit, her neat dress held down with a starched apron. Her knitted stockings spotless white. Her face alight with pleasure over the visit. I like to remember her at our club, as she gave us needed advice and words of cheer. She has only gone on to join little Bama, the sweet little girl that she did not raise to be grown. Gone to meet her husband Jim, that she loved so well. We miss her, but as she said, "I have had my time. My life has been full," and we dry our eyes, as we know she would want us to live our lives to the fullest.

Most of the pioneers who moved to West Texas had roots in the Old South. Some Crosby County settlers had been part of the slave-owning cotton culture before the Civil War. Nellie Witt Spikes was too young to remember the Civil War personally, but she knew many people who had lived through the struggle. Her husband and most of her contemporaries in their new home on the high plains were the children or grandchildren of Confederate soldiers. In her columns she relates family stories and personal memories of life in the Old South, of sufferings during the Civil War, and of the migration in its aftermath from an impoverished and defeated home to a new West, a land full of hope and the promise of a better future.

The influence of Southern culture on West Texas is vividly clear. Nellie's husband Jeff was the son of a Confederate soldier, the grandson of an East Texas slaveowner impoverished by the freeing of his slaves after 1865. Pioneers did not come into a new land free of their past. The immigrants from Parker County and elsewhere brought their religion—most were Methodists and Baptists—their attitudes about liquor, agricultural systems, and preferred crops, and even the inflections of language—their Southern drawl—to the Llano Estacado with them. Southern diets are evident in Nellie's frequent references to meals featuring black-eyed peas, butter beans, and cornbread. Many of those cultural traits persist, handed from generation to generation, making this section of West Texas at least part Southern in its ways of life. But there is much of the West in Spikes's stories, too: cowboys, cattle drives, and homesteads under enormous skies. By the early twentieth century, as time and modernity obliterated the past, people celebrated two of their historical myths in combined reunions of cowboys and Confederate soldiers. The people of West Texas represent a merger of American cultures: Southern roots growing in western soil.

August 29, 1940

Mrs. Littlefield told us bits from her very interesting life. She was born in 1853 in Dallas County, Arkansas, and moved to Texas at the age of two years. Her father settled in Falls County. He once lived in Palo Pinto. His wife did not like it there on account of the Indian depredations. They had a mare called Puss, and Mr. Nix promised his wife when the Indians stole old Puss, he would move away. Mrs. Nix said she prayed every day that they would steal the old mare.

Miss Ophelia Nix was married to Casper Littlefield November 15, 1869. They lived in Comanche, Bosque, and Stephens Counties, Texas, and once lived between Little Blue and Big Blue in the Chickasaw Nation. On September 6, 1891, their covered wagons rolled into Crosby County, where they made a permanent home. Uncle Casper died in 1923. Aunt Phelie, as we call her, one of the two living, is a charter member of the First Baptist Church established in Crosby County at Farmer community. She told of living for three weeks during the Civil War on nothing but hominy. They could not get any flour or meal ground. She told that she, at the age of eight years, spun, carded and

wove material for her father, a suit of clothes, and then cut and made the suit by hand. "There was an old man lived near us that was mean," she said. "He would not help anyone, even in time of the hard war. He died and we children ran through the dark and hid in the chimney corner to see the bad man come and carry this bad old man off on his shoulders. Another time we children were picking up wood and run up on a panther that had killed a calf. The panther screamed, and we all ran home as fast as we could. We had an open lean-to on our house. An old wagon bed on which we slept was swung up near the top. We would look out at night and holler at the wolves and bears that came around." No wonder Aunt Ophelia was inured to pioneer life as she found it on the plains.

"Casper dug us a full dugout. Lined the walls with sod ploughed from the prairie, then he took some sand and made plaster which was smooth to your hand as a crock dish. One time the wagon was left on the north side of the dugout and a snow fell in the night drifting around the wagon and filling the sod chimney. We did not know this till Carol got up and tried to make a fire. The wagon had to be moved and the chimney cleaned out. One morning Casper called to me

Mrs. Littlefield, Mrs. Noble, and Mrs. John C. Sanger, ca. 1935.
Photograph courtesy of Crosby County Pioneer Memorial Museum,
Crosbyton, Texas, 2552.

and said he saw an antelope at the back of the field and if he had his gun he would kill it. I laughed when I saw that it was the mirage, brought a house that was about six miles away, and made it look close and shaped like an antelope."

Mrs. Littlefield has led a busy life, a good life, and has filled it with many friends who love to go and kiss her cheek, as smooth as it was when she was Miss Ophelia Nix.

September 11, 1941

Many years ago we saved seed from some Indian cling peaches that Uncle Jim Witt gave us and planted them. For many years they have had peaches on them, but never before until this year did they have the dark red of the parent peaches. As the peel slips off the red meat and the peach drops in the boiling, sour-sweet spiced juice, some beautiful memories seem to rise from the preserving kettle. Again I see Mrs. Poulson bringing Mother some red Indian peaches, hear the tap of her crutches and the sound of her slightly foreign voice as she greets my mother and me.

More than the peaches she brings, there are talks of the old country and of the settling in the new West. Of planting peach seed in the new-turned sod. Of drouths and disappointments, of happy days, too. She brings a wealth of good cheer and friendly laughter. Oh, how her fine character and brave spirit have stayed with me all these years, released from among my troubled thoughts by the smell of boiling sweet pickles. Time passed. I was a young woman, a wife, staying the day with Aunt Net McDermett. How her strong, white arms stirred the big batches of boiling Indian peach preserves! Jars, big ones, white crocks of five gallons, brown crocks of a gallon or more, held the thick, sweet preserves. There were boys and girls to feed. Neighbors like myself staying all day, a night or a week, feasting on the hot buttered biscuits and preserves. Cowboys to get off of tired, sweaty cow ponies, freighters tired from the long trip to the railroad. All were welcome at the McDermett home. Not enough beds? Well, spread down the thick quilts and make some pallets. None must go away. "Uncle Hugh would not let this happen."

How the Texas phlox loved to grow around the doorstep of this pioneer home! The mockingbirds sang from the wild grapevine over the rock milk house where yellow butter cooled by the side of the morning's milk and the thick white buttermilk. I am not putting up peaches, I am traveling the path again from childhood on to now. A path that was made clear and sweet by the friends that reached out kind hands and welcomed me. A path where green trees held out red, red fruit as I passed, and was bordered with homes of fine people of the new West.

October 16, 1941

It pays to advertise. This we all have known since the first newspaper man put out a sheet of printed material. But how well was exemplified by my putting in my column that Mrs. Smith had hats for sale and I wanted one. Well, the other day she and her husband and my mother drove up with a whole box full of hats, summer, winter and Hallowe'en. Now this Mrs. Smith from Odessa is my aunt, beloved of my childhood days as well as now. Never a critical time that Aunt Mirt did not come to our aid. She washed the faces of the brand new babies, tucked the older ones into bed, cooked us meals to

Henry Hugh (Uncle Hugh) McDermett and Nancy Jeanette (Aunt Net)
Snell McDermett, Crosbyton, Texas, ca. 1902, with sons Charles,
John, Troy, Fred, Henry C., and Linnie and daughters Annie, Ethel,
Nora, and Rosa May. Photograph courtesy of Crosby County Pioneer
Memorial Museum, Crosbyton, Texas, 1786.

eat and saw that we had clean clothes to wear. When District Court was in session and Mother was over-run with work at our little hotel, Aunt Mirt was always there, making crusty apple pies and frosted cakes. We children thought she had the prettiest clothes, her waists had the most tiny buttons down the back and her sleeves were the biggest leg o' mutton. Her petticoats had the most tucks and the daintiest laces. How many times we slipped her clothes on and dressed up to play ladies! If she ever knew she did not say a word. No one could tell as good love stories as she, as we lay still by her side on the fat feather bed in the side room, and were warmly covered with painstakingly pieced quilts. Aunt's flowers were the sweetest that grew.

I remember how the old maids left her flower beds and marched down the side of the path to the cow pen. And the time the horses got in the yard and ate all the cosmos off just before they were in bloom. As the nieces and nephews drifted off there were grandchildren to pet, and there never is a child comes her way that she does not love it. She told the other day of a little girl breaking her beautiful prized vase, "But there will be vases after I have no more use for them," she said.

October 30, 1941

The clear, golden jelly on my shelves is not apple. No, nor peach. It is quince. Now quince is rather an old-fashioned fruit belonging to the pear family, not liked by all, but to those who do like its quaint taste it is highly prized. I found them growing on the side of a dirt tank at the home of Mrs. Lynn Tomlinson near Farmer. There are two trees looking as if made of iron instead of wood to hold up the big, heavy fruit as they hang mellowing for the jellies and preserves. Yellow and smooth when fully ripe, smelling better than perfume, once prized to put in the parlor for its delightful fragrance. Wonder why quince trees have not found a place on many a farm in the West? But I must take you back to the farm home where I found them.

The lovely stucco home of Mrs. Tomlinson sits in a lawn of native mesquite grass. The walk to the door is bordered with roses, spice pinks and dahlias. Tall trees make a park at the back and at one side where chicken barbecues are held. The

largest apple tree that I have seen in this or any other country, for that matter, mirrors its red apples in the tank of clear water. Pecans ripen and fall from the spreading pecan tree. Peach and plum trees have already given their fruit. Pokeberries hang purple black along the walk to the windmill. But the nicest thing I found at this home is the hospitality and friendly manner in which one is met and welcomed by the mistress of the lovely country home, her charming daughter, Gladys, and kindly brother, Elbert. We came away with more than a bushel of quince. Good measures of a happy morning to put away with other sweet memories.

January 8, 1942

It is strange how one will go along for years not knowing much about your fellow man until sickness or trouble brings you closer together. I have in mind Bruce Spencer. For many years we have passed or gone in his drugstore and enjoyed his pleasant greeting. But the other day we stopped long enough to talk about the war and were surprised to find out he saw service in France. Somehow the ones who went over there did not come home to brag about what they did. They did their duty and that was that. Mr. Spencer, like all the rest of the boys who came back, did not remind the ones who stayed at home of what they thought the people owed them for leaving their homes for the hard discomforts of war. Thus, unless they left from our own home town, we scarcely ever found it out, and we are seeing some of our fellow citizens with new eyes and deeper appreciation.

August 13, 1942

Beneath the hot sun of an August day a small group of mourners stood by an open grave in the new cemetery of Emma. Albert Witt, struck down in the beginning of his manhood, lay in the black plush coffin. Why was he there? Why were his old father and mother weeping from eyes that had hardly ceased their tears from the burying of fair Mattie, who was so recently left behind in the post oak–shaded grave near Weatherford. Too, the last, so manly and so lovely.

"Let's go by the mill in the H pasture, I would like to see how it is running." This Frank Jones said to his father-in-law, Silas Witt, as they slowly rode the open range that bleak day in late winter [of 1896]. "I don't see any reason to go by. You can tell it is running from here," Silas answered. But Frank was urged to go, by something he did not then

understand, and hitting their horses with their quirts, they galloped to the mill, almost falling from their horses at the sight that met their eyes. Albert lay helpless and almost frozen not far from the mill, still conscious.

"I was to meet Mr. Detwiler at the mill in the H pasture to work for him," he said as they covered him with their coats, "and he did not come. I climbed the ladder to the platform to look for him. The wheel suddenly turned, knocking me to the ground. I was paralyzed in my legs instantly. All afternoon I lay and suffered. Night came on, dark and cold, water blew from the lead pipe, freezing on me. I tried to crawl to a hole near, caught with my chin and hands. My chin is raw and my hands torn and bleeding. All night I lay. I struck matches thinking the mill might get afire and someone see it or that I might burn to death and cease my suffering." What a pitiful tale. Never again would Albert charm with gay, sweet tunes on his French harp. Never again would his light feet tap to his own music. For he lay on his bed wasting away till the hot day in [July] when his suffering was over.

Tragedy of an early day in the West. Of a lonely mill in a big pasture. Of a young man who did not know the West and of an older man who told him to be at another mill. Going there and not finding his help, he went on his way, not thinking of anything amiss. Heartbreaks of long ago, rising now and then to make one's heart beat with pity, as one stands before a white stone and reads of one so young passing away, before he had given his best to the land he had learned to love.

February 12, 1943

The J. M. Witt family had a reunion yesterday, February 7th, Mother's birthday. All eight of the children were at her home in Lubbock. Two of her sisters were there, Mrs. J. C. Witt of Lubbock and Mrs. R. W. Smith of Odessa: a sister-in-law, Mrs. Ella Jones of Seymour; a niece and two sons; Mrs. Mary Lee Waddell of Odessa; and two granddaughters. All the in-laws did not get to come for various reasons; nowadays someone has to stay at home to keep the fires of defense burning, it seems. We had a grand time, and if dictators could have looked in on the scene they would have better realized that here was a bit of America, one of many reasons why we are fighting to win the American way of life, for families to meet without fear of secret police or that one of the family was a spy to tell on the rest.

Being human, I must brag a little in this column about my family. I am the oldest, but this would not have been true if little Emma Francis had not been laid to rest in the post oak–shaded cemetery in old Parker County, where the lilies still blossom blue as the sky in the spring and the acorns still fall with the red leaves over the small mound in the fall. None of us ever laid eyes on this sister, but we fondle with sweet affection the tiny pink dress and golden lock of soft curl that has rested in the old tin trunk these fifty-six years. Lowell, the next to me, my playmate of happy childhood days, Edna, the last to be born in Parker county—we then rode west in an ox wagon. Then Lois, who opened her brown eyes on a wintry West Texas day. Joe and Guy made their appearance in the Witt Hotel at Emma, and rode proudly in high-wheeled baby buggies in parade, with me pushing the handle before all the district court grandees and the city drummers. Jim broke the smallpox quarantine and got in the family, as Father was quarantined with smallpox at that time. Josephine, the last, cooed and laughed inside a little home on a quarter-section claim in New Mexico after I was proudly holding my little six-month-old son.

The one who takes the pictures of the family group always has my sympathy. They go around looking as distracted as an old hen trying to gather a flock of chickens. All get together, wipe the pie and cake crumbs off of faces, no not all, Guy has gone—the group scatters while waiting; at last all are together, some making faces, others striking all kinds of ludicrous poses, well, you have all been there at some time and know as well as I do how a family of grownups can act at a time like this. We can all work better now that we have been reunited for a short time, as with tears we speak of our father, who is not with us anymore, and say goodbye as each goes to his or her duty—Lowell to defense work at Amarillo, Jim to the same at Houston, Guy to his job of secretary of Plainview Chamber of Commerce, Joe to his place as court reporter at Amarillo, Josephine his secretary, Edna and her husband to a store, a farm and elevator at Bushland, west of Amarillo, and Lois and Mother to their respective homes in Lubbock, myself to the farm.

March 25, 1943

My son writes such an interesting letter from "somewhere" in England. He tells of a business trip he made on which he saw Stratford-on-Avon and the Shake-speare memorial and theatre. "I saw a very picturesque region," he continues, "with low hills, farms, woods, stone houses with thatched roofs. Also visited the ruins of Kenilworth Castle." Thrill of thrills, my son has a rock from that historic castle to one day take its place on my fence. "I am going to make a little garden and plant a few flowers where I am billeted and will mow the lawn this evening. What people these English Allies of ours are, going about the business of living as closely as possible to that of many centuries, even as bombs fall on their land." How life changes. My son making a garden in England; I can remember when he was a boy at home, reading the beloved books about England, always liking the ways of other lands to read about. Now he is at home there, in the land where his great-grandfather, Dr. Fox, lived as a boy, calmly doing his work and at leisure moments planting a small plot where flowers make gay the greens of the vegetables.

July 15, 1943

It is with sadness we read of young Claude Russell Ramseur, formerly of Ralls but now buried on foreign soil as he gave his all to his country. Looking back I see a covered wagon stopping at the white schoolhouse in Emma. My brother and I were riding around and rode up to see the newcomers, to see if they were only passing through, stopping to camp for a night, or aiming to make their home with us. We found a young couple unloading bedding and cooking supplies for an outdoor supper. We saw a boy of our age, Charlie, he told us. He said their name was Ramseur and that they intended making their home in Emma, which they did, adding a vital part to the little community. Mr. Ramseur's hat was always white with the meal he ground on the days the wind turned the gristmill. Mrs. Ramseur brought pleasure and happiness to the women and girls as she sewed gay flowers on summer hats and pinned bright feathers and ribbons on felt hats with sparkling rhinestone pins for the winter's fashionable hats. It was a treat to sit by her as she worked, she was so sweet and made one feel at their best. The children were sent to school, and I remember well just where Charlie and Dodd sat, Charlie working on his lessons while Dodd often found more interesting things to do. Mary and her sister were in the other room, dainty, shy little girls, looking after their brothers, Will and Dave. An honest, happy family, living at peace

with the world, helping establish a land of justice and righteousness. Now a grandson has died to help keep for all the world the things his family had helped establish, given his life that you and I might have the liberty of a free people.

September 16, 1943

In the passing of Dr. Andrews, we of the Old West are made to feel that the early days will soon be only a memory to the youngest and will take their place in the history of the settling of the West. Without doctors even the hardiest pioneer would not have stayed. Although a doctor was only called in the utmost need, Dr. Andrews was one that was called in need, and how well he filled that need. Women in dugout homes held hope when they saw him coming down the steps, a-bringing his satchel and healing drugs. How much his presence and kind words meant to the sick will not be known till the Great Book is opened on Judgment Day. His ears heard the first wails of many a new baby, and his firm hand felt the last beating pulse of the ones on their last call to new horizons. As he measured out so very cheerfully the healing powders on the point of his knife, he measured out hope to the ones whose loved one was sick. Doctor Andrews had chosen a time and place to serve humanity. I doubt if he could have made a better choice than the plains of West Texas in the early days of her settling.

November 5, 1943

As I write I hear the happy laughter of Anne and Carey, my son's children, as they go about the place to see what changes have been made since they were here last year. Tar Baby is not with them to bark and run the chickens, for Tar Baby was killed on last Christmas Eve as he ran after a car, turning the festive day into a child's mourning for a lost pet. Many a mile of salt water flows between these children and their father, and soon a year can be counted since he left, but we carry on, looking forward to the time when a mighty ship will be loaded with returning sons and fathers, to listen to the happy laughter and measure and marvel how much the children have grown in their absence. Carey's maternal grandmother is with them, and many little funny and dear things she tells me about the children. Carey was naughty, very. He needed spanking, badly. So grandmother threatened, he ran shrieking from the room, grandmother fol-

lowed, and slowly he turned back to her. "I will be good," he said, "if you will not spank me this time." "How long will you be good, Carey, if I let you go this time?" "Well, anyway," he suddenly smiled and said, "Till the end of the war."

December 7, 1944

I met Mrs. Collins of Floydada last week and she told me her only son, Pat, was in the conflict zone. We also visited awhile with Mrs. Jenkins, whose only son is a prisoner of war in Germany. I got inspiration from both these mothers as I watched Mrs. Collins figuring up purchases and calmly waiting on customers. Mrs. Jensen was quilting, and I knew as each pound of groceries was weighed and each diamond was neatly stitched on the silk cover, I knew these two mothers were softly saying a prayer to God, and I realized where the two boys got their strength and patience and courage, one to fight and one to remain a prisoner till our country is free from wars and at peace again.

June 15, 1945

Full to overflowing was the cup of pleasure handed out to us last week when Floyd County and Crosby both held pioneer roundup days. Mr. Spikes and I found the fence down, or a little slack, and we crawled through and sat at the dinner for the Floyd County homesteaders. . . . We found Horace Owens, who once drove the mail hack from here to Floydada. Horace's eyes sparkled as he remembered how quickly the harness was peeled off the backs of the tough little mules and a harnessed pair of mules pushed into place. And does he remember that bad tooth. His jaw all swelled up like a cow that had been bitten by a rattlesnake, he made the mules fairly fly. The lady dentist, Mrs. Woods, pried at the old bad tooth and had to call in her husband, who it seemed was never there to help, but out he came. Horace now hears the steam of the cars and sees the steel monsters roll out with loads of freight, but the old white hack and the tough little Spanish mules live on in his memory.

September 21, 1945

We are hearing a lot of laughs these days as men come in to see Mr. Spikes and tell of hurts and wrecks and accidents they have had. After a while even the worst hurt feels all right and is worth telling about. Mr. George Ragle of Ralls told about moving from Alabama to Missouri. He saw a mudhole ahead and tried to make one of his mules go in it, but the mule jumped and missed the mud, a wheel took up a tree, and Mr. Ragle and a child overturned and the child had to be pulled out of the mudhole. Broyles Terrell of Lorenzo said that Uncle Em English once told him that he had another fellow started down the caprock between Ralls and Floydada when the road was pretty steep. They did not have any brake on the wagon and depended on holding the little mules back. All went well for a little while, but the wagon rolled fast and Uncle Em held them back tighter till the collars slipped over the long ears and shoved off the bridles, as there were not any throat latches, and away went the mules and faster and faster Uncle Em and the other fellow went.

July 25, 1947

Seems to me that Grandmother Jones always had the best garden in the world. It was in the sand. Somehow the bugs never bothered her large cabbage heads, and the pepper, hot as a firecracker! Little round beads of pepper that we liked to eat with the cabbage. Long, red hot pods that Grandpa removed the veins from so the children could eat it. And never were tomatoes so big and red. A handful of salt and soon tomato juice was dripping on small hands. We had the run of Grandma's garden, but we never imposed on her; she never scolded. And after dinner there was no time to turn the peaches drying under the fierce sun. So good they smelled, and we looked forward to winter when they would be on the table with sugar and cream to make them unforgettable in our memory. Corn was also drying for the cold months ahead, and usually Grandpa had some strips of beef drying on a stretched wire. He had so much patience with children. He would trim the hard, dry outside of the jerky and give each child a piece to chew. For us he peeled the sweet sorghum stalk and showed us his toes that he cut almost off with an axe when he was a boy in Tennessee. His parents bound them back on, and they were always crooked. He told us about sliding down a tree only to land in a pot of hot water, and he always said, "My skin came off with my clothes." Better than being born with a silver spoon in our mouths was having both grandparents on both sides, and it is a pleasure that my own children got to see all four of them.

April 23, 1948

On many an old photograph of pioneers of early Crosby County days we read the name of the photographer, "Photo by Duncan." I answered an advertisement of Frank Duncan, Terlingua, Texas, which I saw in the *Mineral News Magazine.* I wrote for a price list of rocks, as he makes a specialty of rocks from that part of the state. He answered, saying he once lived north of Old Emma and in Floydada for a time. I sent an order for rocks and asked him if he was a brother to the "camera man." He answered yes. Said he folded up broke in Emma. "Just couldn't take the hard dry years," he wrote.

But I wonder if Mr. Duncan knows about the wealth he left with us, gold that we would not willingly part with. Pictures of Mother and Father as young folks, pictures of brothers and sisters as babies, scenes of the Emma courthouse, with its white walls and shuttered windows, locust trees growing around it and cowboys sitting lazily on cow ponies. We have the Witt and Spikes store, our surrey with its swinging fringe around the sides of the top, Mother and the smallest children inside, Father standing near me with my flowered hat in a cane-bottom chair. Even the bird dog slipped in the picture.

Witt and Spikes General Merchandise, Emma, Texas, ca. 1900. Nellie is seated with the guitar, about age twelve. Her mother, Margaret Jones Witt, and younger siblings are in the surrey and on the bicycle. Her father, John Witt is in the black coat and hat. Standing to Nellie's left, with hand in pocket, is Jeff Spikes, John Witt's business partner and Nellie's future husband. Photograph courtesy of Southwest Collection, Texas Tech University, Lubbock, SWCPC 291 E1 #9.

He took pictures of the school and the teachers and pupils, young ladies with high ribbon collars and pompadour hair, grandmothers and grandfathers. . . . It was not often the pioneers had the privilege of having their pictures "taken." He made beautiful scenes of Blanco Canyon. He did good, honest work as these pictures of some forty years ago will bear testimony. No, Mr. Duncan, we are now pretty late in telling you, but even if you did not make money, you left a lot of what money could not buy to the descen-dants of the early-days settlers. We are proud of these old pictures and we hope someday you can come back and see the country as it is now.

October 1, 1948

Most old-timers will tell you that they either helped dig Blanco Canyon, cooked for the outfit or carried water to the workers. Some even claim to have helped the oxen pull the plow, but Frank Duncan of Terlingua, Texas, is more modest. He waited till it was all finished

then took pictures of the canyon
in all its wild beauty. Mr. Duncan
recently visited in our home, and we
had a fine time remembering this
and that which happened when this
country was new to white settlers.
There are not many families that he
did not photograph one or more of
its members. Some of his pictures
of ranches and cowboys and cattle
are in an old school geography of
Texas. Mr. Duncan has traveled all
over these United States, and he has
been a close observer and tells many
interesting stories of his adventures.
For some years he has lived in the
Big Bend country and has gathered
many fine rocks from the hills and
caverns and from along the Rio
Grande River. He found beautiful
specimens of jade crystals, cinnabar
and agate. Agates with red and black
plumes which polishing brings out
clear. He has many that he polished
by hand. "On long winter nights,"
he says, "I sit by the radio and polish the stones." He brought along
fluorescent rocks and by the light
of his mineral-light lamp they were
exceedingly beautiful. I am more of a
rock hound, as I find they are called
who love rocks, and hope to add
more from time to time to my growing collection.

April 29, 1949

Uncle Jim Witt never passed a pin
on the ground or floor but that he
picked it up and stuck it tidily with
other pins in the seam of the lapel
of his coat when he had one on. I
remember the row of pins, some
shiny, others as rusty as could be.
Uncle had moved near Lubbock.
When anyone told of anything new
or growing or being built at Lubbock, he always pointed out that
Ralls had something just as good and
fine, if not a little better. Uncle Jim
loved beautiful things. I knew, for
one Christmas he surprised me with
a lovely pair of vases shaped like
Easter lilies.

June 10, 1949

The Floyd County settlers gathered
for one short day. . . . Joe Ellis
went with Mr. Spikes and me, and
he enjoyed hearing the older ones
tell of their "days." Mr. Nelson gave
a fine talk on early days in Floyd
County. One thing he said should be
remembered especially. "I think the
schools should have lectures given
about the history of their counties.
Children learn the history of the
world, the nation, the state and it is
only fitting they know that of their
own county." And I agree with Mr.

Nelson. . . . "I brought back some of the broken dishes used by folks who once lived on my place, a long time before me," said Roy Green as he showed me some Indian pottery. Wonder who will show the pieces of the dishes we now break in days to come? . . . The fiddle tunes, beloved music of the pioneers, set everyone's heart to dancing. The horseback riders made all long to get in the saddle again. And didn't you think Mrs. Dan Shipley and Mrs. Miller looked sweet in their old-time dresses? Oh, memories! . . . Pioneer Day at Floydada. Long may it be kept up.

September 23, 1949

Margaret Nell is in school, and she is delighted with everything. Her first school, getting up early and running out to the road to climb the big orange school bus, her new dresses, book satchel, piece of candy or an apple for recess, playing with children, a pretty teacher reading stories—everything is new and fresh and lovely to her six-year-old eyes. . . .

At the old Spikes place on Spikes Prairie we found an oil well going down and two pumping wells just over the fence. In 1890 the Spikes family sold out, left the beautiful trees, green prairies and small cotton patches to come west and ranch. Now the ranches out west are fruitful fields of cotton and grain; the old cotton patches in Kaufman are now a ranch and will be an oil field, or so it looks to the ones down there. Ed and Alma Fox are still lively and full of fun as ever. Festus Priddy and his wife made us so welcome. Marion Fox knows all the family history about the year 1851 when John Spikes brought his family and his well-treated slaves to Spikes Prairie. He tells of Grandfather Fox, riding a yellow horse and carrying his pill bag up and down Williams Creek and Legges Prairie. Once he was gone three weeks, off in another county, being called from home to home as people learned a doctor was in their vicinity. Marion has an old document written on sheepskin. Now the graves of the slaves are tramped by cattle as they switch flies under cedar trees. Grandfather Spikes and Dr. Fox, born in 1800 and both leaving this world in the same year, are sleeping side by side in the Fox Cemetery. An oil well brings up black gold. Cars roar by where ox teams slowly pulled the big blocks of rock for the stately courthouse, which still stands as a monument to the planning of big-thinking pioneers.

November 4, 1949

L'etoile Murphy came to the plains with her family in the eighties when as far as she could see the green native grasses waved in the wind, grazed by cattle from here to Amarillo. She enjoyed the cloud images on the blue lakes, the call of the killdees and the whirring of the prairie chickens. How she loved the picnics and the unpacking of her big loaded basket on the long, spread cloth under the whispering cottonwood trees. She gave her time to church work, was always a leader in the Literary Society, saw that Christmas and Thanksgiving times had a prominent place in the town's yearly calendar. Beautiful material was always on her bed, as she made dress-up clothes for the women and girls. She always had time for the company that loved to go there. I liked to see her walk in the old schoolhouse at Emma, flushed from her long walk but lovely as a queen. L'etoile, a lovely name of French origin, but a name she did not like. L was what her husband called her, and at last it was Aunt Ella to the ones who loved her gracious and beautiful life.

April 20, 1951

You will have to move a bunch of old, old newspapers, books and letters and maybe you can find a place to sit down at our house, for Mrs. Temple Ellis and myself have started in earnest to work on our long-contemplated task of writing the history of Crosby County. Our noses are buried in old tax books of Emma and Estacado town lots. We find queer given names of the Quakers: Cyrus, Pedlina, Uriah, Arwilda, Joshua, Lydia, Sarina, Melesia. We see the gray bonnets and somber gray dresses and suits of the men and women in the bright sunshine of a West Texas day; soft thees and thous mingling with the rustling of a cottonwood tree. We are present at that first wedding when the Quaker minister, Anson Cox, performed the ceremony that made Oliver G. Cox and Cynthia Arwilda Janeway man and wife. We find that the Indians believed there was an immense cave all under these plains where buffalo lived and at times came out upon the prairies for their food, clothing, and shelter. This work is so fascinating I do not want to quit for daily duties. From week to week I may give you something of interest I find. Perhaps it will fascinate you, too; the old, early days when this country was as new as a bolt of blue calico just placed on a merchant's new pine shelf.

What brought you to this country from Fayette, Indiana, back in 1913? I asked Mr. R. E. Heath of Ralls as he lay recuperating at our son's hospital in Ralls while his sister from Indiana, who is visiting him, smiled and listened. "Wife and I came as tourists," he recalled. "She liked this land, and so did I, and when this plains Water Bug bites you, it is fatal and all you want to do is stay and drink of its water all your days. I was a machine tool and die worker. Had charge of machine parts on the CINL Railway at nights. Got tired, and after our trip we moved here. Could not stand to have our cows and horses stand in cold lots, protected only by a three-strand barbed wire fence from blizzards and snows. Wife and I had our headquarters in the front room of our two-room house and made the other room into stalls for our stock. Twice we sold out our stock and left, but each time we came back and tried again and made it. Maybe this will not look so good about this country."

But I think it does. A country that draws the best from a man and keeps him building on and on, regardless of the drouths and depressions, must have something finer than California's famous gold mines to offer. "I did not know I had

so many friends," Mr. Heath's face glowed with happiness, "But since I have been here it has been a revelation to me the goodness and kindness and thoughtfulness of scores of friends."

May 4, 1951

Way back in the year of 1740 two Irish boys landed on the coast of America without funds and without friends. They handed down to generations that have come and gone the name of Spikes. Into new parts of the United States families by this name helped conquer the unknown and untried land. Jack Spikes brought his family to Kaufman and settled on a prairie in that county that was named for him and became known, and is to this day, as Spikes Prairie. His cattle went to the struggling Confederate Army, and he had only a dishpan of paper money, worthless, to show for them. His slaves were free. His sons, Israel, John Wesley, George and Jeff, came home from the war with the stepson, Henry Carter, three son-in-laws, Henry Erwin, Bill Tubbs and Joe Fox. The task before them was to help build a new South over the ashes of the one they had known. Israel rode a horse from Kaufman to Austin and was one of the delegates to write the constitution of Texas. The Spikes

boys married and settled down.
But John Wesley and Sam Spikes,
Henry Carter and the Tubbs brothers still had the pioneer spirit. Wes
put a belt with money on his son,
Jeff, named for the older Jeff, and
started him to East Texas for a small
bunch of cattle. Then the family
moved in covered wagons to Crosby
County, where Wesley soon died.
Jeff, John and Fred Wheeler worked
on ranches.

As I looked in the still face of Fred
Spikes the other day, I thought of
this bit of family history. No, Fred
could not possibly be dead. Just
only away, and memories crowded
in. Fred was young, his face alight
with pleasure, for he was going to
a dance, and he loved to dance. He
was on a bucking horse and it took
a good one to throw him off. He was
driving to Mount Blanco with a mail
bag for a passenger, the little tough
Spanish mule going at a pretty good
clip, for there was seventy miles
to be made that day with the mail,
but more Spanish mules would be
rung in. He was at a reunion of old
settlers, his hearty laugh and firm
handshake making him a center of
friends. . . . He was stopping to see
old friends who were sick and shut-
in. . . . No, he could never die.

July 6, 1951

Well, we hit the trail again this year
that had its ending at the H-V Ranch
in New Mexico and found our host
and hostess, Mr. and Mrs. Harve
Harris, on the welcoming commit-
tee, and was it a welcome! Backed by
all the family of Harrises. Now my
cousin, Cleta Jones, married Henry
Harris, nephew of Harve Harris,
but that was not the only thing that
made Mr. Spikes and me welcome
as guests on this fine ranch with the
white house shaded by tall, tall trees.
But I went to school with Harve at
Old Emma, and Jeff and I knew the
older members of the family. Mrs.
Temple Ellis was Harve's teacher in
Crosby County; Lena Martin Bonine
and Emma Luce Davies, old school-
mates; and Dessie Dennison, friend
and one-time neighbor of the Harris
family near Bronco. So we all six
went together and had a wonderful
time.

As we stopped a few minutes at
Plains, Jeff was wanting to hurry on,
for as he said it was fifteen minutes
after eleven, and we would have to
hurry for dinner. When we arrived
to the tantalizing scent of barbecue
cooking slowly, as it should, on
mesquite grub coals, we felt a pang
of hunger, and the watch said almost
twelve. But nothing happened; cars
kept rolling up and people getting

out. Then all of a sudden I remembered, we were across the state line and it was an hour until twelve. Oh, mercy, our stomachs, used to Texas clocks, had a sinking sensation. But we were repaid a hundredfold as we got our plates and marched by the long tables where barbecue, son-of-a-gun stew, red beans, pickles, salad, cake, pies and cookies soon had our plates piled high. And what barbecue and what stew and red beans! Only the ones who really know how can even begin to cook these old ranch favorites. Prentice Harris was the barbecue cook and we put him in our estimation with our beloved uncle Tom Franklin of Emma picnic days as a meat cook.

We tried to persuade the young lawyer son of the family, who is assistant to the state attorney of New Mexico, to come to Texas and get him a wife, as the girls of California and New Mexico had failed. Major Dalton Harris and wife were there. He is also a nephew of Harve. He did some jumping out over Africa and Italy in a parachute from a plane during World War II. George Fawver and his boys and daughter were there. The Ray Reeds and daughters' families, and Annie Assiter and Teddy Assiter were going down that barbecue line with their plates and tin cans for coffee. Surprising isn't it, how many people claimed a

reason for going to the H-V barbecue? And that coffee must be just right, for I heard a man, Mr. Bailey, that claimed a century of living and coffee drinking, say that whoever made this coffee was sparing on the water. And it was good and hot. Instead of sitting under the tall, tall trees, we took our filled plates to a place sheltered from the cold wind. I had saved a new thin dress for the occasion, and as I got ready at my mother's in Lubbock that morning it seemed about right for another day as hot as Friday had been. But the day grew colder and some of us wished we had been as smart as Lizzie Ellis and Jeff and had taken along a coat, just in case.

The road Harve and wife have traveled in eastern New Mexico has not been too smooth all the way. There have been stops and detours as well as easy going on the H-V Ranch. There was the time 150 H-V cattle died along with cattle all over the country. The loss of that many cattle daunt a Harris? Harve sharpened up his skinning knife and started out getting the stiff hides off the cattle. He skinned his cattle and he got four dollars a day, for he was a good skinner and did not care how hard he worked. He bought and sold hides. He could get as many hides as twenty-five a day. At the end the Harris family had the loss replaced, a new shiny buggy to ride in and a new house to live in. Harve decided he could skin cattle faster than he could raise them. No, the Harris family never sat down and cried over a loss. They turned it somehow to gain, and Saturday friends and neighbors sat with them at the ranch house and enjoyed the fine, old-time brand of hospitality.

July 13, 1956

When the gin whistles blow this fall we will remember John Gray. When he and Mamie lived at McCoy we saw them often. The big gray gin lay to the north of us. As I washed my dishes I could see the gin, and it always looked like a gray battleship, the smoke pouring from the funnels. The shimmering mirage was the ocean, the windmills 'round about were masts of other ships. John was always so nice to Mr. Spikes and me. Once I took a bale of cotton to the gin in a wagon and faced a cold, stiff norther. John helped me get out of the wagon and took me to a warm place in the gin office. This courtesy he always did for Mr. Spikes, having someone to take out the horses and hook them up again while Mr. Spikes rested.

Crosby County Gin, Crosbyton, Texas, October 1911. Farmers used
the high-sided wagon in the foreground to collect loose cotton in the
field. The gin mechanically removed seeds from the loose lint and
bundled the cotton into bales, like those on the loading dock and the
second wagon in this picture. Photograph courtesy of Crosby County
Pioneer Memorial Museum, Crosbyton, Texas, 0051.

Natural History of the Llano Estacado

Nellie Witt Spikes was devoted to the region's people and history, but she loved the land, too. She wrote about the weather, the canyons and plains, the wildflowers and plants. Blanco Canyon, in particular, appears repeatedly in her columns, often in tones of reverence. From her first arrival at the White River at age four, through yearly summer plum-picking excursions, to weekly car trips across the gorge after retirement, Blanco Canyon was at the core of Spikes's universe.

Surrounding that core were the high plains of the Llano Estacado, the flattest part of the Great Plains. There, wide-open shortgrass prairie and brimming blue playa lakes succumbed to Euro-American agriculture during Spikes's adulthood. She was proud of that progress, created by the sweat and hard work of her own people. But she also remembered fondly the natural environment that preceded the plow. Spikes encountered the region before much of it was plowed, she took part in its transformation, and she described the rapidly changing natural environment outside her window. Spikes wrote about her memories of a natural history now receded to the margins of the Llano Estacado. She loved her country, as it was, as it was becoming, and as it would be. The selections below capture pieces of the "first nature" settlers entered in the late nineteenth century as well as aspects of the "second nature" they created in the first half of the twentieth century.

In particular, these pieces describe the efforts of plains people to create a more comfortable plant environment. Spikes describes people planting flowers, ornamentals, garden vegetables, and shade and fruit trees. They brought plants with them from home, transplanted cuttings from one house to another, even, inadvertently, spread weeds back and forth across the landscape. The extent to which settlers remade the floral environment of the southern plains becomes clear in the following selections. The vegetation of today's Llano Estacado is a mixed bag of persistent native species and a multitude of introduced plants and is considerably more biologically diverse than it was in 1850.

August 5, 1937

A turtle dove is calling outside. It makes me think of a day long ago. It was hot. We had been gathering plums in a little sandy draw. The children were under the wagon in the shade. Mother was cooking dinner; biscuits were molded out and put in the dutch oven. Bacon was sliced and put in the skillet. Father opened corn and peeled the onions that would be sliced and put in the pot of potatoes boiling on the fire. A syrup bucket held the fragrant coffee. (The little children were allowed to drink coffee when we were camped out). The hot sun was making sun grins on Mother's face. Turtle doves were calling near. A stillness was over the canyon. Heat waves danced on the hills that were so cool and pleasant when the sun rose over the canyon hills. Tubs and sacks of ripe red plums were in the wagon. Soon Mother would lift the lid of the oven and we would begin a feast. These scenes and days never left the hearts and minds of children that lived in the West in early days.

September 16, 1937

Old Mother Earth is in a gay mood and is flaunting a costume of rich green. Only on country roads is her brown body exposed. Her beautiful gown is woven of luxurious grasses, the shining leaves of cotton and sorghums. Even the weeds are woven in the exquisite cloth and add to the richness of the color. Her dress is encrusted with tiny white pearls of the kaffir. Broad bands made of gold beads of the maize trim the garment. The good earth's bosom is adorned with sapphires—the lakes. She holds gay flowers in her hand, and a wreath of them in her hair; dark green cotton bolls hold her dress together. Around the hem of her garment tiny yellow flowers of the broomweed and the purple Kansas stars make a pleasing pattern. We thank thee, good earth, for your beauty and your rich harvest. Many times this year you have changed your gown. We like the one of white trimmed in glittering icicles you wore last January. The rich dress of gold you wore during wheat harvest gladdened our soul. We look forward to your dress of autumn, the many rich shades of brown, trimmed with beautiful autumn leaves and bands of white cotton. We country people

live so close to you, Mother Earth, our very existence depends on your generosity. May we teach our children to care for you, to love your beauty and to be glad their lives are to be spent in the country.

October 21, 1937

Yes, we must protect the ducks! Must sit by and watch them gobble and scoop up our golden grain, made with hard labor and sacrifice. Sacrifice of good clothing and new cars so that hungry horses and tractors could plow the land. Sacrifice of vacations and rest so the weeds might not grow. I love the beautiful wild ducks, but I do not think it fair the farmer has thousands of them to feed only so that the sportsman may kill them. "Put out flares in your fields at night." Yes, starve the ducks. Why would it not be as well for the farmer to kill them with a gun as to see that they died from slow starvation? But I know the answer. Go ahead and feed the ducks. Ducks are smart. Flares or no flares they will outwit the farmer anyway, as long as there is feed in the fields.

May 26, 1938

My flower garden is becoming a memory book. A honeysuckle from my son's yard in Tennessee flings tiny green arms in the prairie wind as it tries to catch hold of the rock fence. A white iris and a dark red damask rose from the cemetery where Spikes and Fox families have been laid to rest. Blue spiderwort and wine cups from the canyon where I roamed when a child. A mullen stalk from Van Zandt. Our lives and our homes become a part of so many people and so many gardens. . . .

Thursday my husband and I went down in Robertson community in the south part of Crosby County. When he was a bachelor, he had a home down there and lived in a dugout. My good father lived just north of the drift fence that crossed the county down there and reached into New Mexico. At that time the shinnery covered the country to the Yellow House. Today a little shrub oak along the road or a patch in the field is all of the shinnery that is left. How I loved the shinnery when I was a child. The acorns, the plumy sage grass, the flowers dainty and tender as hot house plants, growing in the shade of the bushes. We went there hunting prairie chickens, fat plover and blue quail. Antelope looked at us from a distance, and sometimes we found a tiny baby one. I can remember the smell of the plover frying in the skillet, see my mother lift the lid off an oven filled with tender golden brown sourdough bread, hear the warm summer wind blowing through the bushes. Feel the hot sand on my bare feet. See my father hobble out the horses. Hear my brothers and sisters playing under the covered wagon. Oh, the sandy land looks good now with rows of tiny green things pushing their way to the sun, but I was homesick for days long gone and for the shinnery land.

D espite its classification as a grassland, West Texas is home to the largest stand of oaks in the United States, covering between five million and seven million acres. What's more, these are old-growth oaks, most of them hundreds or thousands of years old. The catch? They grow only waist high and are often hidden by the grasses growing among them. The sand shinnery ecosystem is dominated by shin oak (*Quercus havardii*), a persistent, brushy relative of the better-known species of oak trees. They grow only on sandy soils—the sandier the better—and support a highly diverse assemblage of grasses, forbs, and wildflowers and an abundance of wildlife and birds. The shinnery extends from western Oklahoma through the Texas Panhandle and into southeastern New Mexico.

Shin oak shrubs grow from ancient underground stem systems, a single one of which can spread under two acres of land and last for centuries. The sprouts that emerge above ground rarely live longer then ten years, but the stem puts up new sprouts all the time. The shinnery has existed in this region for at least the last three thousand years, and probably longer. But it has been affected by human activities for a very long time. When Native Americans controlled the Great Plains, they regularly set grass fires that could sweep over thousands of acres at a time. Most of the grassland burned every three to five years. Historical observers in the first half of the nineteenth century described shin oak stands that rarely exceeded eighteen inches high. Regular burning meant that the above-ground shrubs seldom lived more than a few years and did not reach their full height. But the protected underground stems were well adapted to fire and simply put up new sprouts the following year. Today, the shrubs typically grow to thirty-six inches. Since the 1870s Native Americans have not set fires, and Euro-American settlers have suppressed them. The shin oak responded to this change in fire regime by growing taller.

After 1900 the advent of agriculture had a second impact on the shinnery. Farmers plowed large expanses of shinnery for cropland, as Spikes observed in her column. In Texas there were about three and one-half million acres of shinnery before settlement. Approximately one million acres have been plowed out. Most of the rest is on grazing land. Shin oak is worthless for livestock forage and is actually poisonous to cattle for about six weeks every year. It competes with more palatable grasses for water, sunlight, and soil nutrients. Ranchers have tried many ways to reduce shin oak stands, from shredding the plants to burning to herbicides, but none have been very effective. Burning increases shrub growth the following year. Shredding eliminates the shin oak briefly, allowing grasses to increase, but within three years the oaks grow back. Herbicides kill the above-ground portions of shin oak but cannot kill the underground stems, which simply sprout again. Thus, the shinnery that Spikes remembered fondly and that represents some of the most ecologically diverse land in the southern plains persists.

January 12, 1939

New seed catalogs delight us with their beauty of summer flowers and vegetables. We forget the cold. We know this year our gardens will look like the pictures. We pick out things on every page that we must have. If we added it all up, the amount would astonish us. But it costs nothing to choose what we would like to have. I lay down the catalog with its wealth of modern achievements in the vegetable kingdom, my mind goes back to my childhood days, and I remember: a little girl pinching a leaf of rose geranium; the smell of sweet basil in my grandmother's window; a vase of heavenly blue spiderwort, fresh from its home in the lacy mesquite bush; the starry blue flowers of the tame china tree in the courtyard at Emma; acres of sunflowers, their yellow petals turned to the bright sun; a barefooted, freckle-faced boy giving a little timid girl a bouquet of blue flags and sweet peach blossoms; the scent of blue sage flowers and yellow roses a kind old man is giving me. I hear a sweet voice of Mrs. Martin as she gathers gay zinnias and feathery asparagus. I hear the mockingbird singing in the flat lake near Grandmother's home. The yellow and white daisies nod in the mesquite grass to the bluebells and the red wine cups. I see again the cabbage and the Tom Thumb pepper that we loved with its hot flavor, the yellow pear tomatoes. Man has made many improvements over the things of that day, I know, but in memory they were better then than now.

February 22, 1940

I am going to write down about the storm, not that you plains people do not know all about it, but there are readers in other parts of the world that might like to get a shiver or two out of it. What do you think the weather will be? I asked Coleman, the colored man, as he turned the separator handle Thursday night. Now I had missed on recent prophesying, and Coleman had won, so he came out strong that we would have a snow. I laughed to myself Friday morning when it began to drizzle, but the water soon turned to snow that melted as it fell, nice soft flakes filling the air with fleecy whiteness. The wind became higher, tore the nice fluffy flakes into "snow flour," and the ground was soon too cold to melt the snow. The wind picked it up, as a child picks up his toys, and hurled it further on. The dry fields tried to stop it, for they needed the moisture, but it only lay where the cotton stalks were left. The wind shrieked and moaned, bringing to the house the bleating of sheep, the squealing of hogs, cold and crowded in icy pens. The earth was filled with swirling snow that began to find lodgment around the houses, the trees and the barns. Hour after hour the wind filled it higher, packed it more closely, made huge loaves of snow in our yard.

We sat by the fire and wondered about the travelers on the slippery roads, about our stock. The mail came, a blur of moving dark in all that white, a low purr of an engine in all that howling of the wind. Mr. Spikes and Coleman tended to the stock. Long before the night, the pelting snow clung to their jackets and whipped them in their faces with cold, wet whips. The white, shivering cows were milked, helpless chickens carried into shelter. Night came on, the storm increased. We seemed shut out from all the world, but the oil lamp light from the little shack near shone like a yellow blossom in the storm. All night long and all day Saturday the elements raged like wild demons blowing cold and snow from gigantic mouths. No snow fell from the hurrying clouds, but the world was full of whirling snow. With a giant broom the wind swept the fields and the prairies, cleaning them as

a good housewife cleans her floors. The snow was piled higher and higher; four feet, six feet, on to eight feet high the mounds grew around the place. Around and around the windmill went, the wheel a solid disc of ice. No longer the sound of squealing hogs came on the wind; they were buried in deep drifts.

Sunday morning we awoke to a new world, a strange world, a beautiful world. The huge mounds of snow were smooth and white as the icing on Mother's best Christmas cakes; the fields and prairies looked as if the icing had run off the mounds and left a thin layer of white on them. On the north of the house were caves, moulded into beautiful shapes by the cunning hand of the wind. The snow-covered houses around the horizon looked like glittering scenes on tinsel Christmas cards. Long diamond jewels hung from eaves, leafless trees looked like pencil marks on the blue sky. The world was all blue and white, covered with the pale gold sunshine of the rising sun. We heard the chirping of a few birds, the Persian cats came in from the barn, where they had been unwilling prisoners. No longer the wind whined and whistled in our ears—the storm was over.

March 21, 1940

Idly I sat in the car and looked around the horizon while my husband was making a trade. An unexpected vision caught my eyes. I rubbed them to be sure I was not dreaming. To the northwest was an ocean, blue waves rippling in the yellow sunshine, and out in the ocean was an inhabited island. I saw the house, the trees, the point of land that ran sloping down to the deep water. Here and there over the waves were tall, stately ships, sailing along with masts pointing to the blue sky above, smaller boats rocking on the waves. In the west there was another island rising out of the shimmering sea; tall trees shaded white houses. This was not a dream, I was looking at the ocean of the plains, called mirage, distant windmills made stately ships and small boats. . . .

Signs of spring on the plains. A woman takes off the blankets one day, suns them and puts them away. The next night she gets them out again.

June 27, 1940

My husband had to make a hurried trip to town this morning, but to show you how good he is, he let me out in the canyon to gather wildflowers and never even honked the horn for me to quit and come on. Wild sweet sultans, I call the fluffy orchid blossoms. The buds and seed pods are even more attractive than the blooms. Along with the bouquet, I brought home a colony of ants, small black, that were on the flower. They crawled all over me running here and there in the car as if to try to find out what was all about. They seemed so lost on the kitchen table.

July 11, 1940

Saturday we went plum hunting. . . . We put in a loaf of bread, some bologna and cheese, a gallon jug of water, left the baby with Grandmother, rolled our hair in little flat curls and were off in a fast car to be gone some four or five hours. We had changed but the canyon had not. The plum bushes flaunted their red fruit as of long ago. The thorns were still as sharp, the white sand in the draws still as hot. The mockingbird still sang in the old cottonwood tree that had sheltered Indians from the hot sun. Quails slipped, blue shadows, through the bushes. The mourning dove called as mournfully as of old. The hills looked down, not changed through all the years. Crickets droned, flies buzzed and an eagle sailed the blue overhead. Plums gathered, we were soon home. In no time jelly was simmering and boiling on the stove. Butter was being packed into jars. Oh, a glass of plum jelly is better to me than a crystal ball of the fortune teller. I can look in its clear, red depths and see the West when it was new and fresh. I can see pictures of men and women now no longer with us. Pictures of little boys and small girls happy with father and mother in the canyon to get plums for the winter fruit supply.

September 5, 1940

It is strange to me that chiggers (or red bugs, according to where you were reared) can be content to live on vegetation till human beings come along and they then become bloodthirsty and colonize their helpless victims. Some settle in close to one another, many get around the equator, others seek the lonelier spots. Nothing seems to totally discourage them. Night is their best time to torment, and the scratching they demand is never enough.

January 23, 1941

As I write, my thoughts go back many years to a little frame school-house known as LaBarque, which was near where the Robertson school now is. When I go down to that community I cannot place where the little schoolhouse once stood, as the waving prairie grass has been plowed up and even the little lake that once held water for the patient school horses is now planted in cotton or maize. I looked in vain for the shinnery that came close to the south of the school and where the teacher, with the aid of pupils, picked up kindling, loaded it on the rickety topless buggies and carried it in triumph near the house. The wild range cattle that turned and ran as the school hours came are gone, and soft-eyed Jerseys do not look up as the bus passes. The prairie dogs no longer bark defiance as they stand ready for quick entrance into their holes deep in the ground; no longer is the whirr of the prairie hen heard as the hunters shot at them or the buggies scared them up.

April 3, 1941

When I was a child we had a plant called the resurrection plant which was brown and curled up till put in water; then we saw it slowly uncurl and turn green before our staring eyes. In front of our house is a little pasture, once called a "starveout" in

Aerial photograph of Crosby County, Texas, July 23, 1937, shows full and plowed-over playa lakes dotting an agricultural landscape. Photograph courtesy of Southwest Collection, Texas Tech University, Lubbock, SWCPC Aerial photograph no. 3672K 30N 13W.

early days. Yesterday it was brown, slightly tinged with brownish green. Today it is green and seems a miracle brought by the rain. The winter weeds were only waiting, like the resurrection plant, for water to make them unfold and make a green pasture.

August 21, 1941

Someone told me the other day they were told when they came to the plains that there were no mosquitoes in early days. To my certain knowledge they were here, and many a night a cowchip smudge was kept up in the unscreened houses so folks could get some sleep. But the only chiggers I knew anything about were in Plainview. If there were any in the plum patches and grapevines or along the creeks in the canyon I never knew about them.

September 11, 1941

The clouds drizzled around for a while last Friday, slapped the world soundly with torrents of water, then rolled up in long streamers and sailed away to the east, leaving the roads like rivers, the fields, lakes. Some will not admit they are tired of rain; others frankly say they think it has become a detriment. Turnips and mustard greens are liking the frequent showers. Soon the welcome smell of cooking greens will float to the farmer's nose, making him long for the noon hour.

On the Texas high plains there is no natural drainage except around the edges of the tableland. The surface is so flat that water from infrequent rainstorms puddles up in low areas until it evaporates. Intermittent lakes that form in depressions are known as playa lakes. It was these "sky-blue" lakes that early settlers found beautiful and often remembered years later. Playa lakes still dot the Llano Estacado; estimates of their numbers range from nineteen thousand to thirty-seven thousand. Lake beds are greener than the surrounding countryside, usually, as a multitude of grasses, sedges, and forbs take advantage of the extra moisture. Sometimes they are marshy, supporting waterfowl and other aquatic life. Playas average about five hundred acres each, although standing water after a rain usually covers only about thirty acres in the center. Playa lakes are rarely deeper than ten feet. They host standing water for a few weeks after sudden summer thunderstorms and year-round in wet years. In the heat of the summer they are often completely dry.

The depression ponds are a frustration to farmers. Water deposited in playa lakes is hard to transport to thirsty crops nearby and usually evaporates into the air. And the ponds take up acreage in the middle of farms that might be put to profitable use. Many farmers plow and plant their playa lakes, gambling that rains will not flood their growing crops. By the 1950s, with the expansion of irrigation technology, farmers began to drain playa lakes to make more land available for crops. The drainage and plowing of playa lakes to expand crop acreage removed multiple islands of plant and animal diversity from the midst of high plains farms.

October 9, 1941

When will it frost? Will it stop raining? Questions asked not only by
the farmer, but by the merchant, the
baker and the automobile seller. On
these two weather questions hinges
the money crop of most of the plains
country. If frost will only stay off
'til November. If it only will quit so
the feed can be saved and cotton
open. If, if, if. Well, time goes on so
swiftly. These questions will be answered one way or the other. Lewis
T. Nordyke of the *Amarillo Globe* is
putting on an interesting program at
8:45 Sunday morning from KGNC.
He calls it the Exchange, and it is a
friendly review of the newspapers of
the plains. He is collecting reasons
by which the first frost questions
are based. My husband goes by the
white flower in bloom everywhere
at this time. It is a kind of an aster,
I believe. It is snow white with
small starry blossoms. Jeff says he
has noticed it always matures seed
before frost. That will give us several
weeks, yet, if true this year. One
thing I have observed is spiders spin
webs all over every bush, the grass
and anything they can reach a couple
of weeks before the first frost. I have
not noticed any webs this fall. They
are so aggravating, wrapping across
your face, webbing all over your
clean wash on the line.

December 25, 1941

From the pioneers of the Plains who
bore so many hardships together
I feel such a warm welcome from
your hearts as I slip in your door
this Christmas. You have given
me so much—lessons I shall never
forget—and if I, in a small measure,
can tell what you mean to me, I shall
be content. . . . You taught me the
love of the beautiful, for you planted
long, slender-limbed willows and
cottonwoods to fan your homes
with their green tiny fans; you set
out roses that make yellow pools of
gold by your door, planted stately
hollyhocks to march to the gate;
made Christmas a delight with red-
berried cedar, fresh and fragrant
from the hazy blue canyon hills, and
trimmed it with strings of popcorn
linking like strands of tiny white
roses. You taught me faith in the
resurrection as I saw you leave your
loved ones, after they were let down
in the cool mother earth by the stout
ropes from a cowboy's horse, and go
to your homes, knowing the warm
summer winds would sweep over
the grass-covered plot and scatter
the scent of flowering mesquite and
red wine cups. You knew the blizzard
of winter would cover the rounded
mounds with a soft, white blanket
knit in the gray clouds above. And I
knew when you sang the "Unclouded

Day" as all stood at an open grave that you knew God would not forget where your loved one was when the Resurrection Morn dawns.

April 16, 1942

Gardeners new to the making of a garden are peering at tiny plants pushing up under small clods to the sun, wondering what each new one might be. I remember my first garden, especially a tomato bed planted in one corner for plants. How long the fuzzy flat seed had to stay in the ground. And how much like the long, slender leaves of the tomato is the buffalo burr's first ones. Inexperienced eyes could tell no difference till the burr's sticky leaves appeared. There was a careless weed come up; yes, believe it or not, there was a time on our place when we had no careless weeds. I just knew it was some kind of a flower even if my more experienced neighbor laughed at my ignorance. The time came for blooming, then I resignedly pulled it out. Then one spring I visited my people in New Mexico. The Russian thistle was just getting a good hold on that country. I brought two plants home, wrapped in wet rags to show my husband. Now do not be too hasty and blame me for the thistle getting here. As soon as my husband looked at those innocent looking plants, he ordered them burned.

The Russian thistle (*Salsola kali*) that Spikes refers to from time to time also goes by the name "tumbleweed." Russian thistles are not native to North America. They arrived from the Eurasian steppes in the nineteenth century and quickly established themselves as an iconic if despised weed in the American West. Russian thistles grow in spindly globes, sometimes only knee-high, sometimes as tall as a grown man. They are covered with mild thorns. When their seeds ripen, the single stem breaks off, and the lightweight plants roll across the land, pushed by prairie winds. They drop seeds as they travel, ensuring new crops of tumbleweeds next year. Typically, Russian thistles lodge against barbed wire fence lines, where their seeds take root in long rows. Tumbleweeds are a curse to farmers, a menace to drivers, and an enduring symbol of the wide-open spaces of the arid American West.

July 16, 1942

Like the magic everlasting plant of the desert, mesquite grass has the power to grow green overnight after a good rain. This is one of the many delights of the prairie, quick changes that make a brown world green and growing.

September 2, 1943

Around the place: The mimosa tree is very lovely this summer with its long, fernlike fronds waving in light breeze. Well I remember the late afternoon when Anne and I walked up the tree-lined railroad track to the home of Della, the colored maid, to get seed of this tree. Dark was coming on with deep, dark shadows as we came home, and we were glad when we got in the deep pools of golden light at the hospital. I find the mimosa tree grows as well and feels just as much at home here as its parent tree did in the Missis-sippi Valley at Memphis, Tennessee. Last fall the box elder tree was only as high as my head; now I cannot tiptoe and reach the top limbs. This tree has an interesting history, as it came from seed of the trees that the Quakers planted near their treeless homes in historic old Estacado. The pecans are not so handsome this year, as the freeze broke out many big limbs, but the side next to the house is full and green, and there are young pecans. The Chinese elm looks all right; they make such quick growth that a thing like being broken up does not hurt them long. The old peach trees are done for; the young ones with good luck may bear next year. A few grapes hung, purple and black, from the vines, a dozen or so peaches may be gathered soon.

October 22, 1943

Without much warning the first frost of the fall slipped up the morning of the sixteenth, blackening the tops of the tomato vines, and green leaves of fodder now hang brown and stiff. As it has been so dry there was not too much green stuff to be killed and to be grieved over. Cotton farmers will find it a relief to get cotton leaves out of the way. Feed had either made or burned up. As the new maize does not fall after frost very much, no particular harm has been done by an early frost.

When cotton bolls full of white lint burst open in the fall, they are ready for harvest. Through the nineteenth and the first half of the twentieth century field laborers—including slaves, free Southern blacks, and Mexican immigrants at various times in Texas history—harvested cotton one handful at a time, walking through fields and pulling lint from each boll, putting it into sacks they dragged behind them. It was slow, back-breaking work, and in West Texas the cotton harvest extended from October through December. A hard frost would drop leaves from the plants, making cotton picking easier. Cotton plants were tall in the early twentieth century, sometimes growing shoulder high to an adult. With those sizes harvesters didn't have to stoop so low to collect lint. When farmers finally mechanized the cotton harvest—decades later than other crops such as wheat and corn—they needed shorter plants to accommodate the machines. Researchers developed new, shorter cotton varieties, and today most cotton fields grow no more than knee high. When plants are ready for harvest, farmers no longer wait for a hard freeze to drop the leaves; instead, they spray a chemical defoliant on the plants to remove leaves and ready fields for their machines.

April 7, 1944

The taste of home-grown fruits from our own trees has been changed to one of bitterness by the loss of the fruit in the last bitter cold spell. There may be grapes, but they have not bloomed, nor have the canyon plums. We always have had winter sometime in the year on the plains, and this year is no exception. The young willow leaves still sway and wave, but now they are brown and rattle in an early death. The tender new leaves everywhere are frostbitten. There is a sadness about the young green things of spring being killed, although we know more will come later.

May 26, 1944

Not many of the seed did the settlers have to buy, for they had seeds of red beans, and seed corn for roastin' ears, and seed of the little white soup beans we all called the Detwiler's in honor of Mrs. Detwiler first planting them. Also there was never a scarcity of black-eyed peas and kashaw punkins.

In the next column reprinted here, Spikes uses deeply offensive language to describe a common plains wildflower, the coneflower. Elsewhere, she does likewise with a slang term for a slingshot (see p. 223). To modern ears, this casually racist language appears out of place coming from a woman who otherwise seems gracious, kind, and respectful. Why would Spikes consider it acceptable to use such language in her common conversation, let alone to publish it in a newspaper? So deeply embedded were racial prejudices in Southern culture in the early twentieth century that people used such terms routinely and with little thought. The Civil Rights Movement of the 1950s and 1960s changed that, as blacks and whites challenged the discriminatory policies of Jim Crow America and the racist attitudes and language that supported them. Racism did not disappear in the nation, and the use of offensive language continues. But no longer would respectable people publicly employ offensive terms thoughtlessly, unconscious of the hurt and anger such words would provoke.

The late twentieth century was a time of transformation in American attitudes toward race, and since language reflects culture, terms of racial reference underwent rapid change. When Spikes wrote about particular African Americans in her columns she called them "colored" (see pp. 77, 162, 163, 195, and 203) or "Negro" (see pp. 31, 71 and 76), terms considered polite at the time—think of the titles of Civil Rights organizations created during this era, such as the National Association for the Advancement of Colored People or the United Negro College Fund. By the 1960s some activists argued that the term "Negro" had come to imply passivity and acquiescence to oppression, preferring "black" as a more powerful signifier. In the 1980s "African American" emerged as a preferred polite term. Racial language continues to be controversial. When the 2010 U.S. Census forms asked participants about their race, one of the options was "Black, African American, or Negro." Protestors complained that "Negro" is a derogatory term, and the director of the Census Bureau publicly apologized.

Wagon team and horses coming up the Caprock Escarpment, Crosby County, ca. 1890. Photograph courtesy of Crosby County Pioneer Memorial Museum, Crosbyton, Texas, 0605.

June 30, 1944

When a child I always liked to walk up and down the long, rocky caprock road. The driver would stop the team on the top and call out, "All who want to walk, get out," and mother-hubbard women, gingham girls and blue denim boys would crawl out from under the tied-up wagon sheet and the team would get the get-up signal. Mother was afraid, "your papa" would let the team run too fast down the hill or the children would need to be seen after, but the children knew no fears, only deep joy to run after the long ride in the jolting wagon. Flowers were what I loved and drew my almost undivided attention. The stiff "nigger-head" [coneflower], the fuzzy pink flower on the thorny bush, the yellow daisies; soon my hands were full, and with a tired, happy feeling I crawled back in the wagon at the foot of the hill to admire my bouquet. Coming back home again there was the climb up the hill, more flowers to gather and wilt on the long ride home. How cool the breeze felt at the top of the long hill! And how restful was the bed in the back of the wagon!

November 3, 1944

Nothing gives me more strength and peace than a visit to the canyon. I feel the presence of God, the eternity of time in the hills. The beauty of nature in the trees, always changing but never ugly. Gray as an old person's hair in the winter snows, pink and green and soft yellow in the spring, fanning with grown green leaves all summer long and glorious with color in the fall.

November 9, 1945

Wilma met a coyote in the road the other day as she had to walk back from her car that had run out of gasoline. It is not so far from the canyon over where they live. Mr. Spikes told us that when they moved west, one night when camp had been made, he hung his bridle on a fence post, and the next morning it was cut to pieces and looked as if it had been done by a knife. He said it took him a long time to figure out how it had been done, and he decided it was cut by a coyote.

November 16, 1945

One of the nicest "shock absorbers" I have had in quite a while was the visit I made with the women of the Home Demonstration Club of the McAdoo neighborhood on the East Plains. I did not see how I could leave Mr. Spikes and go, but Wilda and his sister, Mrs. Ellis, said they would look after him. I always get a thrill when I catch a glimpse of the canyon and every bit of the crossing was delightful. Indeed, "My strength cometh from the hills." Smoothly down the winding paved road rolled the car, and I remembered the jolting of a wagon down a rough road. Swift as the flight of a bird I seemed to go across to the hilltop on the east side; again the memory of a long drive behind lagging horses. I had on my new black dress; other days, I felt the roughness of a checked gingham apron. Then my eyes had the clear gaze of a child; now, rimmed glasses helped me to see. But the years between the new black dress and the checked gingham apron seemed nearer as well-remembered scenes unrolled. The roaring of the falls, the shadow of an eagle across the car, the old Rock House, the unchanging hills with the gray rocks and the faint green of the dying grass. I checked them on my fingers—the hazy blue of the hills, the color I loved so well, the cedar shrubs with recollections of Christmas greens, the days of picnics under the cool shade of the trees and the feel of running water on hot bare feet.

August 13, 1948

There are some beautiful birds down at our lake which has some water in it. Margaret Nell and I call them the geek birds, as this is the call they seem to make. They look like a large snipe, white bodies, black wings and soft deep rose necks and heads. They run along in the water and scoop up bugs with long, slender bills. When we go down to the lake they fly swiftly towards us, make a swoop as if going to hit us but get scared and fly away, angry and calling, geek, geek.

April 28, 1950

The weather is jumping from hot to cold these April days. Seeds planted are having a hard time coming up. The ground is being covered with long, green hairs of the hated Russian thistle, and goatheads are showing up in spots. The well maker's fence is being hung with green lace of the grapevines. Blue lilies are making one "consider the lilies of the field, how they grow; they toil not, neither do they spin." Farmers are busy watering fields, plans are being made for old settlers reunions, and mothers are busy getting ready pretty dresses for the end of the school year. Warm days call for picnics; summer is at hand, even though the news is for colder weather the next several days.

June 16, 1950

And speaking of honey, did you know that Matt Kirkey near Lorenzo has hives of bees which make fine honey of Crosby County flowers? He gave us a pound, and how good it is. I can taste the wildflowers I loved so well. The white daisy, the red winecup, the mesquite yellow curls—and some honey from the fragrant, waxy white locust blossoms. And I think I know just the reason why Matt likes to have honey on his table. Bertha is a good biscuit maker, and my, how honey goes with hot buttered biscuits.

Silver Falls on the White River in Blanco Canyon near Crosbyton,
Texas, October, 1911. Photograph courtesy of Crosby County Pioneer
Memorial Museum, Crosbyton, Texas, 0021.

The Modernization of Farm Life

The day-to-day lives of farmers changed considerably between 1890 and 1960. These changes included at least two separate processes. First there was the conversion from frontier to settled farm country, a process that took citizens of the southern plains from tents and sod huts to frame houses and even brick construction. Second, there was a general modernization that happened throughout the United States during the twentieth century. Both series of changes happened with lightning speed, in this case over the course of a single lifetime. Nellie Witt Spikes experienced, participated in, and wrote about both of these processes.

In particular, she wrote about changes within the household. Since women were typically responsible for the home and for subsistence production, modernization affected them considerably. Spikes wrote about these transformations as they occurred around her. She described the installation of plumbing in the house. She compared the challenges of rendering lard at home to the ease of purchasing it from the grocer. She wrote about the impact of automobiles, remarking on how many trips to town she took each week in her middle age compared to the rare trips of her youth. Perhaps nothing was more dramatic than the arrival of electricity in farm homes in the late 1930s and early 1940s. These changes had an enormous impact on how people experienced their everyday lives, the scope of their activities, even the standards of cleanliness expected by society. Spikes described all of these transitions and others as they appeared to common people over the course of one lifetime.

August 5, 1937

We have sold the old car. A new shiny one is in the garage. I miss the old car as I miss a friend that has been near and dear to me. The car took me to church, to town picnics, to the club and to my neighbors' homes. I knew its faults and its good points. The new car is a stranger to me. When I look at it I think, "You are not going to be any better than I am. You can take me to places and help me do things that will make the world better or that will make for more misery. You can be an instrument of life as well as a bringer of swift death. You can carry me to the lands of beauty. Swifter than the winged horses of old you can go." In time this new car will be like a friend to me.

November 25, 1937

My husband has his first zipper coat and wonders what makes it zip and unzip. Sometimes he cannot get his coat off and has to call for help. At a friend's home near are three old people. One of the men bought a zipper coat. The clerk zipped it up and the man wore it home. That night, none of the three could solve the mystery, so my friend slept in his coat. Could someone perfect a patent to put zippers down the sides of cotton sacks? This is an idea I am passing on; I am not an inventor.

February 3, 1938

Whether to, or whether to not, is the question that is with many. Of course, I mean about the oil propostation as you all know. Shall we lease or would it be better to wait?

Would an oil field in the good farm-ing country be better for us than things are now? Would our lives be enriched by the oil as our pocket-books would likely be? Would we gain the whole world and lose our souls? Oh, let us pray for wells of happiness and peace that will gush out of our hearts and lives and bring the riches to the world that are so badly needed.

May 26, 1938

We were in a broom factory recently and were told brooms were not used today as much as in the past. I remembered pine floors being scrubbed with a broom, hot water and lye. Now we use a mop on the pine floors covered with linoleum. There is not so much hard work for a broom to do and they last longer.

July 28, 1938

We drove from the little city of the Croton breaks. If you have not driven that way, you have missed something; "rough" is how it is called. But that does not begin to tell it: deep gorges that cowboys long ago could not get cattle from, hills covered with huge rocks, red rocks, white gyp rocks, rocks that are flat and almost black. We watched with fascination as the road crew built in the new highway; two huge cranes scooped up rocks from the hills, swung out their long arms of steel and dumped the load into waiting trucks. Men fed the rocks into a mighty crusher whose iron jaws tore each mouthful into gravel. All this that we might glide over a smooth highway.

One red hill that had half of it cut away wore an intricate design on its red side, a design picked out in minute detail with white rock. We wished for a Kodak, but what would one tiny bit of this majestic spread on each side of the highway mean on a small picture shown to the ones at home?

Why do we long for the sights of the world when beautiful scenes are in sight of us? As I looked, I could envision scenes of the past, see the giant mastodon as he fed on the green hillside. Giant wolves and a species of camel, now extinct, roamed these brakes. Dainty three-toed horses and the giant lizard. And Indians dressed in war paint and plumed bonnets shot their arrows at the herd of grazing buffalo.

August 4, 1938

The new house is started but is now just at the tearing down stage. It is not very interesting. Piles of lumber, of dirt and rock. Ladders and nails strew the lawn. We have moved the kitchen and most of the things to the shack. But when I get over there I find I have left most of the things I needed at the house and the other way around. So I traipse back and forth. I feel lost and confused. And a while ago the cellar got lost. It has always been north of the two rooms at the back. I had forgotten the rooms had been moved to the west and went behind there to hunt the cellar.

August 11, 1938

The sound of the saw and hammer are heard; clouds of dust stream away in the wind as old shingles are pulled off. The two back rooms are moved to the west of the two front ones and the new rooms are taking shape. For the first time the old house sits on a solid foundation. Meals are prepared and eaten at the shack. I like to cook for working men. They enjoy eating so much. There is a great deal of friendly banter at the table. Something of the old house-raising spirit still lingers.

August 18, 1938

The pile of lumber and bundles of shingles are disappearing from the lawn. Walls of new rooms are rising, new pine floors are being laid. Perhaps I shall never see the spicy-smelling red cedars of Washington, but red shingles, cut from their stout hearts, will shelter me from the heat and the cold. I may not hear the wind sighing in the tall pine trees, but yellow planks made from them will make my house tight and warm. I did not intend to get into any of the work of building, but my husband suggested that I help him pull out nails. Then there were the old shingles to pick up that had fallen in the house. Then he needed someone to pull the flooring up close to nail. I have an easier time when he goes to the field to plow.

September 1, 1938

It is not easy to sit down and write this column this week. Hurried trips to town for more paint, sheet rock and groceries. Everything in disorder. My pencil at the shack, paper out of its usual place and "Where do you want this door?" and "Is this the way you want this closet?" I go from the two old south rooms out of familiar doors only to be hemmed up by the new rooms, or I go into the pantry. I must feel somewhat like the British must have felt when the American army caused them to play the music "The World Turned Upside Down." How long will it take me to feel that I am not a stranger in my own home?

September 8, 1938

The house is nearing completion. Lumber and nails, paint, paper, kalsomine screws and glass knobs are at last getting in their places. The lawn is clean, the rock fence going back in place. We will soon be gone from the little shack where we had happy dinner hours together. I have been in a quandary about what color to paint the screens to go with the white house. I bought a can of vermillion paint but was still doubtful. "Paint the screens white," advised Mrs. Maud Hollums, "and put the red on your lips." Thank you Mrs. Hollums, I will take your advice, but I'm afraid it will take a long time to use up that quart of red paint on my lips. . . . Sam Jones, the carpenter at work here, was deploring the fact that he was not educated, had never had the opportunity to go to school. But to my way of thinking Mr. Jones is an educated man. His hand has the cunning to make wood into

beautiful things, can build a house that will stand staunch and true, make furniture and fine cabinets. His heart is educated to serve and love his fellow man. He reads and remembers many interesting things of the world, and of the Bible. He writes letters to his mother, who is old and lonesome for her family of children she has raised. We are glad to have known Mr. Jones.

September 29, 1938

For the last thirty or forty minutes my daughter has been reminding me about writing this column in time for the mail. But I was busy washing windows, a task which I dislike very much and wanted to finish before I quit. Paint had to be scraped off, and the screeching sound makes one's flesh crawl. The finishing up in the house takes much time and patience. I will be glad when all the things are in their place and I learn all the new ways of keeping my things. The new house, a house the friends can come and feel at home in, is not fine, just comfortable. Doors are not alike, only that they have a coat of white paint. Old-fashioned doorknobs keep company with new-fashioned ones. My kitchen has sheet rock walls enameled white. The carpenter made a large, convenient cabinet. I put things in one compartment and then change to another, childish ways denoting age. Kitchen and dining room are in one. And in a corner I have a writing desk. Red trimmed curtains and gay pictures brighten the room. From my work at the sink I look through a window north and remember.

December 8, 1938

Do you remember how we had to dress when we first got cars? Dresses of khaki trimmed with brass buttons made an ideal costume, a cap with large bill over which we tied a long chiffon veil that floated back in the wind, a pair of long gloves to the elbow of soft leather. We got the first car in the neighborhood, a Buick. A. W. White bought a Ford, the McDermetts a Glide, and the Hamiltons another make which I have forgotten. Not for the world would we have had cars alike, and the farther we had to go to get repairs, the better we thought them. We made a cover of muslin to cover our car with when it was in the shed. (We thought it affected to say garage.) Our horses ran and snorted every time we drove the new car out. The children always wanted to drive with the muffler wide open, because they liked the noise it made.

(Wonder why they were made to open and close the muffler?) The curtains flapped in the cold air and flapped out the warm, the tires held seventy-five pounds of air and it was not so free then—not free of work, at any rate. We had to own a tire tester, catch rainwater in crock jars to fill the batteries. We gave away twenty-five dollars to get a battery remade, and tires cost twenty dollars. Gasoline was twenty-five cents a gallon. We pulled her wide open and made forty. When the wind blew we let back the top and took it, but we felt grand. They were indeed magic carpets to take farm people to see the world.

February 16, 1939

Everything on the place is being upset again to put water in the house. It is a trying time but I look forward to the enjoyment of not having to carry water in and carry water out. In the book *My Country and My People*, Lin Yutang says, "In contrasting the happiness of the Chinese with the American people . . . the modern world, with its over-development of machinery, has not taken time to insure that man enjoys what he makes. The glorification of the plumber in America has made man forget that one can live a very happy life without

hot and cold running water, and
that in Germany and France many
men have lived to comfortable old
age and made important discoveries
and written masterpieces with their
water jug and old fashioned basin."
And I could add to what he said. The
farmers of America have added so
much to their country and have had
as much lack of hot and cold running
water as France and Germany.

March 9, 1939

We got the water pipes all in and
connected up. Put the water tub
on the tower, put new leathers on
the mill and turned it loose. All
the afternoon the mill turned,
but no water—the sucker rods and
pipes had to be drawn, the bottom
cylinder replaced. There was a nail
too that had fallen inside. Windmill
trouble does not come often, but
when it does the farmer has real
worry and hard work. Perhaps soon
when we turn the faucets we will
have water.

March 23, 1939

In the northwest corner of Stone-
wall County were the salt flats, from
which many early-day settlers got
their supplies of stock salt. A branch
of the Croton was strong with salt,

and when the summer sun dried up
the water, there lay a lake of white
salt, shining like snow. Can you see
the pioneer man with his wagon and
team all ready for a trip? All bolts
and taps were made tight, for salt
would rust them. A flour sack of
biscuit, salt pork, canned corn and
tomatoes, and coffee in the chuck
box. A two-days trip before him,
across the grass-covered prairie,
down the rock canyon hill, across
mesquite-covered flats. When the
salt flats were reached, a hard day's
work was before him, shoveling up
the thin layer of salt into tubs and
emptying them into the bed of the
wagon. His eyes would smart and
burn, his feet would feel like they
were on hot glass. Then there would
be the hard pull on his team to get
the load out of the flats. A three- or
four-day journey home. Now when
we want salt for our stock, we drive
up to a grocery store, and while we
sit in comfortable cars our salt is
loaded in the back for us.

Charles Hart and Charles Parr built the first tractor in 1902. Unlike the situation in most of the United States, tractors were present on the southern plains from the very beginning of sod-breaking for crop agriculture. The C. B. Livestock Company used large steam engines to plow new land for small farms. These early tractors required several men to operate them: a driver, a steam engineer, and one or more men to feed coal, wood, or even straw into the voracious engine. They were large, unwieldy, difficult to turn around, and expensive. Only farmers with many acres of land and a lot of capital could afford them. One of the reasons steam tractors found more use in the Great Plains than elsewhere in the country was the long, straight, flat stretches of farmland with few hills and infrequent turns.

Small farmers, including most of the settlers in Crosby County, did not seriously consider adopting tractors until the 1920s, when innovators created gasoline-powered engines that were small enough to cultivate row crops, easier to maneuver for light farm work, and inexpensive. Even then, many were hesitant. The Texas high plains made the transition from horses and mules to tractors during the 1930s, five to ten years later than the rest of the nation. Ed Holmes, farming in Floyd County, for example, resisted buying a tractor because he believed they put people out of work. He finally gave in and bought a used tractor in 1942.

Probably more important was the cost. Few farmers could afford to pay for a tractor all at once, and while most carried debts routinely, they knew borrowing was risky. Farm incomes were notoriously unstable. Any given year could see a bumper crop and high prices for cotton, or a drought, crop failure, or low commodity prices. It was impossible to predict the next year's income, and that made many people hesitant to commit to loan payments years into the future. Those concerns decreased in 1933 when Franklin Roosevelt's New Deal government introduced federal farm subsidies for the first time. Those farm programs have brought a large amount of money into the county every year since. They guaranteed farmers a basic income each year, regardless of rainfall or crop prices. Farmers had more money in their pockets and a reasonable expectation that they would have money to pay debts in the future. The number of tractors in Crosby County nearly quadrupled during the decade, from 273 in 1930 to over 1,000 in 1940. At the same time, the county's horse population plummeted from a peak in 1930 of over 8,500 horses on farms to fewer than 2,000 in 1940. What had been an essential element of every farm became little more than an expensive hobby in only a couple of decades. For the rest of the twentieth century horse numbers in the county hovered at 350 as tractor numbers drifted upward.

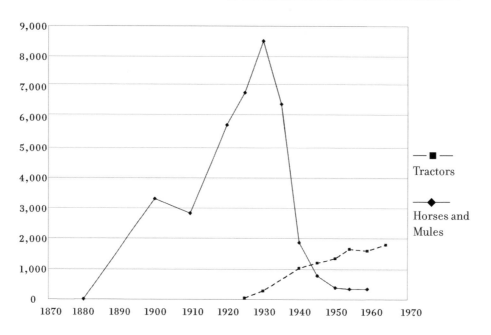

Number of horses and mules compared to tractors, Crosby County, Texas, 1880–1964. The rising number of horses and mules matched increasing human population through the 1920s before plummeting with the advent of tractors. Source: Myron P. Gutmann, "Great Plains Population and Environment Data," On-Line Extraction System, Ann Arbor: University of Michigan, 2005. Drawn by Geoff Cunfer.

Large, eighty-horsepower steam-driven Case tractors, pulling eight-gang, fourteen-inch plows, breaking sod near Crosbyton, Texas, for the C. B. Livestock Company, February 2, 1912. Compare to the mule-drawn breaking plows on C. B. land shown on page 51. Photograph courtesy of Crosby County Pioneer Memorial Museum, Crosbyton, Texas, 0058.

"Tractor on large farm near Ralls, Texas," May 1939. Photograph by Russell Lee. Library of Congress, Prints and Photographs Division, FSA-OWI Collection, LC-USF34-033334-D.

February 29, 1940

Grown people were so particular about what kind of chips we children had to gather up. As a boy once said in telling of his load of fuel he was trying to sell to a housewife, "They are hard, brown medium." Fastidious people now may shudder at this kind of fuel, but it kept me warm, and Mother cooked good, honest food over its quick, hot blaze, and today there is nothing that makes me long for my childhood days as a whiff of burning cow chips. It seems to me when I see the soft, misty-blue haze on the canyon hills, it must be from the smoke those brave pioneers made in long ago days from the "prairie coal."

March 7, 1940

A trip to the city always gives me a thrill, even if I did have to spend most of my time at the yards where my husband was selling hogs. This was a busy part of town, trains switching, whistling shrilly for the crossings, and puffing out thick, black smoke; the hogs squealed and grunted as if in their pens at home. (Did you ever hear of a homesick hog, if he got plenty to eat?) Near us were the stockyards, where fat yearlings and cows waited their turn to be sold for tender steaks and juicy roasts. Golden grains of wheat were turned into soft white flour to make flaky biscuits and pastry. The smoke poured from the big smokestacks at the mill, where cotton seed was being crushed into oil to season the biscuits and fry the steaks. One thing I noticed, the man who once was clad in blue gingham shirt and blue denim overalls had given place to the man clad in suits of soft tan. Farmers were bringing heavy cream cans that the world might have butter on their bread, boxes of eggs that they might have cake, also. Chickens squawked as they were brought in, their legs tied together; mighty engines purred as they did their work; a sour smell of grain, cotton lint over the ground where lay heads of maize with the grain gone—these sights and sounds told of a nation being fed from the farms and ranches.

March 21, 1940

Seems like country people have to run to town as often in a week as they once did in a year. Three times last week we had to go, twice in one day. While on the road to town we remembered when we were first married and went to Floydada in a wagon. We had a buggy, but it would not hold a load, and things had to be bought in large quantities to last from one trip to another. The sun was hot that long-ago day; my hat scarcely shaded my warm face. The road ran through a lake that had some water in it. Somehow my husband decided to go through the water; he slapped the horses, and mud and water began to splash on my Sunday hat and Sunday face. Tears of anger and aggravation ran down my dirty face as my husband roared with laughter. Then we made the trip in a Spaulding hack, which now rests with dignity and honor in the Museum at Texas Tech. . . .

The first words I ever heard over a radio: "President Wilson died this evening." The others in the room were laughing and talking as these sad words poured into my ears alone, as I sat with the receivers to my ears.

April 17, 1941

Brother Guy, wife, and daughter, Junelle, came from Plainview bringing three little girls for an Easter egg hunt. We made ice cream. Guy brought their electric freezer and said it made him feel foolish to bring an electric freezer to the country. Many a year he has come to this place when there was not even a dream of electricity, and no wonder it makes him feel queer.

Whereas most towns installed electrical systems about the turn of the century, rural areas were without power into the 1930s. Private electricity companies could not make a profit delivering service over long distances to relatively few customers. A handful of farmers generated their own electricity: windmill generators could produce enough energy to power a few light bulbs and a radio in a farmhouse. But most farms relied on oil lamps for light. Early in Franklin Roosevelt's New Deal the federal government determined to revolutionize the electrical industry in the United States. It undertook a number of big hydroelectric projects intended to increase dramatically the supply of electricity in places with ample rivers such as the Pacific Northwest, the Tennessee Valley, and the desert Southwest. Strings of dams went up on major and minor rivers across the country, including along the Colorado River in central Texas, where Lyndon Johnson, a newly elected New Deal Democratic congressman, brought federal funds home for his district. Roosevelt wanted to bring public electric generation to the nation. He felt that privately owned electric companies charged too much and had failed to bring service to large parts of the country. Now the government would go into the electricity business. The cost of electricity plummeted.

In May 1935 Roosevelt issued an executive order creating the Rural Electrification Administration (REA), which Congress authorized in 1936. The REA offered low-interest, long-term loans to rural communities that set up electrical cooperatives. The co-ops generated electricity locally, built transmission lines along rural roads, and provided electricity for the first time to hundreds of thousands of farm families. Farmers could borrow directly from the REA to wire their houses and to buy electrical appliances. Repayment cost three dollars per month over twenty years, and many took advantage of the program. In 1930 almost no rural homes had electricity. In 1950 more than half did, and by 1960 virtually all American homes were electrified. One Crosby County observer commented that "The REA has been the greatest boon of any of the many services rendered the women of the farming communities. The telephone and electricity provided the rural home with all the conveniences of her city sister and has made living on the farms a pleasure rather than drudgery that it was before the advent of REA."

April 24, 1941

My husband does not think he can shave unless his shaving things are on the dining table in the kitchen, although we have had a bathroom for over two years. We become creatures of habit about ordinary things.

May 15, 1941

We put a doorbell on the door last week. So far it has been too muddy for anyone to come and ring it. I always have such a funny feeling about pushing a doorbell button. You cannot hear it ring and stand there wondering if your call is being announced in the back or the bell is out of order. When I am in the kitchen I cannot hear anyone knock at the front door. Now please push the button.

October 16, 1941

The time of year has come to put up stoves. This year it will not be a hard job on this farm, as a gas stove is quickly brought down from the attic and connected. But I remember the times when I was a girl and for many years in my own home when putting up the stove was an agonizing time. No matter how careful the woman was to hold tubs and scatter down papers, the soot would sift all over the room. Somehow the stovepipes would never fit. My father was the freest man I ever knew to use no kind of a by-word but one. . . . He would say "plague-take-it" when he was too aggravated. This word always came out at putting-up-stove times. The emphasis he put on it made it sound awful as he stood on a cane-bottomed chair and tried to couple up the black pipes.

November 13, 1941

Well it seems that tapioca shall be absent from the tables this winter. Not a sigh from a single man have I heard. Give them a bread pudding or one made from rice, good old American dishes that staved off starvation when the West was new. Sparkling cellophane will slip out of our hands to go into defense. Back to the plain things of yesterday. To use our old aluminum cooking vessels makes us feel that we are not being very patriotic. Back to the good old black skillets and pots. Back to the good old plain thinking and plain ways, too, in many things might be best for us.

January 8, 1942

If there had been a limit put on the rubber supply when I was a girl at Emma, the way it would have affected the inland town would have been to put a stop to the grand old game of town ball, not having the small bouncing rubber ball. The little boys would not have had their nigger-shooters [slingshots], the little girls and big girls would not have had pretty pink and blue garters with satin bows to hold up their black cotton stockings and teachers would have had a blacked out paper of mistakes for the lack of erasers on examination day.

January 22, 1942

In the early days Amarillo and Emma were connected only by the old freight road that ran a straight course between the two towns. On this road loaded wagons slushed and rattled, according to the weather, and the gray ashes from the cow-chip fires marked the camps, not only of the hardy freighters but of the drivers of herds of cattle staying for a night and bedding down the weary herd or stopping for a short rest at noon. One must not forget the carrier of Uncle Sam's mail, who whipped up his tough little Spanish mules into a run from one station to another, braving the rain and the bitter cold that the few citizens of Emma might have connection with the outside world. The old road was cut deep into the prairie sod, the old ruts left to fill again with grass but looking like old scars on the earth, new ones cut clear of grass by the hoofs of many animals and the turn-ing of creaking wagon wheels. Now the pavement, smooth as the middle of the old grindstone that stood by the windmill, does not show a print of the soft rubber wheels that now carry the loads of goods, the cattle and the mail from Crosby County to the town of Amarillo, which grew big and rich from the old wagon roads from the smaller towns.

Amarillo, the pride of the north plains, sitting in beauty and dignity and honor on the plains and looking to the hazy blue Canadian breaks on the north, connected now not only by pavement but by tall pine poles holding wires that hum with busi-ness and news and even by the waves of the air as the radio broadcasts to the four corners of the world. Imagine how I felt, talking to friends I could not see but who I knew

were listening, my voice traveling hundreds of miles as quickly as it did when I talked to my brothers and sisters as we jogged along in the bumping wagon. What a happy privilege was mine, a pioneer of the plains connecting my beloved home to a busy city with the wonders of the radio. . . .

My brother Joe says he got tired of hitching up eighty-five horses to ride to the Amarillo courthouse where he is court reporter, so he bought a bicycle, saving time, rub-ber and gasoline. Now, believe it or not, once I could ride a bicycle. My brother Lowell and I owned one at Emma, and we thought it quite a feat to ride out to the sandhill a mile west of town and back. If I remember rightly we spent most of our time pumping up tires. No, I do not suppose I will ride a bicycle into town soon, however many things will change.

February 12, 1942

As the government has put a ban on weather predicting, the good old subject of weather has given way to that of time. It takes some minutes for everyone to understand just what hour is set for a meeting. The old time, war time or what have you? And anyway just how does the

Ernest Witt on his freight wagon at Emma, Texas, 1906. Photograph courtesy of Southwest Collection, Texas Tech University, Lubbock, SWCPC 291 E1 #18.

new time save? Endless topic for discussion. Do you remember how some of us fought railroad time? We were so accustomed to the good old sun time. We could always look in the almanac and set our clocks by the rising or setting of the sun.

My husband said I could run up our clock, but he did hate to go to bed at eleven, and he did not want dinner any earlier. I am only thankful he does not call me at five o'clock war time to prepare breakfast.

Until the late nineteenth century, time was a local matter. People set their clocks by the sun, and precision was unnecessary. The first institution that required greater time precision was the railroad. In 1883 all U.S. and Canadian railroads instituted Standard Time across North America. People began to distinguish between "sun time" and "railroad time." War prompted further changes. In

1918, in the midst of World War I, U.S. law made railroad time official across the country and also created the first Daylight Savings Time as an energy conservation measure. With the end of the war, in 1919 Congress repealed the unpopular Daylight Savings Time but retained Standard Time. When the United States entered World War II, Daylight Savings Time returned to stay, beginning on February 9, 1942.

January 14, 1943

I have been thinking this morning of a trip I made to Portales when I was a young woman with a son of two and one-half years and twin babies of six months. Mother and Father came down from their claim in New Mexico one spring in a covered wagon to see the grand twin girls. Father decided to stay awhile, and I was to go home with Mother, who had a boy of eight years, one of five and a girl of two. Such a trip. We got my cousin Mary, a young girl, to go with us and help me back with my train journey. The weather was cool, but with bedding in the wagon we kept warm. The twins cried; we thought they did not like to ride. When we stopped to camp, they cried louder than ever. Wilson and Josephine got into mischief, spilling the talcum all in the wagon, getting perfume into drinking water and cups, opening a box of black pepper. We lost our way; all day we journeyed a little to the

northeast when it should have been northwest, making our trip a lot longer. The last evening we rode into a storm, dirt and lightning and roar of thunder. We stopped at a little house till the storm was over. It was dark, but we were in five miles of Mother's home. We started to the wagon, me carrying the twins. A sudden flare of lightning lighted the whole universe. I was starting to step off into an old cellar with my girls.

We took the train home after a two-weeks stay. The girls did not like that way of traveling; they cried even more about that. We stopped for a night at Hereford. Next morning we were waiting for the train, trying to keep up with Wilson and see after the babies. Mary handed me the one she had to corral Wilson. I heard the shriek of the train, and I rushed up to Mary, saw that she did not have a baby in her arms. I fairly yelled, much to the amusement of the onlookers, "Mary, where in the earth is that other twin?" me standing there excitedly holding one in each arm. . . .

My husband has been telling the family about the time "bob" wire came into use in his boyhood. People on the prairie bought some of this new fencing. Cattle and horses, running, would not even stop. Many were cut and folks were enraged. Fences were cut. He told of one fence being cut between every post, every wire. Legislators were alarmed, laws were passed in favor of the fence and it became a penitentiary offense for one who cut a wire fence, which law is still in force. Mr. Spikes said it was the law then that a plank or pole should be put longways between every post. A man in Kaufman county fenced a league of land and put long poles between every post. Stock could then see the fence. The barbs were long and sharp and closely spaced. On many an old fence in this country one sees a strand or so of this wire, which almost caused a revolution and changed the old way of letting stock run on the outside ranges.

February 25, 1943

No, Mr. Shine Phillips of Big Spring, your hankering for a good old hog killing time on a bitter freezing day cannot be fulfilled any more. Step right this way and see a modern hog killing. No special day is set, but on a warmish cool morning the man of the house gathers up the old dull butcher knives, dull since last year's hog killing, the children go to school as usual, the man gets a target and goes to the lot and shoots down a hog or so, loads them in a trailer and thirty-fives to the nearest gin. Knives are sharpened on an electric emery, steam is turned on the hogs, soon they are scraped and in the trailer again, back to the farm, where they are washed and deprived of their innards, then carefully wrapped and on their way to the locker in town. The man returns home, knowing his hog will be sliced, sausage made and put in rolls, the fat waiting a few days in the cold room, when it can be gotten and rendered up. No, Mr. Phillips, it isn't the same, not anymore. Buying oatmeal is not the same anymore, either, that is since the children got grown. I remember coming home from town, the children going through all the packages as they sat in the back seat of the newly owned car while my hands gripped the steering wheel. They would always open the oatmeal to see what would be the gift inside. It always irritated me like stepping on sugar, but nothing I could do about it, unless stop the car and see to the mischief in the back. Oatmeal would always spill as the gift was pulled out, and usually the box overturned as I swept around a corner.

September 16, 1943

If my grandmother had awakened some morning and found her floor covered in pretty, smooth, shining linoleum, would not she have shouted and told her neighbors that fairies had been good to her in the night? And if she could have . . . turned a knob and seen a blue blaze flare up round and hot for cooking, she would have shouted "Miracle." So I still believe in fairies and miracles and after the war we are promised more and more. Why, only the last war Mother had been reading an article in the *Saturday Evening Post* by Floyd Parsons, and he told of the coming radio. Mother told the family, only to be laughed at and asked, "Why, Mother, do you really believe that?" . . .

Still thinking about magic and miracles—the combine goes down the rows with long, sharp and gleaming sickle, cutting off more heads in a second than our hoarding knives did in hours. I can see myself now, by the side of the wagon, going down the same spot of ground, a maize crop ahead that looked as endless as the waves on the ocean, my husband just ahead with his wagon and team. My bonnet slouched over my hot face, endless showers of maize chaff fell over me, much of it finding its way down my neck. My arms ached from reaching for the swaying goosenecked heads, turned in every direction, bending my sore back for the heads that had fallen on the earth, cutting my way on and on, a jungle of heads to fight through to the end of the row. A brief stop for knives to be sharpened and to swig long draughts of hot water from the jug, then back again. Throwing heads over and walking around the wagon to pick them up, hollering at the horses, seeing that the children did not get in the way of the wagon. Aching and dirty, stinging and sweating. Of course I believe in magic. Who wouldn't when they watch the combine snatch red-gold heads from the straight stalk. Shaking out the grains from the chaff as clean as we once beat it out with a stick for seed maize, piling it in waiting trucks, me cool and clean at the house.

October 22, 1943

Do you ever sigh for the good old days of the middy blouse? Whether tall or short, thick or thin or young or old, we rolled up the bottom of those white blouses at the top of a long wool skirt, pinned them close to each side, tied on a gay bow of red or blue or black at the neck and felt ready for sport occasions. How hard they were to wash and iron. Droopy if not enough starch, hard as a plank with too much.

November 10, 1944

Just as I had convinced myself and I hope my husband, that never, never, would I help scrape another hog, I find this in a paper. "The traditional scalding and scraping of hogs in butchering may soon be replaced by a new scientific method. The Hercules Powder Company has produced a liquid plastic which does the trick. Hogs are dipped into the sticky stuff. After the plastic cools, it is peeled off taking all the hair and dirt with it. Plastic can be remelted, cleaned and used again."

December 7, 1944

Since Sunday night we have not had electricity. Now we can do without the lights tolerably well, but the electric separator is a different matter. There is the job of disconnecting the motor. Screws stick and defy all pressure. The stand is so low one has almost to stand on his head to turn the handle. Of course there was not but a tinsy bit of oil in the lamps, and the chimneys were not clean. I should have had all this attended to. The candles I had seen all summer long were not to be found high nor low. The sewing machine belt took this time to wear out—of all times to do a thing like that. The house is too dark in daytime to see how to read or do hand sewing.

My goodness I must stop. Looks like I am piling up complaints into a mountain. Why don't I remember that water still comes into the house, that the butane fire burns warm and bright, that I am having time to think about some things, that Joe Ellis and Wilma and Paul had time to come yesterday and spend the day. I believe I could keep on till the mountain of complaints could be overshadowed by the mountain of blessings.

The first telephone service reached Crosby County in 1902 in the form of a row of short telephone poles that stretched straight across the open prairie from Floydada south to Emma. The wires hung neck-high to a person on horseback and were not popular with local cowboys. The following year another line connected Emma with Dickens to the east, allowing for the first telephone connection between Amarillo and the eastern part of the state. Each line connected to a telephone box at the Witt and Spikes store. The store clerk answered calls and served as message-taker for the whole county. When someone from Floydada or points north wanted to connect through to Dickens or points east, the clerk used a piece of metal to close the circuit between the two lines.

Rural residents took advantage of their preexisting network of fences to extend telephone service into the countryside. They ran telephone cord along barbed wire fences from one farm to another, establishing a party line for multiple households. Each home had a unique ring pattern and only picked up if their ring sounded. Families were responsible for maintaining the telephone line along their own fences. This relatively simple and inexpensive technology diminished the isolation felt by rural families. Nellie Witt Spikes and Temple Ann Ellis commented in their county history that "the women who had been so isolated, because of distance and poor transportation, were overjoyed, when their housework was done, to sit down and visit over the telephone with neighbors they had only known by name. . . . The rural telephones of today, established on the electric lines are only the wire fence phones revived, but they can never bring such joy to the housewife as did the barbed wire line. . . ."

July 27, 1945

Now once upon a time the farmer's wife and children went to the stack lot and broke off good heads of maize and kaffir and hegari, piled them on a sheet and whipped out the grain, the mother having to do most of the whipping of the grain and threatening to do the same to the children. Then the grain was emptied into a tub, water carried and the bad grains and chaff floated out with many washings and pourings. Then the water was carefully drained off and the wet seed spread evenly on a wagon sheet to dry in the sun and wind so the farmer would not have to stop the planting. Now, and this part reads like the end of a fairy tale, the farmer takes the dressed up family to town, goes 'round to the feed store where white sacks of grain seed are loaded in the car and he is ready for planting.

January 10, 1947

"Yes, it has been cold and some snow," the old-timer admits, but, he adds, "You just orter been here when I first come, then you would have seen some bad weather." 'Twas bad then, I admit. I was a little girl and we lived in a house, the only protection against the northers were the thin box walls stripped with old outworn shirts and dresses down the wide cracks, and sometimes thin canvas and wallpaper, but more usually the many times read newspapers pasted on. I learned about President Cleveland by reading the writing on the wall, as it were, and could quote ads about castoria, liver regulator and pink pills for pale people. And if you ever tried to keep warm by a cowchip fire or even one of green mesquite, or from scanty piles of coal hauled the long, weary freight road from Amarillo, you know what I mean.

Of course, the men wore under-shirts and drawers; now don't get excited, you say shorts now and no one cares. The only difference in the two is that older generation wore those an inch thick, and it took a week of good sunshine and a sandstorm to dry when washed, and those garments covered one up so well that it only took a long beard, a long nubia twisted round the head, a pair of wristlets, knitted by mother or sweetheart for Christmas gifts on the wrists where the gloves could not reach, a pair of knit socks covered with a pair of brogans or boots, a homemade shirt and blue pants to finish a complete covering. Not to be outdone, or for the reason the cold had to be kept out, the women and children wore a thinner kind of underwear, some three petticoats, all showing under a long skirt, a fascinator, which I see is popular now as such a handsome head covering should be, and a cape which the wind had a good time blowing up around one's neck. But how pretty the beads were on the trimming. Good old thick cotton flannel was the fashion for underthings and baby's wear. It got good and cold in those days. High-topped shoes and black thick stockings pulled carefully over longies; no, not pretty, but oh how warm!

Well, if I started out to prove or

disprove anything about the difference in the weather now and then, I have forgotten it as I sit comfortably by a butane fire which doesn't have to be replenished every few minutes, wear a short-sleeve dress and, as we used to say, slippers, and remember how cold it was when we came here. The first REA ever to be had in these parts was when Si Smith, now of Ralls but first living near us, brought his family out from Louisville, Kentucky, in the spring of 1910. He brought a motor with him and lived in a big barn till his house was built, and he lighted up his barn with electricity which was the forerunner of REA.

February 28, 1947

We welcomed our son's wife last week when he brought her to Ralls, after they were married in Dallas. She has come a long way, some five thousand miles, and we hope she will feel at home and be happy in the country she has adopted. She is pleasant and friendly, a bit of the England we have always loved to read about, and her sunny nature delights in our sunny climate. "If I had only made one connection sooner," she says, "It would only have been a week from Cheltenham, England, to Dallas, Texas, and if I

had come by plane it would have been quicker." I smiled to myself as I remembered the Spikes family spent two months coming to Crosby County from Kaufman.

November 21, 1947

Somehow I can't throw away a pretty bottle, or a plain one for that matter. I remember when I was a child I would have given worlds for the ones we get now most every day. They would have been so very handsome on the old rusty five-gallon can covered with a clean piece of newspaper in our play houses. We treasured pieces of burnt glass, bits of broken dishes, and a little sliver of mirror was happiness untold. But we could play like ladies as well then as little girls can now with more finery than we ever dreamed of. And perhaps we had as good a time, but—still, I can't throw away the bottles.

February 27, 1948

I spent three days in my son's hospital at Ralls last week. As I lay there I thought of how many times I had attended him when he was sick, and now he was seeing after me. True, the methods I used when he had a cold were far different from the ones he used on me. I found a heavy flannel cloth, greased it good with lard, then sprinkled it with turpentine, camphor, and kerosene oil, warmed it good by the fire, and put it on his chest, with loud protestations from my son. I gave him a good dose of castor oil, he more vigorously protesting, but then I thought it had to be done so he got it; even had to lick out the spoon, insult to injury. And for high fever I once made a poultice of hot cooked onions and put it on his stomach. Well the fever left after a time, anyway. Seemed the worse we made anyone smell and the more uncomfortable, the better chance the patient had of recovery. How tender is the touch of my son's long fingers, I thought, as he gave me soothing drops to stop my headache; how fine it is to have him near us again. And he never put a greased cloth on me or gave me castor oil to get even.

April 9, 1948

The first cooker I remember was one Mother bought when I was growing up. It was a round, tall, tin affair and had a whistle to blow when the water was running low. Then when I first was keeping house a neighbor went to Louisville, Kentucky, for a visit and brought home a fireless cooker. I simply had to have one.

Of course I could have taken a deep wood box, stuffed hay in the bottom and round the sides with a deep hole in the center to put a cooking batch of beans, but I wanted one just like Mrs. White's, so she ordered me one. Some $15 it was, but the long box was shiny with dark varnish, and two hinged lids opened at the top to put big aluminum vessels of cooking food in. First you started the food to cooking and put the sandstone on the fire to heat. This was lowered into the deep hole by wire hooks, and the boiling vessel put on it. Then the lid was let down and the food kept cooking and cooking while you went to the field to hoe or run the binder. Rice and beans, puddings and fruit cakes simmered away in its depths, but changes brought on other methods of taking all work away from cooking and one just had to have a waterless cooker of aluminum and cook a whole meal at one time on top of the range, discarding the once much-desired fireless box. Then someone had a happy thought, and the canner was on the market and every woman wanted one, putting away the waterless cooker. Now we are to cook whole meals and store them in a deep-freeze. What next, quien sabe?

December 10, 1948

I am writing in the room which we first built in 1907. Then it was our kitchen. Today the window in the south lets in big squares of yellow sunshine. I remember it then. The sunshine came in and made eight small squares on the white pine floor. A small dining table and chairs stood between the window and south door. A coal stove on the east side, a homemade folding bed on the north on one side of a window and a washstand on the east side. Yes, we had another room, but this was the room we used. A flowered curtain hid the bed when it was let up. I covered a yellow square with a piece of lace curtain and put it in the center to hang over the side of the mantle of the bed. A little alarm clock ticked the happy hours away.

September 2, 1949

George Jones wanted a house. He hooked up several yokes of oxen, pulled out to Colorado City over rough roads in the breaks and brought back enough lumber to build a two-room house. This house must have been a forerunner of small modern homes, for it had no eaves. In my mind, at that time, it was deplorable. He put the ceiling on top of the joists and thus made a floored attic. Many a night before the light was out I lay in Grandma's good bed and read the words stamped on the bottom of the ceiling: M. T. JONES LUMBER CO. Fifty-nine years later we needed a small house for cotton picking hands. We drove to Lubbock in a car, looked at houses already built, and in a few days the house will be delivered. The 1949 version: "Lady, will you take your house along, or shall we deliver it?"

January 12, 1950

There is something about a door that opens as one approaches that make me feel kinda funny. What if it does not open? I can hardly hold my hand off the handle. But that would make me look foolish as if I had never had a door open at my approach. So I hold my hands stiffly at my side, step up as if every door I enter would open and close by hands unseen, as it were. You remember in the good old fairy stories all one had to do for the door to open was to say, "Sesame," and it would open, even a secret door. Maybe it would help feelings to say, "Sesame," to the doors of business houses in Lubbock. Anyway I like them much better than I do the revolving doors.

July 7, 1950

I have such a peculiar feeling when I am watering the garden and the wind stops blowing. For many, many years on the farm I watered from the windmill when it was turning, having to quit when the wind stopped. Now it is almost a shock that the water keeps right on running.

July 21, 1950

In the days when a palmetto fan was the only air conditioner on the market, when you drove to a man's house in the summer and the doors were shut or in the winter when no smoke was coming out the stovepipe, you knew at once there was no one at home. Not so these days. No smoke comes out in winter and the doors are shut so the air conditioner will cool the house.

December 8, 1950

The other morning we went into the Ford house and a lady pinned an orchid on my coat. Now I was not paying too much attention as we had had a little engine trouble and were waiting for it to be repaired. I went over town and not till I got home did I realize I had a really truly orchid, my very first, and I had been so indifferent and in my mind

I had always visualized getting my first orchid and the thrill and the admiring envy of orchidless others. But the thrill did come, and proudly I wore my first orchid with the word "Ford" pinned to my coat. Wish I had compiled all the jokes on the Ford car we heard in the days when Henry put the world on wheels. We recall the two little boys watching a man spread a blanket so his radiator would not freeze up, then telling the man, "No use covering it up, mister, everyone saw it was a Ford." Now the jokes are on the people who joked about the Ford, and we do not blame Mr. Bishop and Mr. Cooper for being very proud of the shiny cars in their showrooms and the lovely orchids which told of triumphs of not only people being on wheels but easy-riding, fast-moving wheels, ready at the turn of another wheel to take one on magic carpet trips.

February 23, 1951

This morning as I look out the north window, white and gray fleecy clouds float northeast. . . . Storm-feeders, we used to call them. In these days when we depend on the weatherman to tell us the coming weather, we are just too plum' lazy to watch the signs in the heavens and be our own forecasters. Of course, we used to fail, but does not the weatherman do the same? When we saw the northern horizon blue and smoky we brought in cowchips and mesquite wood, filled extra buckets of water and waited for the blizzard. If any ever traveled east and missed us I do not recall it; they hit and how! Our children will not even know it is in their power to tell the weather. They get it out of a radio like they get milk out of a bottle, without a thought.

January 25, 1952

This was a time of year we got ready for the new year's work. . . . Mr. Spikes was getting rope line in readiness for the harness, new hame strings were put in, plows and wagons greased . . . a box of axle grease, new lines and harness patched up, maybe a new horse collar or so, plowshares sharpened or replaced, some new bolts, and the spring work was getting ready to be done. No income tax return to worry over! Were those the good old days? But there might have been a drought the year before, and maize would have to be bought to feed the work team or the plowing would go slow; "plowing on the grass," the horses would not be able to do as much work. We did not have electric lights, or butane or radios. The *Semi-Weekly News* told us the news of the then-peaceful world, or at least America was out of the wars. Now that we have many luxuries I am reminded of the lines, "We can do without any article of luxury we have never had; but when once obtained, it is not in human nature to surrender it voluntarily."

November 4, 1955

I see in a gift catalog a contraption to hold up the covers off one's feet. Our grandfathers solved that problem long ago; they just put their younguns at their feet, and they kept the covers held up. I can just see my Aunt Ella pulling out the trundle bed from under her and Uncle Frank's big bed. The two older boys slept on the trundle bed, the little ones at the grownups' feet. . . .

I have always been kind of a weather barometer as far as northers are concerned. I feel them a day or so beforehand. My children did not like for me to forecast one, for as they said, "Mama can always tell." Now we are not told we will have a "norther." It is a "cool wave" or a "cold wave" and before I even have time for any symptoms for a change in the weather, it is taken from me by some weather forecaster and I do not have to bother. . . . I miss the word "norther" from our western vocabulary, but I do not care if the blue northers do not come again, do you?

A Poetry of Place

Nellie Witt Spikes wrote in a distinctive style, often flowery, but evocative of her era. On occasion she lapsed into "poetic prose," painting vivid scenes of color and texture using similes, metaphors, and other figurative language. This short chapter excerpts small pieces of writing that tend toward the lyrical, most of them celebratory of place and the natural world.

Spikes was deeply interested in poetry. She read it avidly and routinely reprinted short poems within her weekly columns. None of those poems are included in this volume, but it is clear that poetry was often on her mind. More than one column included the line, "Oh, I wish I were a poet!" One suspects that in her heart of hearts she thought that she was poetic. In honor of that impulse, she occasionally allowed her prose to flow freely in the direction of imagery. These pieces are not poems, and they are pulled from the context of longer passages. Still, they are gems, brief pieces from which vivid images spring brilliantly to life.

November 4, 1937

We have had a taste of the beauty of the woods this fall. The gold of the apricot vies with the red splendor of its neighbors, the ash. Virginia creeper waves scarlet leaves to the pear tree, dressed in soft yellow. There are enough dead leaves for me to scuff with my feet. I gather up the beauty around me and store it away for the days to come. I love the sea gulls flashing in the sun, now soft blue, then white as the winter snow. The call of the curlews, the gay whistle of the field lark as he warns that "laziness will kill you," mingle with the gobbling of fat gobblers, ready for the Thanksgiving table, and the piercing whistle of the gin.

May 19, 1938

Twilight in the courtyards at Emma. A little girl gathering starry blue flowers of the China tree, branches of waxen, white, fragrant flowers of the locust trees. The first star shines clear. "Star light, star bright"; the little girl is making a wish. The sound of a key turning the lock of the store door, the steps of the merchant going home, the good feel of the soft night breeze, the dying song of the cowboy's galloping horse. Neighbor children laughing and shouting, playing hide-and-seek. The smell of fresh brown biscuit, fried bacon and potatoes. Water making music as it falls from the iron pipe to the cypress tank. The sweet voice of a little girl's mother singing a lullaby to the new baby, the rocking of the cane-bottom chair as it keeps time to the music. The girl's father calls, "Nellie," and with a reluctant look back to the flower-laden trees, Nellie gathers her fragrant bouquet in her stiff, starched gingham apron and goes across the hard dirt street of the little prairie town, to her home.

June 23, 1938

The windmill makes a pleasant sound as it turns, but to me one of the best sounds is that of water running into the water barrel. Water clear and cool and pure. Water for the thirsty gardens and gay flowers. Water for the wooly sheep, the tired team, the soft-eyed cows, water running into a little pool where downy chickens stand on the edge and drink while baby ducks skim over

The Johnsons, a family of black farm laborers from the South, help
with cotton harvest on the Terrell farm near Lorenzo, Texas, ca. 1935.
A. B. Terrell stands on the right with a pipe, while J. R. Terrell stands
on the trailer to the left. Transient Hispanic and black families hired
from outside the region brought diversity to small West Texas towns
during the fall cotton harvest. Photograph courtesy of Crosby County
Pioneer Memorial Museum, Crosbyton, Texas, 0558.

the water and stand on their heads,
their little black paddles waving in
the air.

October 6, 1938

The maize looks like a golden stream
as it pours from the combine. No
rain on it to blacken its beauty this
fall. And the cotton is as soft and
white as the clouds that pass over it.
Many hands are working to save the
feed and the cotton. Streets of the
towns look like Mexico or way down
in East Texas.

January 26, 1939

This morning, I have acres and acres
of diamonds, blue sky paper to wrap
them in and silver ribbons unwind-
ing from the eaves of the house to tie
the packages with. I will dip my pen
in the gold of the sunshine and write
each reader's name on a package. It
is a wonderful morning.

February 23, 1939

The world is a study in gray this morning. Nature got out her colors, but decided on gray. She flung soft gray over the sky, painted the trees a darker gray, so that one could see every slender twig outlined against the sky. The prairie is a tannish gray, the turned furrows a dark oxford. I look for a bit of gay color. My neighbor's windmill supplies it with its tower of dull red. Even the birds that fly in formation to the ground for the golden bits of maize are gray. Outside it is cold, but in the house warm fires burn. The smell of freshly baked spicy fruitcake comes from the kitchen. The cats sleep by the fire, the baby bawls from his high chair. My husband sleeps in his chair, his paper fallen to the floor. The farmer works in the heat and the cold, but days like this when the work at the barn is done, he has a few hours of nothing to do.

March 30, 1939

Spring is coming to the prairie country. Not with a breathtaking parade of beauty as she does in the timbered country, but shy as the antelope and the blue quail. She spreads a cover of pale green on the pasture and starts the wildflowers; gives the haze on the canyon hills a deeper blue; entices the killdeer back to call "dee dee dee"; swells the buds of the cottonwood trees, promises them millions of tiny fans. She waves her wand and peach trees are dressed in pale pink, pear trees in white satin; gives the freshly turned furrows a fragrance dear to folks on the farm; pins a corsage of sweet wild plum blossoms on her brown dress.

April 6, 1939

Every day for a week there has been something different. Rocks were hauled from the canyon hills and a new fence across the west side of the yard was made. Somehow these rocks bring a part of the canyon to me. They tell me of endless time, of the Indians who shouted war cries from the hills, of dark brown mothers who sang strange lullabies to tiny black-eyed babies. They whisper of cowboy romances and of a swift-thrown lariat and the smell of burning hides. They bring the roar of the thundering feet of the thousands of buffalo as they rushed over the unbounded green prairie blending against the blue heavens. They saw the world carpeted with an endless expanse of curly mesquite grass. Some of them might have been the seat of some of Coronado's ragged, tired men as they hunted for the silver and gold that Spain wanted so badly. Just a plain stacked rock fence to some, but history, romance and love to me.

February 8, 1940

Each window in the house this beautiful morning frames a picture which holds my interest till my housework is slowed up. The picture in the east window: Brown, slender limbs of the graceful pecan trees, etched against a pale blue sky; smoke rising like a long, white plume from the house of my neighbors, the Crimps. I can almost smell ham frying and coffee bubbling in its pot, see brown biscuits, tender with homemade lard. Near our barns the little herd of woolly sheep lie on the ground, made warm by their bodies; they chew so funny, and their breath looks like steam on the cold air. A huddle of ducks, chickens sitting on red feet to warm them; the horses and cows eating the dry sorghum with crunching sounds; the old gobbler struts and gobbles at a sudden loud noise; a bank of dark gray clouds hugs the sky near the ground, but they are edged with shining silver, and the rising sun hunts the torn, ragged places in

them to put on patches of flaming red from the south. Many houses are drawn on the horizon as if with huge charcoal pencils; the brown fields lie resting in the early morning, waiting for the plow and the seed; windmills clank and glitter like mirrors as the sun throws its giant spotlight on them; birds feed on the seeds of the broomweed; the rock fence separates the yard from the road, where so many friends have driven in to see us. The pictures change from day to day, from year to year, but they are always of interest and delight to me.

September 5, 1940

Like a herd of frightened wild mustangs the rain dashed across our fields yesterday. On to the lake, up the hill to the draw it raced, a flash of lightning, a roar of deafening thunder, and all was still as before. Only half an inch the old cream-colored churn in the garden held, but there is a faint hope of new green stirring in the mesquite grass, and the cane and hegari seem to be taking on new life. Little pools were left in the pasture, and my little grandson had his first lesson in wading in cool rainwater where his mother had waded when she was a child.

December 19, 1940

I think the weather man must have looked in the stores and the homes, seen the lovely decorations for Christmas, and then decided he must do something about the old world he had made so brown and somber. So nothing better to work with, he spread a gray, misty cloud over the prairies, shook the weather thermometer to below freezing, then told Father Time to go ahead and tick off a few hours of time. Trees and houses, roads and fields were soon covered with glittering ice. My rock fence was wrapped in sparkling clear ice like cellophane. The weeds along the roadside, which had looked so ugly, were as beautiful as the trees and the winter shrubs. When all was ready, the weather man snatched the clouds away with a brisk north wind, switched on the sun again, turned a blue bowl over the plains and was ready with his Christmas decorations.

January 23, 1941

Today, Monday, a great nation witnessed the inauguration of a president. The ones of us not fortunate enough to be present in the capital of the United States will sit and listen over the radio. This morning as the strains of that mighty song,

"The Star Spangled Banner," poured out in all its sweetness and beauty from the Marine band, my throat constricted and my eyes filled with tears. Tears of gladness that we live in a nation at peace, tears of sorrow that we might be called to help fight the battle of democracy.

As the music filled my ears, another scene, another room where the music of the nation's song filled a schoolroom at Emma, Miss Lillian Brockman leading, her pupils singing. The United States was going to war with Spain; the Battleship Maine was lying at the bottom of the ocean with its dead soldiers appearing to be "remembered." A call for volunteers blazed on the headlines in the papers. How lustily we sang, how we squeaked at the high notes! Patriotism was born in the hearts of the singing boys and girls. I trembled as I sang; my young uncles, whom I adored, might have to go. I could almost smell the smoke of battle, hear the piteous cries of the wounded as they cried for water. How many times I had my grandpa tell of his adventures in the Civil War. A horror of war filled my heart with patriotism. The war was soon over, peace seemed to have come to stay in our dear land. But in 1918 again the "Star Spangled Banner" stirred our patriotism to new heights and we thought and prayed and fought that war might be outlawed. Sweet peace again hovered and alighted over our land. War was surely no more.

But we did not figure with the enemies of peace and goodwill to men. The time for peace for all has not come. Again the strains of the "Star Spangled Banner" swell to the American breezes and our duty seems to be to help the men and women desperately holding back the forces of wrong.

October 23, 1941

Today is a lovely day. The strong wind is sweeping the mud and water away. The farmer has taken new heart and is out seeing what he had better do first. There is so much to be done. Sunshine and dry weather will pop open the cotton. Soon the fields will look like long white sacks going down the row by themselves as the pullers are hidden by its full sides. Big yellow heads of maize will hit the throw boards of moving wagons pulled by horses filling up on every head they can snatch. Headed bundles will fall from moving binders, then set up in straight rows, looking like the Indian tepees that once covered the plains. The McCoy gin has taken on the appearance of a steamboat. The hazy weather, the mirage, the battle gray of the gin, the

tall, smoking smokestack and the shimmering of the horizon make it look as if a ship was steaming up a broad blue river.

Summer has passed. The blue haze on the canyon hills has taken on a tinge of purple. The ash trees in our yard that were so shiny green all summer now wear a dress of cloth-of-gold. Leaves are beginning to fall and sweep across the green lawn, making patterns of gold and brown. Ducks, tired from rising and falling on the waves of the lake, sit on the shore oiling their feathers and thinking, if a duck thinks, and I believe they can, of how good the farmer's maize will taste at night. This is dahlia time, chrysanthemum time and cosmos time. As these beautiful flowers are cut and brought in the house, the roses we gathered last spring do not seem the loveliest of flowers as we thought them. The dahlias raised from seed are all in bloom and are as pretty as the ones grown from tubers. Remember next spring to plant a few papers of dahlia seed.

October 30, 1941

Today the plains sat under the dryer of a bright, hot sun after her beauty shampoo of the last few weeks, while the northwest wind combed her wet

Picking cotton on the Ellison farm near Crosbyton, Texas, ca. 1910. The urgency of the cotton harvest brought all members of the family into the field, even the baby in its buggy. Photograph courtesy of Southwest Collection, Texas Tech University, Lubbock, SWCPC 291 E4P.

tresses with long, sweeping strokes. We hope the lady is content and does not need another shampoo for many moons.

November 6, 1941

There are times in one's life when things are dull and prosaic. The new moon ceases to be a gypsy's gold earring and is just a plain old moon lying on its back, holding water that no one wants at the present; the wind, usually so confidential in its whisperings of romance and beauty at the far corners of the world, is a whining old woman, telling of a tragedy and sorrow; the garden, holding yellow gold and ruby red tomatoes, crisp butterbeans and tender string beans in its green lap, becomes a tiresome old place to bend one's aching back and tired arms; the flower garden just another place to weed; the beloved books, pictures: more dusting. But along comes a fairy godmother in the guise of a cheerful friend, a letter in the mailbox, a flower of soft yellow in the window as I come to the house or little white arms 'round my neck and a sweet voice saying, "I love you," and life is a wonderful adventure with no telling what nice things may surprise one around every corner.

November 13, 1941

I stepped out early this morning and saw Autumn, her dress covered with white frost, warming her cold hands by the fire of the blazing pear tree. The sumac also held out red flames as if to thaw the white mists of the day. I thought the president called in all the gold and it was buried safely deep in dark dungeons, but I have found this not true. Someone has hung gold leaves on the apricot tree, and I see gold dollars, fresh from the mint, hanging on graceful poplar and spreading cottonwood trees. This proves that gold cannot be kept from the eyes of man, even though he buries it deep from the sun.

November 20, 1941

I never saw as many browns. From the lightest tan to the darkest Vandyke, all the in-betweens, the golden, the reddish, the gray-brown. The country looked like a home demonstration agent had had women making a hooked rug of fall colors.

January 15, 1942

I like the picture brought away from a visit one day in Floydada. A picture of a woman making a rug from old clothes. The soft blues were the lovely haze on the distant hills and the lakes of water; the green was the waving grass; the pinks, the roses in the cheeks of our mothers; the yellow, the gold of their hearts. No, she was not only making a rug, she was weaving old dreams and old scenes as she sat in her pleasant room, remembering faces only seen in memory. Recalling a brown-eyed, merry little girl, sitting on a spring seat in a covered wagon by the side of her one-legged Confederate father and pretty, plump mother as the lean horses climbed to the top of the plains and came to rest at the new town of Estacado, where Mr. Hammack unloaded his boot-making machine and a big brass dinner bell, for the new citizens were to feed the hungry cowboy as he waited for his shop-made boots. Orlie, the brown-eyed girl, rode a mustang pony, wild and fast as the prairie wind, danced the fast-stepping polka and the gay breakdown in the handmade red Morocco shoes.

May 14, 1942

Sweet, fragrant, waxy white blossoms of the locust tree, swaying in the light of a clear moonlighted night, a mockingbird pouring out his thanks to the world, a couple of little boys, softly stirring in their beds, a golden-haired little girl whispering to grandmother, the pyracantha white with misty bloom, these are defense stamps to paste in our soul-books, in time growing into bonds, the enemy of all peace and freedom cannot break or destroy.

September 17, 1942

The South Plains is all dressed and ready to go—but how to get there is her problem. Her full skirt dress of green is embroidered with the pink and white of cotton blooms. Around her neck and arms are a chain of golden maize beads from a cornucopia. In her hands are fruits and vegetables of every sort and of rainbow colors. Her fields of tall, waving sorghums, red heads of wheatland maize and white of hegari and rows of cotton with full bolls ready to burst and spread snowy cotton to dry are enclosed with lanes of yellow bloom and autumn weeds. Fat cattle graze on her green pastures, yellow cream pours into waiting tin cans. She is ready to go, and somehow the farmer will see that she gets there.

September 23, 1943

September, like an advance agent for a circus, has been plastering up many signs of the coming autumn all over the farm, while from his pipe a smoky haze settled all 'round, thinly veiling the gay placards with soft blue. Today a north wind is whistling around him as he works, making the brown leaves rustle and fly across the deep summer blue of the sky to a faded blue gray, where not long ago were clouds like bales of cotton burst open and fluffing higher and higher. Browns and grays are the background colors for the signs, but here and there he adds a bit of flaming red of late-blooming red hollyhocks, a daisy of flaming gold, of zinnias, flecks of starry white of the fall aster, speckles the trees with dabs of yellow and orange. I watch him as he works, listen with sadness as he whistles a tune in a minor key, smell the gray smoke from the humming gin, knowing that the signs that he is painting and plastering up all around are the signs of chilling winds and of drab days to come.

July 14, 1944

A dark cloud fans out across the western sky, hiding the sun and giving promise of much-needed rain. Streaks of lightning come and go, as a child turns on a light switch, distant thunder rolls as if the same child rolls a wooden ball along the floor. The wind is busy, turning the mill which brings water falling into the wooden tank with a pleasant splash. The cottonwood leaves dance on their slender stems, singing a song of the West as they whirl and turn.

April 13, 1945

One morning last week I awoke, pulled the covers tighter around me and hated to get up, for I could feel it was very cold. Just how cold I could not tell, but when I did get up I went outside to see what the weather was up to. What a sight. Only yesterday the fresh green leaves had waved with the wind, the blossoms promising much fruit. Now the same green leaves were stiff and looked as if made of green plastic, myriads of green leaves to be strung for necklaces. The flowers were of pink plastic, thousands ready for the thread and needle to make more necklaces,

or so I thought to myself. But when the sun came out the necklace material turned to rags. The vision of juicy peaches, red plums and orange pears faded and was lost as of so many years past and gone. April needs to weep over what she has done, tears so plentiful that will seep to the roots of the trees she has tried to destroy, tears that will gurgle and go down to the roots of the wheat and in the land that is plowed and ready for planting. Yes, April needs to weep and weep aplenty.

October 12, 1945

Beauty of the autumn on the plains is not heaped in trays of sparkling jewels in a jewelry store, silver and gold, rubies and diamonds and emeralds. Only here and there we catch a gleam of gold, a sparkle of silver, the red of rubies and the green of diamonds. It is in the heavens above on the prairie lands that you find the colors that nature puts in the leaves of the trees and the rolling hills at this time of year. Redder than the red leaves of the forest, the color flames in the west of a declining day. She heaps more gold there than the trees that turn golden as if by the hand of a Midas. Here in the skies you find the blues of the lakes among the hills, the white in the clouds that lay cold and gleaming on the high mountaintop. Nothing obscures an inch of the sky from your pleasure when the clouds are away.

September 5, 1947

Weeks have slipped from wild, snowy white plum blossoms and grapevines with shining leaves to heavy gold, red and purple fruit. I try to capture the joy of each hour's wealth of flowers and trees, so soon to be over for another season. Blue damson plums hang like purple pendants around the neck of slim young trees; peaches smell like only ripe peaches can, making one's mouth water; a few wild plums hang on slender stems, red as the lips of the little girl that eagerly pulls them. Late-planted peas and pinto beans are fresh and beginning to bloom. The okra holds on, only wanting to be gathered each day to make more and more. The tomatoes this year are large, round and as smooth as glass and delicious to eat. Plenty of everything to eat from the garden I have loved and cared for, from greens and potatoes, lettuce and radishes and onions to beans and peas. Now the butterbeans, which have been busy climbing to the top

of the fence, are filling thin green pods with buttery beans. And there has been plenty of space for flowers which Margaret Nell and I love to give away and give away and which still bloom in abundant beauty and fragrance. Reminds me of love: the more you give away, the more you have. The pot plants are taking hold and will fill a need for flowers when cold northers come sweeping across the gathered fields.

October 21, 1955

These are surely days of pure gold. Gold is the sun which rises in the eastern skies, gold is the same sun as it sinks in the west. Golden sun rays glitter all day, and cottonwood trees are slowly turning to gold as if a giant Midas is touching them with his gift, which proved fatal in the story of old. Fall of the year is usually the most beautiful time of year on the plains. Spring does not come timid and flower-laden as it does in other parts of our land. Summer sometimes brings hot winds and drouth-stricken flowers and lawns, but after early rains of autumn the grass is green, flowers take on a new, deeper beauty. The leaves are tender and tinged with the colors of the flowers themselves. We gather a few green beans, some turnip and mustard greens; sweet potatoes are there for the digging, still a few tomatoes. This Monday morning I am making up a batch of pie-melon preserves as we did in early days when this melon was used for pies and preserves. I have added some apples to one part and a can of pineapples to the other. I cling to the peace and beauty of these days, try to take time to appreciate each hour of the day. Thank our Father above for all he does for me and all His children. Days of pure gold, the October days.

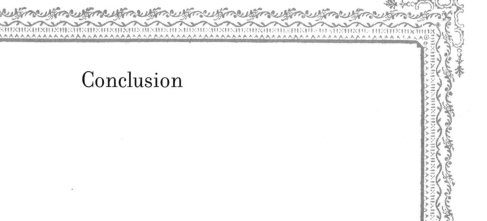

Conclusion

Nellie and Jeff retired from farming in 1950 after Jeff, then aged eighty-two, injured himself riding a cultivator in the fields. That year they left the farm and moved to a house in nearby Floydada. They lived there for two years before moving to Ralls. Nellie continued writing her column for another eight years after leaving the farm. Jeff died in 1964, and Nellie lived alone in Ralls until her death in 1977, at eighty-nine.

Nellie Witt Spikes's columns ran for some twenty-five years, averaging thirty-five columns per year, nearly nine hundred articles in all. Their topics span contemporary events from the 1930s through the 1950s, but also retrospective descriptions of county life back into the 1890s, drawn from her own memories and conversations with other "old settlers." Some of her neighbors and friends were a generation or two older than her, and through them our historical vision extends back into the 1850s in the Old South. Nellie received her education in the rural school system of early-twentieth-century West Texas. She was well read but never went to college and did not train as a journalist. Yet her stories flow with life and color. They are vibrantly evocative of the rhythms of farm life, as seen through a woman's eyes. They celebrate a close-knit community, a proud pioneer history, and a deep-seated sense of place. That commitment to locality is what entices the reader from another place, another time, to become engaged with the personalities and landscapes that Nellie deeply loved. She was not shy about proclaiming her devotion to a place that many today deride or dismiss. She wrote of endless plains dotted with sky-blue playa lakes shimmering under a vast West Texas sky. She described fondly the arrival of spring, with its wash of flowers across Blanco Canyon. In her youth in the 1890s she enjoyed plum-picking excursions into the canyon with her family. In her old age she retired to town but chose a location that allowed her to drive through the canyon regularly. Nellie Witt Spikes wrote from a bioregional perspective before the word existed.

Her bioregionalism was not limited to landscape and environment, though those elements were often present. Nellie's sense of place also emerged from her local community, the farm neighbors and townspeople, their culture, and, especially, their history. In these columns the personalities of early Crosby County, from seventy-five or one hundred years ago, spring to life. We meet neighbors stopping in to visit, attend a bustling weekend market day in Ralls or Floydada, wait in line at the Lubbock stockyards with other farmers selling their cattle.

These stories are heroic, reflecting the first half-century of apparent progress and the rise of "civilization" on the Great Plains. The essays do not turn a critical eye on the region's history. They do not address, for example, the destruction of Indian cultures that preceded Euro-American settlement. The Indians had been gone for some fifteen years—dead or removed to reservations in Oklahoma—when Nellie's family moved to Crosby County, and she dwelt little on that legacy of tragedy and injustice. Much the same was true of the natural environment. The pioneers destroyed the very thing they celebrated as they plowed the wide prairie, drained the playa lakes, and exterminated or crowded out much of the wildlife. Spikes's attitudes were contradictory, both lauding the beauty of the plains as she had first found them and congratulating the pioneers for transforming that beauty into economic power and civilized institutions. Her articles omit or gloss over troubling aspects of local history. For example, she makes almost no reference to the black population that worked in the cotton fields every year at harvest time and only passing reference to the Hispanics who were always present. Reading her articles, one might think this was a uniformly white culture, but in 1950 10 percent of the students enrolled in Crosby County schools were black. In these regards Nellie was a woman of her times, and we should read her articles with care. What she wrote about was true and accurate, but there are omissions and blind spots, too, and we should not take this portrayal as the whole of southern plains life during the era.

Nellie did not grapple with the defining trends of the second half of the twentieth century: the grow-ing concern about environmental degradation, the depopulation and decline of rural communities, the uncertainty about the region's economy in the face of a diminishing Ogallala Aquifer, or the general cultural reassessment of the 1960s. She was seventy-two when she wrote her last column in 1960; most of these concerns arose later. The emerging generational divide appears only in a gratuitous swipe at "beatniks" by the editor of the *Ralls Banner* in a 1958 article about Jeff Spikes's birthday: "The new, lazy, and decidedly beaten generation won't receive this news calmly, but J. J. Spikes spent his 91st birthday chopping weeds out of his garden." If there was a "generation gap" developing in the 1950s, it is clear on which side of it Nellie, her husband, and her editor stood. Partly as a result of the cultural upheavals of the 1960s we now see plains history in more complicated ways than did Nellie's generation. Her stories reflect the optimism, hope, and confidence of her times, and that sense of unlimited possibility may be why many of us look to an earlier era with nostalgia, as an antidote to our jaded perception of modern life.

Further Reading

Abbe, Donald R. *Lubbock and the South Plains: An Illustrated History*.
    Chatsworth, Calif.: Windsor Publications, 1989.

Andreadis, Harriete. "True Womanhood Revisited: Women's Private
    Writing in Nineteenth-Century Texas." *Journal of the Southwest* 31
    (1989): 179–204.

Armitage, Susan, and Elizabeth Jameson, eds. *The Women's West*. Nor-
    man: University of Oklahoma Press, 1987.

Atkeson, Mary Meek. *The Woman on the Farm*. New York: The Century
    Company, 1924.

———. "Women in Farm Life and Rural Economy." *Annals of the American
    Academy of Political Science* 143 (1929): 188–94.

Biles, Roberta Frances. "The Frame House Era in Northwest Texas." *West
    Texas Historical Association Yearbook* 46 (1970): 167–83.

Blodgett, Jan. "Crosby County's Year Old Baby: Julian Bassett and the
    Development of Crosbyton, Texas." *West Texas Historical Association
    Yearbook* 62 (1986): 43–51.

Bogener, Steve. *Lubbock: Gem of the South Plains*. Encino, Calif.: Cherbo
    Publishing Group, 2003.

Boswell, Angela. *Her Act and Deed: Women's Lives in a Rural Southern*

County, *1837–1873*. College Station: Texas A&M University Press, 2001.

Boulding, Elise. "The Labor of U. S. Farm Women: A Knowledge Gap." *Sociology of Work and Occupations* 7 (1980): 261–90.

Branscum, Virginia Miksch. "Some Aspects of the Life of Women in Eastern New Mexico and the Texas Panhandle-Plains Area From 1875 to 1905." M.A. thesis, University of Texas at Austin, 1952.

Brooks, Una M. "The Influence of the Pioneer Women Toward a Settled Social Life on the Llano Estacado." M.A. thesis, West Texas State Teacher's College, 1942.

Brown, Pat. "Dugouts, Dooryards, Dirt Tanks and Daffodils (Crosby County, 1877–1936)." *West Texas Historical Association Yearbook* 57 (1983): 71–83.

Burnett, Georgellen. *We Just Toughed It Out: Women on the Llano Estacado*. El Paso: Texas Western Press, 1990.

Caffey, David L. *The Old Home Place: Farming on the West Texas Frontier*. Burnet, Texas: Eakin Press, 1981.

Cashin, Joan E. *A Family Venture: Men and Women on the Southern Frontier*. New York: Oxford University Press, 1991.

Churchill, Frances M. "Notes on the Native Grasslands of West Central Texas Since 1854." *West Texas Historical Association Yearbook* 31 (1955): 54–64.

Cloud, Kathleen. "Farm Women and the Structural Transformation of Agriculture: A Cross-Cultural Perspective." In *Women and Farming: Changing Roles, Changing Structures*, ed. Wava G. Haney and Jane B. Knowles, 281–99. Boulder, Colo.: Westview Press, 1988.

Coltharp, J. B. "Reminiscences of Cotton Pickin' Days." *Southwestern Historical Quarterly* 73 (1970): 539–42.

Corder, Jim. *Chronicle of a Small Town*. College Station: Texas A&M University Press, 1989.

———. *Lost in West Texas*. College Station: Texas A&M University Press, 1988.

Cowan, Ruth Schwartz. *More Work for Mother: The Ironies of Household Technology from the Open Hearth to the Microwave*. New York: Basic Books, 1983.

Crosby County Pioneer Memorial Museum. *A History of Crosby County, 1876–1977*. Crosbyton, Texas: Taylor Publishing, 1978.

Cunfer, Geoff. *On the Great Plains: Agriculture and Environment*. College Station: Texas A&M University Press, 2005.

Denney, Susan G. "It Was No Place for Women: Women on the Texas Panhandle Frontier, 1876–1900." *Panhandle-Plains Historical Review* 74 (2001): 23–46.

Downs, Fane; Nancy Baker Jones; and Elizabeth Fox-Genovese. *Women and Texas History: Selected Essays*. Austin: Texas State Historical Association, 1993.

Elbert, Sarah. "The Farmer Takes a Wife: Women in America's Farming Families." In *Women, Households, and the Economy*, ed. Lourdes Beneria and Catharine R. Stimpson, 173–97. New Brunswick, N.J.: Rutgers University Press, 1987.

Ellis, Temple Ann. *Road to Destiny*. San Antonio, Texas: Naylor Publishing Company, 1939.

Faragher, John Mack. "History from the Inside Out: Writing the History of Women in Rural America." *American Quarterly* 33 (1981): 537–57.

Fink, Deborah. *Agrarian Women: Wives and Mothers in Rural Nebraska, 1880–1940*. Chapel Hill: University of North Carolina Press, 1992.

———. *Open Country, Iowa: Rural Women, Tradition and Change*. Albany: State University of New York Press, 1986.

———. "Sidelines and Moral Capital: Women on Nebraska Farms in the 1930s." In *Women and Farming: Changing Roles,*

Changing Structures, ed. Wava G. Haney and Jane B. Knowles, 55–70. Boulder, Colo.: Westview Press, 1988.

Flora, Cornelia Butler. "Farm Women, Farming Systems, and Agricultural Structure: Suggestions for Scholarship." *Rural Sociologist* 1, no. 6 (1981): 383–86.

———. "Public Policy and Women in Agricultural Production: A Comparative and Historical Analysis." In *Women and Farming: Changing Roles, Changing Structures,* ed. Wava G. Haney and Jane B. Knowles, 265–80. Boulder, Colo.: Westview Press, 1988.

Flora, Cornelia Butler, and John Stitz. "Female Subsistence Production and Commercial Farm Survival among Settlement Kansas Wheat Farms." *Human Organization* 47, no. 1 (1988): 64–68.

Flores, Dan. *Caprock Canyonlands: Journeys into the Heart of the Southern Plains.* Austin: University of Texas Press, 1990.

Furnish, Patricia L. "Women and Labor on the Panhandle Plains, 1920–1940." *Panhandle Plains Historical Review* 68 (1995): 14–36.

Gracy, David B., II. *Littlefield Lands: Colonization of the Texas Plains, 1912–1920.* Austin: University of Texas Press, 1968.

Grant, Michael Johnston. *Down and Out on the Family Farm: Rural Rehabilitation in the Great Plains.* Lincoln: University of Nebraska Press, 2002.

Graves, Lawrence L. *A History of Lubbock.* Lubbock: West Texas Museum Association, 1962.

———, ed. *Lubbock: From Town to City.* Lubbock: West Texas Museum Association, 1986.

Green, Donald E. *Land of the Underground Rain: Irrigation on the Texas High Plains, 1910–1970.* Austin: University of Texas Press, 1973.

Haley, J. Evetts. *The XIT Ranch of Texas*

and the Early Days of the Llano Estacado. Norman: University of Oklahoma Press, 1967.

Hall, Claude. *Early History of Floyd County.* Canyon, Texas: Panhandle-Plains Historical Society, 1947.

Hampsten, Elizabeth. *Read This Only to Yourself: The Private Writings of Midwestern Women, 1880–1910.* Bloomington: University of Indiana Press, 1982.

Haney, Wava G., and Jane B. Knowles, eds. *Women and Farming: Changing Roles, Changing Structures.* Boulder, Colo.: Westview Press, 1988.

Hayter, Delmar. "Pioneer Women of West Texas in the Early Twentieth Century." *West Texas Historical Association Yearbook* 65 (1989): 78–92.

Henderson, Caroline. *Letters from the Dust Bowl.* Ed. Alvin O. Turner. Norman: University of Oklahoma Press, 2001.

Hill, Pamela Smith. *Laura Ingalls Wilder: A Writer's Life.* Pierre: South Dakota Historical Society Press, 2007.

Hoffert, Sylvia D. "Promise to the Land: Essays on Rural Women." *Southwestern Historical Quarterly* 96, no. 4 (1993): 626.

Holt, Marilyn Irvin. *Linoleum, Better Babies, and the Modern Farm Woman, 1890–1930.* Albuquerque: University of New Mexico Press, 1995.

Hoofman, Judy. "A Day in the Life of a Texarkana, U.S.A., Homemaker from 1900–1917." *East Texas Historical Journal* 32, no. 1 (1994): 12–26.

Hudson, John C. *Plains Country Towns.* Minneapolis: University of Minnesota Press, 1985.

Hunt, George M. *Early Days Upon the Plains of Texas.* Lubbock, Texas: A. G. & C. E. Hunt, 1919.

Hurley, F. Jack. *Portrait of a Decade: Roy Stryker and the Development of Documentary Photography in the Thirties.* Baton

Rouge: Louisiana State University Press, 1972.

Hurt, R. Douglas. *The Dust Bowl: An Agricultural and Social History*. Chicago, Ill.: Nelson-Hall, 1981.

Jameson, Elizabeth. "Women As Workers, Women As Civilizers: True Womanhood in the American West." In *The Women's West*, ed. Susan Armitage and Elizabeth Jameson, 145–64. Norman: University of Oklahoma Press, 1987.

Jellison, Katherine. *Entitled to Power: Farm Women and Technology, 1913–1963*. Chapel Hill: University of North Carolina Press, 1993.

——. "'Sunshine and Rain in Iowa': Using Women's Autobiography As a Historical Source." *Annals of Iowa* 49 (1989): 591–99.

Jenkins, John Cooper. *Estacado, Cradle of Culture and Civilization on the Staked Plains of Texas*. Crosbyton, Texas: Crosby County Pioneer Memorial Museum, 1986.

Jensen, Joan M. "Canning Comes to New Mexico: Women and the Agricultural Extension Service, 1914–1919." *New Mexico Historical Review* 57 (1982): 361–86.

——. "Cloth, Butter, and Boarders: Women's Household Production for the Market." *Review of Radical Political Economics* 12 (1980): 14–24.

——. "'I've Worked, I'm Not Afraid of Work': Farm Women in New Mexico, 1920–1940." In *New Mexico Women: Intercultural Perspectives,* ed. Joan M. Jensen and Darlis A. Miller, 227–55. Albuquerque: University of New Mexico Press, 1986.

——. *Promise to the Land: Essays on Rural Women*. Albuquerque: University of New Mexico Press, 1991.

——. *With These Hands: Women Working on the Land*. Old Westbury, N.Y.: Feminist Press, 1981.

Jones, Anne Goodwyn. *Tomorrow Is Another Day: The Woman Writer in the South, 1859–1936*. Baton Rouge: Louisiana State University Press, 1987.

Jordan, Terry G. *Trails to Texas: Southern Roots of Western Cattle Ranching*. Lincoln: University of Nebraska Press, 1981.

Karolevitz, Robert E. *From Quill to Computer: The Story of America's Community Newspapers*. Freeman, S.Dak.: Pine Hill Press, 1985.

Key, Zela Mae Cornelius. "A West Texas Childhood." Ed. Ellen Ruth Key-Clark and Edward Hake Phillips. *West Texas Historical Association Yearbook* 71 (1995): 127–43.

Kincaid, Naomi H. "Anniversary Celebrations of West Texas Towns." *West Texas Historical Association Yearbook* 32 (1956): 135–48.

King, Evelyn. *Women on the Cattle Trail and in the Roundup*. Bryan, Texas: Brazos Corral of the Westerners, 1983.

Kohl, Seena B. "The Making of a Community: The Role of Women in an Agricultural Setting." In *Kin and Communities: Families in America,* ed. Allan J. Lichtman and Joan R. Challinor. Washington, D.C.: Smithsonian Institution Press, 1979.

Lewis, Willie Newbury. *Between Sun and Sod: An Informal History of the Texas Panhandle*. College Station: Texas A&M University Press, 1976.

Mackintosh, Prudence. *Just As We Were: A Narrow Slice of Texas Womanhood*. Austin: University of Texas Press, 1996.

Maret, Elizabeth. *Women of the Range: Women's Roles in the Texas Beef Cattle Industry*. College Station: Texas A&M University Press, 1993.

——, and James Copp. "Some Recent Findings on the Economic Contributions of Farm Women." *Rural Sociologist* 2 (1982): 112–15.

Matheson, Rebecca Jumper. *The Sunbonnet: An American Icon in Texas*. Lubbock: Texas Tech University Press, 2009.

McArthur, Judith N. *Creating the New Woman: The Rise of Southern Women's Progressive Culture in Texas, 1893–1918*. Urbana: University of Illinois Press, 1998.

McGonagill, D'Aun. "Women on the Ranching Frontier: The Early Settlement of Ector County, Texas." *Permian Historical Annual* 21 (1984): 11–24.

McNall, Scott G., and Sally Allen McNall. *Plains Families: Exploring Sociology through Social History*. New York: St. Martin's Press, 1983.

Mercer, David. *The Telephone: The Life Story of a Technology*. Westport, Conn.: Greenwood Press, 2006.

Myres, Sandra. *Westering Women and the Frontier Experience, 1800–1915*. Albuquerque: University of New Mexico Press, 1982.

Neth, Mary. *Preserving the Family Farm: Women, Community, and the Foundations of Agribusiness in the Midwest, 1900–1940*. Baltimore, Md.: Johns Hopkins University Press, 1995.

Neugebauer, Janet M., ed. *Plains Farmer: The Diary of William G. DeLoach, 1914–1964*. College Station: Texas A&M University Press, 1991.

Nye, David E. *Electrifying America: Social Meanings of a New Technology, 1880–1940*. Cambridge, Mass.: MIT Press, 1990.

Opie, John. *Ogallala: Water for a Dry Land*. Lincoln: University of Nebraska Press, 1993.

Peterson, Roger S., and Chad S. Boyd. *Ecology and Management of Sand Shinnery Communities: A Literature Review*. USDA Forest Service General Technical Report RMRS-GTR-16. Fort Collins, Colo.: Rocky Mountain Research Station, 1998.

Riley, Glenda. *The Female Frontier: A Comparative View of Women on the Prairie and the Plains*. Lawrence: University Press of Kansas, 1988.

Riney-Kehrberg, Pamela. *Rooted in Dust: Surviving Drought and Depression in Southwestern Kansas*. Lawrence: University Press of Kansas, 1994.

——. "Separation and Sorrow: A Farm Woman's Life, 1935–1941." *Agricultural History* 67, no. 2 (1993): 185–96.

——. "Women in Wheat Country." *Kansas History* 23, nos. 1–2 (2000): 56–71.

Rodenberger, Lou H. "West Texas Pioneer Women: The Wilder, Stronger Breed." *West Texas Historical Association Yearbook* 77 (2001): 38–53.

——. "Presidential Address: Texas Women Writers and Their 'Usable Past.'" *West Texas Historical Association Yearbook* 72 (1996): 201.

Rosenfeld, Rachel Ann. *Farm Women: Work, Farm, and Family in the United States*. Chapel Hill: University of North Carolina Press, 1985.

Sachs, Carolyn E. *The Invisible Farmers: Women in Agricultural Production*. Totowa, N.J.: Rowman and Littlefield, 1983.

Salamon, Sonya. *Prairie Patrimony: Family, Farming, and Community in the Midwest*. Chapel Hill: University of North Carolina Press, 1992.

Salutos, Theodore. *The American Farmer and the New Deal*. Ames: Iowa State University Press, 1981.

Schwieder, Dorothy. *Growing Up with the Town: Family and Community on the Great Plains*. Iowa City: University of Iowa Press, 2002.

Schwieder, Dorothy, and Deborah Fink. "Plains Women: Rural Life in the 1930s." *Great Plains Quarterly* 8, no. 2 (1988): 79–88.

Sharpless, Rebecca. *Fertile Ground, Narrow Choices: Women on Texas Cotton Farms,*

1900–1940. Chapel Hill: University of North Carolina Press, 1999.

Smith, Loren M. *Playas of the Great Plains*. Austin: University of Texas Press, 2003.

Snapp, Harry F. "West Texas Women: A Diverse Heritage and a Succession of Frontiers." *West Texas Historical Association Yearbook* 72 (1996): 21–38.

Spikes, Nellie Witt, and Temple Ann Ellis. *Through the Years: A History of Crosby County, Texas*. San Antonio: The Naylor Company, 1952.

Stapp, Dawn Lucas. "Surviving Depression and Drought: The Farm Women of Martin County, Texas." *Permian Historical Annual* 35 (1995): 3–16.

Strasser, Susan. *Never Done: A History of American Housework*. New York: Pantheon Books, 1982.

Vanek, Joann. "Work, Leisure, and Family Roles: Farm Households in the United States, 1920–1955." *Journal of Family History* 5 (1980): 422–31.

Wallace, Ernest. "Anniversary Celebrations in West Texas." *West Texas Historical Association Yearbook* 33 (1957): 147–55.

Wandersee, Winifred D. *Women's Work and Family Values, 1920–1940*. Cambridge: Harvard University Press, 1981.

Webb, Walter Prescott. *The Great Plains*. New York: Ginn and Co., 1931.

Westin, Jeane. *Making Do: How Women Survived the '30s*. Chicago: Follett Publishing Company, 1976.

Wik, Reynold M. "The Radio in Rural America during the 1920s." *Agricultural History* 55 (1981): 339–50.

Williams, Robert C. *Fordson, Farmall, and Poppin' Johnny: A History of the Farm Tractor and Its Impact on America*. Urbana: University of Illinois Press, 1987.

Worster, Donald. *Dust Bowl: The Southern Plains in the 1930s*. New York: Oxford University Press, 1979.

Wunder, John R., ed. *At Home on the Range: Essays on the History of Western Social and Domestic Life*. Westport, Conn.: Greenwood Press, 1985.

Index

Page numbers in italics indicate images.